The Paros Commune of 1971
to 2021 & Beyond

The Paros Commune of 1971 to 2021 & Beyond

The Paros Commune of 1971 To 2021 & Beyond

Jubilee Imagings of Soul and Community

Martin Gibson

UniServEnt, PO Box 2358, Southern Pines, NC 28388
UniServEnt.org
martin@uniservent.org

UniServEnt
ISBN 978-1-958488-02-7

The Paros Commune of 1971 To 2021 & Beyond

Dedication

This work is dedicated to

All the Souls

throughout history, now, and in the future,

who show Fortitude in the face of adversity,

choosing

Love over fear and Wisdom over ignorance

in the pursuit of

the Spirit of Truth in their Lives and

Justice in their interactions within the Community,

through adherence to the

Principles of Faith and Science

in the cultivation of an attitude that is

Liberal toward Opportunity and Conservative toward Risk,

as found in the Love of my Life and Wife, Molly.

The Paros Commune of 1971 To 2021 & Beyond

The Paros Commune of 1971 to 2021 & Beyond

CONTENTS

The Paros Commune of 1971

ΠΡΟΛΟΓΟΣ

ΓΕΝΕΣΙΣ

I

ΧΗΡΨΣΤΑΛΣΙΣ

ΔΙΑΣΠΟΡΑ

ΕΠΙΛΟΓΟΣ

2021 & Beyond

PREFACE to The Paros Commune of 1971

Some Personal Context for this Writing

<u>The Paros Commune of 1971</u> was written in early to mid 1973. It was not finished at the time of this photo, taken in Vermont during a spring ski outing that year. If anyone recognizes themselves in this photo and is still alive, good luck. Drop me a note and I will be happy to remove the anonymask if you so desire. Ed doesn't get one.

That's me in the red sweater trying to sneak into the photo on the right, helped by Ed, my Canadian friend and Howard Stern doppelgänger, I comment on a time or two in the book, then there are five friends of Ed's whose names I don't remember from, you guessed it, 'Oh, Canada', disappearing off into the beer haze at the other end of the table, before coming back up the left side with Carl, a good friend from North Carolina who had come with me on the trip, peeking out from behind a deer-in-the-headlights looking Bilbo, Bilbo being a another name for Carl wearing the cap and one of the Communards from Paros as was Heidi, furthest left, and Molly, leaning over in the foreground.

My friend and fellow Communard, J.C. took the polaroid, I guess. 48 years on, things are a little hazy now—as seen in the photo. Everyone was full of good cheer, well, except maybe for Bilbo, who must have been caught off guard by the camera.

The next year J.C. and Heidi moved to Washington and bought some land up in the hills near Chewelah in the eastern part of the state. Ed, his girlfriend of the time whose name I don't remember, and I drove out to visit them so that I could help them build their cabin, and I could write. Here is a photo of J.C. on the right with me at a campsite in British Columbia shortly after we arrived. After a year, with the help of many friends we got the roof on their cabin, and I came back to North Carolina, primarily for family reasons and to work for the winter.

The following summer I went back with my brother and cousin to build a cabin of my own on a corner of J.C. and Heidi's property. A photo is included of the front of my cabin, the result of efforts of several friends, with substantial help from Heidi on the stone foundation. J.C., lounging on the stoop, blends in well with the woodwork.

X

Those were heady times, full of promise. The Vietnam War was becoming history, civil rights and voting rights had become law, along with sexual equality and sexual rights, at least on paper. With the end of the Jim Crow era in the South—an era and area into which I was born, while managing to escape indoctrination by its darker values—the optimism and perceived capacity of the American experiment to accommodate the basic needs of everyone drew me away from the left-wing programs and unfulfilled promise of the Paris Commune of 1871 that had motivated me the last couple of years of my university studies.

It led me away from the programs, but not from the promise of their ideals for social justice. It led me toward an inclusiveness of the spirit and away from the divisiveness of the politics based on greed on the one hand and corrupting desire for retribution and redistribution on the other. Having finished my undergraduate degree work from Duke in economics in 1969, at the time I faced the possibility of being drafted into the morass of Vietnam, and my path to graduate school was forestalled—permanently.

From my earliest memories, I had two primary motivations that the Greeks and Freud would recognize; the first was to grow up and find a woman like my mother to marry and the second was to find a way to make my way in the world and take over the reputed professional position of my father. Then, as now after almost 40 years of wedded bliss, I disproved the myth of Oedipus and did neither. Instead, after college I went home to work for a year with my dad in the design and construction business, to save some money and plan my next move.

For me that move was to take the opportunity to see the world. A friend from high school, J.C. was finishing up his stint as a corpsman in the Navy, which had included a year at a base in Naples. He wanted to go back to Europe when he got out of the service, so we decided to travel and work and go on from there. Many long hours were spent planning the trip in some detail, none of which included the name 'Paros', though 'Paris' entered our consciousness for various reasons many times.

Despite all the talk of revelry and debauchery in this book, the process of living those few weeks involved plenty of introspection. It was, for me unrecognized at the time, the start of a spiritual quest. Within a month of leaving Paros and traveling up through the Soviet Union and into Scandinavia, I had an epiphanic episode that removed from my psyche any notion that we humans were anything other than spiritual beings, souls. My life since that episode has been an attempt to figure out just what the revelation meant for me individually and collectively as a responsible fellow sentient life form; as a soul.

While most of us coming out of the campus new left of the time never had an affection for the USSR, the rational 'materialistic' analysis of Marxism nevertheless had an elusive, contradictory appeal. It explained well the reality of socioeconomic inequalities found in the US and around the globe in terms of the material, capital motivations generated by neoliberal economics. But it appeared to avoid or ignore the fact that those same material motivations were necessary in any ideal solutions to the problems proposed by the left or that any material solutions required the ideal capacity of human capital of all types, including some of those on the right.

I remember my first break with that appeal when I returned to campus a year after graduation in response to student calls for mobilization against the invasion of Cambodia by the US and South

Vietnam. In a strategy session, some of those present were contemplating a tactic designed to provoke the police to attack members of the general public in order to 'radicalize' them. I responded with a comment that we were supposed to 'love the people,' not try to get their heads beat in. The 'what are you talking about' look I got from some of my comrades in the room was a clarifying moment for me.

As far as our trip through the USSR from the Black Sea to Finland went, I still recall the outburst of Ed in the lobby of a hotel in Leningrad, now once again Saint Petersburg, where we had gone to board our bus tour of the city scheduled by the authorities merely the day before. It was as succinct an appraisal of the Soviet system as possible, announced by our neutral Canadian with moral rectitude and certitude. After a very early rise and departure from our campground near Vyborg some hundred-thirty kilometers north of the city and most of the way to the freedom of Finland, in order to catch our tour, we found on our arrival at the hotel that the tour had been canceled because of a scheduled naval holiday.

Ed responded as only he could, in full fury, to the chagrin of those in the lobby. "Red Menace my ass! I'll start worrying about a Red Menace when you folks learn how to build roads!"

This last comment was a response to the perception that on the road between Odessa on the Black Sea and Leningrad, we could count on one hand the number of paved roads that we crossed in the countryside outside the confines of any metropolitan area, which were themselves few. Of course, to their credit they had but recently emerged from the struggle against the fascists and perhaps had more important things to contend with. Still, the absurdity of Stalinist, fear imposed, autocratic government as an expression of idealistic intent was pertinent.

The epiphany I experienced on a ferry from Turku between Finland and Sweden a few days later culminated in a more profound experience a few years after that, shortly after I got my cabin in Washington in the dry. For those of you who do not have construction experience or at least have access to HGTV, 'in the dry' was a state where I could keep out the elements and keep in some heat in order to further my career as a writer, whatever that otherwise might entail. It gets cold in eastern Washington in November, at least it did in 1976.

I am at the end of a period of life that began for me early Thanksgiving morning in 1976, some 4½ years after the epiphany in Scandinavia. I have written about this in some detail in the blog of my UniServEnt.org web presence, started a few months before the start of the Covid pandemic and quoted in 'Letter to a Friend' in the companion to this writing, The Paros Commune – 2021 & Beyond.

That website is in part a result of my frustration with the more polite approach at trying to reach the experts in the fields in which I have some experience, political economy and theoretical physics, as documented on the website. This led to the development of Ergodidiocy as a tongue-in-cheek portmanteau—well part of the tongue is bitten anyway—with possibilities as a work in progress in commenting on the idiocy of the truth-statements of parties to both sides of almost any contentious subject, particularly of those identifying with the extreme cultural and economic perspectives of US life. This bit of drollery is derived from my recent encounter with the use of ergodicity in the statistical modeling of thermodynamics as coined in the 1800's.

From the Greek words for work, *ergo*, and roadway, *od*, ergodic thinking posits that, for any constrained collection of individual elements as microstates of some quality and position which are free to move along a variety of paths based on some quantifiable metric, the average value of each microstate over the lifetime of its trajectory will be equal to the average as a macrostate value of the entire ensemble of microstates at any given point in time.

With Paros in mind, a simple way of looking at this is to assume we have a jug of retsina that is half full, with enough wine for everyone to have a drink. The average measure of a drink is the depth of a jug full of retsina measured at the midpoint, divided by the number of drinkers, which we have to keep shaken so the resin won't all sink to the bottom of the jug. Provided we shake the closed jug vigorously and long enough, everybody's drink of retsina will at some point pass through the midpoint of the sealed jug satisfying our ergodic condition.

This is a simple enough concept, sort of, except when it is applied to politics and economics, since it is used to imply that everyone has an equal opportunity for their drink of the beverage, which is a sip for some people, while for others, it apparently requires a gulp.

The problem is that you can't drink from the jug while it's being shaken and only those positioned at the front of the line get the pleasure of their drink when the shaker stops the shaking to allow for a sip. There is nothing wrong with some people having to drink first, in fact it is inevitable. But if there is no method of gauging the rate of consumption, as the average amounts already and yet to be consumed, there are likely to be some people near the end of the line who would like a gulp, but can only afford a sip, if that. This is particularly likely to occur when the gulpers get to go first—especially when they are inclined to take two or three.

Even though it is understood that more retsina is being made as we pass the jug around, only an ergodidiot would think that some divine, neoliberal hand of the free marketplace is there to ensure that everyone, on average, gets their appropriate gulp as their fair share of the coveted beverage. On average, some get nothing, since they are expected to wait in line and accept a small sip if it is available, like in Jim Crow days; but I am not talking about just race here. There are plenty of white folk that have never been allowed in line with the gulpers and end up having to sip along with the majority of our swarthier brothers and sisters. Of course, those that are insistent get more, even though sated.

Another extreme of ergodidiocy is to think that appointment of a keeper of the jug is a good idea, someone to divvy out the retsina in equal sips to one and all given the difference in people's appetites and capacities to imbibe, not to mention insistence. It may be a noble concept, but as the number of individuals waiting for the jug increases, so does the range of thirsts about the average, and the feasibility of an egalitarian solution to the divvy decreases.

Ergodidiocy incorporates a number of related notions. One is that because an individual has average expertise in one field of experience, absent similar experience they have similar average expertise in any other field. Another is the notion that the individual's consciously adaptive capacity can be modeled as a function of mindless material interactions using deterministic inertial or stochastic probabilistic methods to explain the ensemble's sentient adaptive capacities, without acknowledging the conscious effort that set up the parameters of the model in the first place. Another is the ergodidiotically absurd notion that the way for experts to address a public problem that requires a real solution is by playing make-believe and lying to oneself and the public about it. Another is the belief that proclamation of ideological purity of any type makes one enlightened. Another is ...well, perhaps that's another book.

It is when it is applied in questionable manner to economic and other social modeling that ergodicity deserves to be called ergodidiocy. Idiocy, also from the Greek, is derived not as a measure of innate lack of intelligence, but as an indication of a level of expertise yet to be achieved, as amateurism of an individual or group posing in the public arena as an expert; hence the term ergodidiocy. I have attempted to live up to this level for most of my life.

In the process of hosting this website, I remembered The Paros Commune of 50 years ago and had the notion to dust it off and see if it still had any life in it.

I was pleasantly surprised, but what was more surprising was that my wife of almost 40 years, who had never read it and is not usually curious about most of the stuff I write—which tends to be of a technical nature—thought it was a good read, as did my sister and my sister-in-law. Perhaps it's a chick book. So here it is.

Cheers to you, Fellow Communards, Souls, Friends, Sisters–Brothers, Citizens, Comrades, Experts, and fellow Ergodidiots!

June 17, 2022.

PREFACE to 2021 & Beyond

The content of <u>The Paros Commune of 1971</u> speaks for itself. It is the heart of the book, a young soul's celebration of Life, of self-discovery and friendship; an aspiration of the time for open inclusion in community over any type of exclusionary social status. The second portion, <u>2021 & Beyond</u>, builds on this heart using the head, reflecting on 50 years of experience, working to pay the bills but with a primary interest in developing non-market based human capital through an understanding and expertise founded on both faith and science, born of a mix of success in dealing with risk and opportunity, my own and of others in the community. These reflections start with personal experience and related insights in 'The Hourglass of Space and Time Funnel', followed by the 'Glossary', 'A Communion of Souls', 'A Dream', 'Contemplation, Service, and Communion', and ending with 'Letter to a Friend'.

The experience of 50 years has resulted in a difference in voice between the heart and the head, so that someone who picks up and starts reading and enjoys the voice of <u>The Paros Commune of 1971</u> may at first wonder what is going on as they get into <u>2021 & Beyond</u>. On the other hand, some may think, "finally, no more sex, drugs, and rock & roll." The first six of these are essentially a collection of commentary involving personal transcendental experience—transcending in perception and identification with any established religion or philosophical school of thought—followed by four related essays based on insights provided by this experience.

I have done this as a testimony to the reality of Soul and its relationship to Community in this current period of widespread doubt, fear, and ignorance about the scientific nature of spirituality and the undeniable economic constraints of materiality, both of which subjects I have studied in detail using axiomatic monism. It is included as a link between the 'heart' section of '1971' and the 'head' section of the last four essays of '2021 & Beyond' for individual investigation of any interested reader. These sections are a series of three 'Contemplations' and a 'Communion', intended to give the reader a notion of the monistic material-ideal-spiritual-soul nature of humankind in line with that of the Neo-Platonist, early church thinking of Plotinus and Origen, while referencing aspects of the spiritual thinking of Marx and the material thinking of Christ.

'A Communion of Souls' is a brief overview of personal psycho-spiritual experience in the first few years after returning to the U.S. in the fall of 1972 following the apogee of our trip to Europe—to Paros—and the epiphany on the ferry from Turku. This period was marked by an increase in the occurrences of lucid and hyper lucid dream with psycho-physical experience and the eventual permanent recognition of continuity of consciousness as recounted in the three chapters that follow this one. As a result, the notion of a permanent soul as distinct from the individual's personality becomes fully recognized as seamlessly integrated with Soul in a Community of souls, or as I eventually came to think of it, as the Soul Nature. The mortar that holds us all together in that community is Love, or to differentiate it from any notion of a personal or romantic emotion, Goodwill.

This is followed in the three Contemplation chapters by a series of meditations on the ideal Form of the Essential Trigon, a triangle considered as a polygon which includes the area between the three boundary lines, defined as an intentional, inertial, and formal or form producing capacity. These three boundaries which focus and

XX

define the tripartite nature of the Soul, as the intuitive, logical, and innate capacities, are understood as three equally important and necessary aspects, which are developed with the aid of Venn type graphic representations of the model.

CONTEMPLATION I concerning Life as Essential Principles, studies the Intentional Capacity of Spiritual Nature to initiate and effect purposeful change in the forms & processes we encounter in our field of experience, in the formal (mental) and the inertial (physical) capacities of the mind and body, intuitively, logically and innately understood to exist in both form and formless manner, on a scale from the most particular to the most universal in scope. It is understood that these three aspects are each all-pervasive, in varying degrees of actual strength and intensity in the existential world, in full as infinite potential for the essential capacities in all worlds.

CONTEMPLATION II concerning the Appearance of Physical Phenomena, studies the observed Inertial Capacity of Material Nature to resist change and thereby maintain forms & processes, objectively as assemblies of quantum components, and subjectively as groups of individual souls of the community observing these material natures, as a means of understanding experience in the world according to the axiomatically consistent, logical capacity of the soul to recognize these forms and processes as specific purposeful instances of ideal natures. This is supported by links to independent modeling of the emergence of physical phenomena of rest mass and photon interaction as a localized wave mechanism of an inertial substrate. This is mathematically modeled as a function of isotropic expansion stress which is quantized by rotation of torsional oscillation as quantum gravity, particle spin, and quantum electromagnetic fields. Based on this modeling, it also provides links to a theoretical understanding of the potential for the technological and economical development of cold fusion. Such modeling of wave phenomena was the only way that I could envision the emergence of quantum phenomena and still maintain consistency with an underlying axiom of continuity, generally recognized in the physical sciences as conservation of energy. In fact, the correct axiom as a conserved property responsible for all phenomena is the conservation of power, the capacity to produce activity or energy.

CONTEMPLATION III concerning the Quality of Political Economy, studies the Formal Capacity of Ideal Nature to direct the economical flows of the energy of Life from the solar systemic Source through creative and evolutionary change using axiomatic logic to give objective structure to the intentional capacity of Life in sustaining all life forms and the human community. The soul does this through the innate capacity to recognize ideal Forms and Processes in the material forms and processes observed, to intuit the purpose and function of the qualities of the material forms of Nature, to form mental images based on a technologically ideal understanding of the material nature, and to apply the mental formulations in a logical manner to change the material forms and processes for community purpose. This study is supported by links to independent modeling of macrostate economic dynamics of human capital, both market and non-market valued, as an ergodic function weighted by the market position of microstate decision makers. It also includes links to spreadsheet modeling for comparing three options for the funding of public sector needs through taxation, borrowing, and fiat issuance of electronic currency in keeping with the basic thinking of Modern Monetary Theory and Universal Basic Income as a citizenship dividend.

COMMUNION of Love, Wisdom, and Community is summarized in the final section with a graphic depiction of the Essential Trigon, showing the essential unity of all faiths in light of this Neo-Platonic modeling, all of which is based on an understanding that the personal ego is a developmental feature of the constitution of the soul which must be transcended by the individual realization of each soul as an existential feature of the Essential Nature of the collective Soul. This is followed by some observations concerning the current state of public political discourse, particularly as it relates to notions of 'conservative' and 'liberal' in the polarization that has occurred due to the lack of insight into the nature and means of reconstituting a viable public money supply.

In light of this confusion, particularly in the U.S., in this final section we consider in brief form; 1) public versus private problem solving, 2) abortion and religious liberty, 3) guns, and 4) race and a public safety net.

Substantive feedback to this writing is welcome, though I am not currently in a position to guarantee any responses.

Peace to you, dear reader. We are all Souls that share one Community, one Earth, if not in perpetuity, at least for a very long while as we disperse as souls across the Cosmos... before we are drawn back in together for another Breath of the Great Cosmic Spirit.

World without end, Amen, Amen.

The Paros Commune of 1971

The Paros Commune of 1971 To 2021 & Beyond

ΠΡΟΛΟΓΟΣ

PROLOGOS

The following things did not more or less happen in 1971. They more or less happened in 1972. But what's a year, more or less. This kind of thing has probably always been happening and always will. Less in the past and hopefully more in the future. It could just as easily have happened in 1971 and no one would have known the difference. Except for the people to which it more or less happened, who would have been misplaced in space and time many miles and a year. It would have been quite a shock to me, to have awakened for work in Sanford on the 17th of June 1971, and stepped outside into the boiling sun of the Aegean. I would not have been ready to handle that.

I have used 1971 instead of 1972, because it is more poetic. It rhymes more nearly with 1871. I also used it to fake out all the people who want to read about 1871 as if it happened in 1971. I used to do that until I realized it belonged to the past century. I am now more interested in 1971 and beyond. I know I may not trick but one or two, but I hope some of those who start reading this accidently in 1871 will follow through and come out tomorrow. That is the reason I used 1971. More or less.

ΓΕΝΕΣΙΣ

GENESIS I

BEGINNINGS ARE 100 YEARS TOO LONG

It doesn't come easy with my soma in Raleigh and my psyche some 7000 miles away on a Greek island. Greek islands are noted for capturing unwary travelers. I had no wax for my ears, and there was no mast on the Elli, so I was driven to the rocks of Paros. Now I sit in Raleigh, my mind locked in a bottle, washed up on a beach of Paros, another would-be Odysseus caught by the Sirens of another age. And Penelope sits in a suburb of Detroit, taken by other suitors, and thinking that the Trojan War must have been a dream.

I have aged a century in the last year. When I arrived in Europe wrapped in a Red Flag, I thought it was still March and in 1871, but it was May and the reaction had set in like suburban sprawl along the Seine. By the time I reached Greece it was 1971, and I was wrapped in nothing at all among the sand and rocks of Paros.

ISLANDS WITH WATER – ISLANDS WITHOUT

Islands are successful because they are surrounded by water. That is why Paris is no longer an island and is no longer in 1871 and is a favorite place for people like Henry Kissinger and Georges Pompidou. Of course, you may say that Notre Dame is on an island, which is perfectly correct, but religion and islands don't mix. Pretty soon people begin building bridges. There's a high admission to God these days.

Islands surrounded by land give people strange ideas. Before long they start imagining that their island has no bounds and they start to extend their happiness everywhere, like a used war, even to people who don't want or need it. It is said that an island of democracy can't exist in a sea of fascism, but I think it has a better chance if the sea is not made out of land

WHY DID COLUMBUS CROSS THE WALL?

When we arrived at Paros, we did not expect the island to greet us the way it did. The last island we had stopped at had been friendly enough, but the trees decided they could not grow more than a few feet high without being watered regularly. They strained to see over the low stone walls, but never could quite make it. I didn't have the time nor the heart to tell them that it didn't matter, since the trees on the other side presented only a mirror image of themselves. Besides, they never would have believed me, thinking that the walls were Atlantic Oceans, and they were all Columbus searching for a quick route to the East.

Paros looked at least as friendly, but the trees did not appear to have heard of the Orient. Perhaps they had heard of it but were not interested. In any event, the trees were not as strong willed as on the previous island. Perhaps that was because the walls were not as high on Paros.

HE WAS HUNGRY

A great green, pointy-headed lizard, Paros basked before us on a sunbaked rock in the hot, still Aegean. The Elli steamed toward it, her head perpetually squinted to one side to get a better view of her objective. The heat does strange things to one's perception, even after being out there for years and years.

The lizard opened its mouth, and the Elli turned toward the dazzling row of teeth along the far shore. The happy remnants of previous repasts stood in colors along the waterfront, waving slowly in the warm breeze of our arrival. The chattering groups of fresh particles queued up along the gangways, the tin can opened and the new fare of international flavoring poured out amidst the alabaster blocks which are the main village of Paros.

Reptiles are not the only ones with large appetites. "Let's get some souvlaki before we find a beach," Ed said. His appetite is greater than any lizard in the Aegean.

"And maybe some beer or wine," said J.C. His appetite is equally large but runs in a somewhat different direction. Together they consumed vast quantities of food and drink, leaving behind not so small islands of burnt-out umber up and down the coast of the Mediterranean in testimony of their voracious passing.

"Pull Gertie over, and I'll go look in this café," I offered. I was hungry and thirsty, too, but I was a little leery of more souvlaki.

My stomach carried uneasy memories of Athenian souvlaki binges, feeling like the grease pit of an all-night diner.

The waiters weaved in and out of the tables on the awning covered patio, serving beer, retsina, ice cream, and some white mush with brown powder on it. People chatted lazily, new arrivals greeted old friends excitedly, and a few freaks sat at a table drinking expensive Scandinavian beer and wondering where to crash as they gazed out over the Aegean.

"Hey man, where do you crash around here?" one of them asked me warily. He feared a rip-off.

"I just got here. We're going to crash on the beach out of town. But you can get a room in town for about 75¢." I wanted to be helpful. This gave me a chance to slide into the old at-home routine like an old broken-in easy chair.

"That's cool," he replied. "How much is that in Greek money?"

"Oh, about 22 or 23 drachmae," I answered, once more helpful. "Do you know if this place has souvlaki?" It was his turn to be helpful.

"No, man, I don't. Just got here." I don't know why I asked, when I already knew the response. If he didn't know about drachmae, he wasn't likely to know about souvlaki. But these help-games ease the entry to a new place, like gestalt talk before a new woman.

"Well, take care," I said, moving toward the interior of the café. I always say "take care" as a few people who know me will testify. I carry it behind me everywhere I go, like a wagging tail. It has a mind of its own, wagging out behind my control. The other day I said "take care" four times to a friend in one and a half minutes. Each time I said, "take care," he said, "I will", the last time with special emphasis. I thought he was about to get mad or something. And I know he won't...take care, I mean. He has no more control than my tail.

The freaks nodded and said, "Yeah, man," and I entered the café. The interior of the café looked like the set from a Humphrey Bogart movie, the big fans turning slowly so that you didn't know whether they were starting or stopping.

The good-natured looking man beamed on from behind the counter, with teeth that put the lizard's to shame.

"What you like?" he asked in broken English.

"Souvlaki?" I asked. I wanted to be polite, but I could never remember the Greek for please.

"No, sir," he said. "At the end of the street. Toward the other windmill. Only place in the village."

"Poly calo." I remembered, 'thank you'.

"Thank you, sir." He won the language contest, but I didn't mind. It was another easy chair for me.

Like a lure on a fishing line of an unsuccessful cast, I left the smiling, gleaming toothed man and the Humphrey Bogart movie, wove through the tables, waved to the freaks, crossed the road, and hopped into Gertie, reeled up for another try.

"No souvlaki?" J.C. questioned.

"They ain't got no souvlaki here, but there's a little place down by the windmill's got the best souvlaki on the whole island." I attempted the gravelly, nasal singsong like a bogus Hollywood star. My attempted humor was lost on them.

"It's good souvlaki?" Ed didn't fool me. He was interested in quantity not quality.

"I don't know. But it's the only place on the island that has it." They looked at me in disbelief.

GENESIS II

A TREATISE ON THE ISLAND MODE OF PRODUCTION

They were somewhat new to islands. They did not realize that mass-production is not a necessary attribute of islands. Islands are best recognized by virtue of their singularity. They may and do exist in pairs and every conceivable multiple and no doubt exert a complementary and beneficial influence upon each other, but this is not their chief concern or aim. This is but a pleasant side effect of their primary mode of existence. And that mode is to express to the best of its ability its unique and individual island-ness. Mass-production is anathema to this mode. Mass-production would build bridges between all islands, until the time is reached when all islands are but reflections of each other, like the view from a barber's chair. Then all islands would be shorn of their island-ness in one quick clip.

I am sure my socialist as well as my capitalist friends will be quick to take exception to this. From different sides they will support each other. One will say that all islands are basically alike and should be treated the same. True, they are all surrounded by water, but this is what makes them different. The others say that if they are all bridged together, they can all receive the greatest benefits that all have to offer. Hum. I am sorry I do not have a greater faith in these sublime schemes of my fellow travelers, but islands have been around a while longer than their schemes.

My friends forget that islands are not completely separate. The same ocean touches all their shores. And there will always be ships.

Some people will be eager to point out that islands are all connected under the seas and that they merely convey an illusion of separateness. They suggest that we should bring to light and make immediate this underlying reality. I cannot disagree with this basic premise. There will be a time for that, but it need not be forced, for it will assert itself at the proper time. As for me now, I am not quite ready for it. The ocean exists in purpose, and part of that is the creation of island-ness. I do not look forward to the subsumption of islands and their diversity at present. I love them as they are, individually diverse.

It is alright with me if there is only one souvlaki joint on Paros. I hope it remains that way as long as I return my thoughts to it, even if those thoughts bear with them the knowledge that that souvlaki is not the best in Greece.

I did not, of course, have all these thoughts in mind as J.C. pulled Gertie back onto the street, and we headed down the quay, through the groups of ambling people, toward the windmill and my last souvlaki for a while.

GENESIS III

"Jesus, am I hungry. I'm going to eat six souvlakis!" Ed said, gleefully. I knew he wasn't boasting. His Little Orphan Annie hair was electric, and his eyes went white like two search lights as we entered the shop.

"Three souvlakis, please." J.C. got in ahead of us in the excitement.

"You're going to eat three of those things? You haven't even tasted them yet," I reminded him.

"Yeah, I'm hungry, man." He looked at the price list for beer. "Beer's about as much as it was on the ferry! I'm drinking retsina."

I was more cautious. I had tasted the turpentine wine once before and was not thinking about money.

"I guess I'll start out with three, don't want them to get cold." Ed grinned at us with his characteristic food chuckle.

I was busy looking for the alternatives. By the door, four lambs' heads were roasting on a spit over open coals. At each turn of the spit, their skinned heads grinned and stared at me in unison. "Come try some of the exotic Greek cuisine. Souvlaki is like a Big Mac compared to us."

I waivered no more.

"Two souvlakis, please. And a beer."

15

The three of us took our orders across the street to the tables on the quay. I bit into my first one, as I watched Ed swallow a big wad of dough, lamb's meat, and lettuce, then pick up his second one.

"They're not too bad," the connoisseur replied.

"I guess not, you swallowed it before you could taste it," J.C. retorted, as usual laying bare the truth.

I forced down the last bite of the bland, gristly Greek answer to the taco and guzzled some beer. "You want my other one, Ed?" I said, deciding to quit while I could still keep the one down.

"You're kidding? You don't want it?" His search lights gleamed white once more.

"It's yours. No charge." I handed Ed the souvlaki and turned my gaze out to sea.

GENESIS IV

In the veiled and distant past, Saturn ascended the throne of our world, bringing order and stability out of chaos. It is he that gave us the islands. Saturn—I should have said Cronos since he was really a Greek— made his capital on the peninsula that has become Greece. From there he could look out over the calm, but at that time empty, Aegean.

Saturn was put in a position which none of us would envy. He was informed by his parents that one of his own offspring would one day dethrone him. This was an exceedingly sad prospect for Saturn, for although he would have loved to experience the natural joys of fatherhood, he highly valued his throne. He had achieved and maintained it at the expense of great effort, and he had no desire to have it usurped by some brash upstart, even if it was his own son. After much internal debate he arrived at a somewhat distasteful solution to his dilemma. He purposed to return his children from whence they came by devouring them at birth.

This habit continued for quite some time and through many children, until Rhea, Saturn's wife—oops, that should be Ops, if we're sticking to the Roman gods while here in Greece—feeling the children to be as much her concern as her husband's, set about devising a plan whereby she could put an end to the distressing fate of her offspring. At the birth of her next child, Jupiter—that would be

Zeus in Greece—she was prepared. Ops substituted a rock for the young Jupiter, and in his feverish haste to elude the prophecy, Saturn failed to realize the true contents of the swaddling clothes. Jupiter was quickly spirited away to Crete, where he grew to manhood, waiting for the time when he could fulfill the prophecy of his father's doom.

The day finally arrived, and Jupiter went forth to Greece to avenge the tragic fate of his siblings. Saturn was put to the point and forced from the throne, but Jupiter did not quit him until Saturn had disgorged his offspring and Jupiter's brothers, spewing them out into the Aegean.

Although I cannot appreciate the loss of a throne, I could well imagine the probable relief of Saturn, as I fought down again and again the rock in my throat and tried to force back the image of his ordeal recreated in microcosm along the beach of Paros.

"You guys just came in on the Elli, didn't you?"

We looked up at the Bronx accent straddling the bicycle behind us.

"Yeah, you were on it too, weren't you?"

"Yep. Does the pavement end up ahead? I brought the bike with me, but there's nowhere to ride it," he said in a detached way, his head slowly rocking back and forth as if it had gone on to the next island and was still at sea.

"I think it does. Why don't you sit down and have a souvlaki?" Ed likes to spread his joy and contentment to all around him. He eats his way into your heart.

"What's that? I just flew into Athens yesterday with my bike. I haven't eaten a lot of Greek food yet," still rocking, head cocked back slightly to check out the last of my second one disappearing into Ed's bottomless pit.

"Kind of like a constipated taco. They're a real treat."

"Okay." He leaned the bike up against a neighboring table like a lame stork and sat down beside us.

"Let me see, you must be Stick from the Bronx?" J.C. said, once more with a good grasp of the situation.

"I went to school in the Bronx, but I live up the river a way. I'm not Stick yet. That comes later. I'm Richud."

"Hi," we all said, introducing ourselves.

"Hi. How much do those things cost?"

"Five drachmae… and retsina is only six. Good stuff. You have to go get it yourself." J.C. was the helpful one now. I was consoling my stomach.

"Well, I'm ready for two more, heh, heh," Ed grinned across the table.

We all got up one at a time and crossed the street to the shop, Ed for more souvlaki, J.C. for more retsina, and I for another 12 drachmae beer.

"Man, you've got to get into the retsina. It's so cheap and really gets you going. Arriba! Arriba!" J.C. said with a swallow.

J.C. is always looking out for my best interest.

RETSINA AMIDST SURPRISES

We sat back down at a table under the canopy in front of the shop. Richard had settled for one souvlaki and a beer. The sun moved slowly toward the horizon. Not content on 100 degrees for the day, it lingered on, drawing our anticipation of the coming night out pink against the evening sky. A small ferry labored toward the port, racing the sun for home. A few freaks walked by in the direction of the beaches that we assumed must be out there somewhere, waiting for us to invade and establish our colony of new social forms.

Richard calmly chewed on his souvlaki, non-committal on the new delicacy. He nodded his head a few times, surveying the scene.

"This place is alright."

"I don't know," I said, "It's awful dry. And there's hardly a tree in sight, or at least not one that would give any shade. I bet it's hot as hell in the daytime."

"Yeah, at least Corfu had some shade. I don't know about this place. It's not exactly what I had in mind," Ed backed me up. I waited for the response.

"You guys are never satisfied. This is exactly what we are looking for. Just like I had imagined. Man, it's so easy here. No people. You've got to slow down to a crawl." J.C. was in heaven. There was no budging him now.

"You've got to get into it. Here, try some retsina." He handed me the bottle, and I reluctantly raised it to my lips. The bitter pine resin went down like cold lard, raising the sleeping souvlaki from its fitful repose and chasing it halfway back up my throat. I forced it back down and took another swallow, this time letting it trickle down my throat. It worked.

"I guess it takes a little while to get used to it. But it's not too bad," I ventured.

J.C. was all smiles. He always gets a kick out of exorcising my squeamish hang-ups. "It's good, man. You'll get into it."

To the left, from the direction of the beaches, came a tractor pulling a trailer load of hay. From under a wide straw hat, the driver's leathery face caught the sinking sun. Behind him in the trailer were two western looking girls.

A shrill cry went up from Ed as he took to his feet like a startled flamingo. "I don't fucking believe it! It's Fuck-Stick and Annabelle!"

GENESIS VI

WE ARE A BIT LIKE ISLANDS, YOU AND I

We are a bit like islands, you and I. Although the myriad differences of background have led you there and brought me here, we all have felt the pounding of that same vast tempestuous sea of custom and culture, assaulting us wave upon wave to beat us back into the submerged world of uniformity. It is one of the more difficult aspects of island-ness that we each must weather the storm alone. I have tried. I have reached the point when I could stand no longer to the hurricane of forces striking left and right. I have retreated into dreams and let the world do what it will. You may have done the same.

That is when it starts. You open your eyes from the refuge of the fantasy to find a world more fantastic yet. The dream stays on, but the waters have subsided, the wind has blown over, around, through, carrying off the tattered remnants of your fears. Your mind is clear and calm, and then begins, almost imperceptible at first, the ever-growing chain of synchronicity. With no expenditure of effort, indeed because of it, the same great ocean that so late you thought to be your doom, brings all your needs gently to your shore.

It scared me at first, this hallucination of a madman. But I learned to take it with the rest. After all, it has led me here, and that is not so bad. And it led me to Paros. Like some occult pole of the earth, it drew me to the rocks and sand of Paros. When at first I felt the pull, I thought it was to Paris that it drew me, the thought and hope of the new age. But not content to leave me at the Sorbonne, it drew me further, to a deeper source, to an ancient wisdom, more subtle and abiding.

If you have seen the islands of the Aegean, you will know what I mean. Their parched countenance stands as a sacrifice endured for the privilege of serving as the center of an enormous force. The blistering sun daily pours its life into the vortex of some mysterious power that spreads unseen but not unfelt throughout the world.

The Communards of Paris, for all their noble intentions, were out of step. Their bright and promising venture was but an eddy of isolated time. But Paros is at the mainspring of the great terrestrial clock. That is why it should not have been too surprising to see Suzanne and Annabelle on the back of a trailer of hay on the main street of Paros.

GENESIS VII

We had known they had been in the Aegean. A month before in Rome we had received word that they were there somewhere, but we assumed they would be gone by the time we arrived. Anyway, with scores of Greek islands, what were the chances?

"Do you think we'll run into Fuck-Stick and Annabelle?"

"No way, man. With all those islands?"

"Wouldn't that be too much? What a bummer!"

For all the positive things that can be said about islands, there are still a few drawbacks that are often overlooked. There is still an illusion of being untouched by the rest of the world, a false sense of security. In the fervor of the revolution, the Paris Communards forgot about the Sea of France which came rushing back in upon them, trapping them like drowning rats.

We thought our islands would erase past and future with one clank of the gangplank, but like all islands, its link with the present, though tenuous, was nonetheless real. So, we were surprised indeed when Suzanne and Annabelle's faces exploded like V-2 rockets in the evening sky over Paros.

Not that we weren't glad to see them. Just very shocked. We had talked about the possibility so many times, that now the reality had the effect of déjà vu seen in advance. And Suzanne's other appellation, though edged with hostility born of sexual frustration in the high Alps, carried a great deal of affection.

She had traveled with us several weeks from Amsterdam to Switzerland. I courted her briefly but put her off and was put off by her coquetry, while J.C. just sat back and was his usual affable self. She dug his act, and they had a brief but humorously passionate thing down the Rhine in the back of the bus. I pouted. She decided to stay with us and work in Switzerland. I detected and detested the way she insinuated herself into our plans, but said nothing to J.C. Their relationship quickly cooled, and J.C. saw it too. Paul was just lustful, as usual, and didn't mind being direct with Suzanne or being rebuffed. She teased him in return.

All four of us came to be stuck 2000 meters up in the Alps, in Chandolin, a beautiful old village of 102 people with a magnificent, if cockeyed view of the Matterhorn. We worked our asses off during the day, at least at first, skied a little, came home at night and got drunk as was possible on the Swiss beer. There were no English-speaking people in the village—that we knew—so the four of us sat in our one room with four beds, a table, a couple of chairs, an old cabinet and one 40watt light bulb. There was a stove and sink, but no hot water, and a closet with a commode with no seat. The accommodations were alright by us, but they brought out the latent tendencies to be slobs, at least on the part of the guys.

Suzanne is Canadian and speaks French as well as her English, so she quickly charmed some of the local inhabitants, who asked her over for dinner. She would come back at night shocked by some of the propositions she was getting from a few local men to a room full of three drunk repressed men, who would get their substitute gratification by being as verbally vile as they could possibly be.

So it went for some four weeks, until the three guys moved to roomier quarters and left Suzanne in the basement room. That wasn't enough distance for me, so I came back to the States to collect some money and work at a more lucrative position for three months. Paul left later, but Ed, who we had met before in Germany, came to work, and Annabelle came to live with Suzanne. Things were more even then, but no better, and when the girls left in March, Ed and J.C. were still sexually frustrated, a bit embarrassed, and awfully glad to see the girls go. Never to be seen again.

I returned to Switzerland in May, and J.C., Ed, and I headed South, away from the harsh winter in the Alps and the even harsher celibacy and its sordid memories—toward Greece, to sunshine and cheap drink, to endless water and beaches, to lovely naked bodies, tanned all around.

It wasn't Suzanne and Annabelle as much as a repeat of Switzerland, that we wanted to avoid. So our emotions were very mixed when we saw them skiing down the streets of Paros on a mound of hay.

NEW DIRECTIONS

We didn't know whether to yell at them or not. They hadn't seen us, and were headed on down the street, two playful victory goddesses on their triumphal march, riding high on the spoils of harvest. Perhaps they were working at a ski resort on the other side of the island. We didn't want that. Perhaps they had found a good beach, having come to Paros to get away from Switzerland. That was alright.

The pause.

The decision.

"Hey, Suzanne! Annabelle!"

They looked around and blinked the snow from their eyes, as we got up and moved toward the trailer. I suppose some of the same things went through their heads that went through ours.

We gave a brief explanation to Richard. He sat and nodded his head in the evening breeze.

The girls were down from their mountain now. Big smiles on their faces. Hugging. Kissing. That's what Paros can do for you.

"I didn't think you'd make it back from the States," said Suzanne.

"I know I'm moody and impulsive, but there are better things than working in North Carolina in the summer," I said. "It's good to see you." I was sincere. Things are different in Paros than in the Alps.

28

"We've got a house down on a little cove about a mile from here."

"Are there many people?"

"No, and there's a well in front of the house. We've been here six weeks."

"Nice, aye?"

"Yes, but we' re leaving tomorrow."

"Really? We just got here."

"Well, our plane reservations have been made, so we have to leave. We're going back to Canada."

"We've got to get our tickets for the Elli now, but we'll be back in a little while. We'll tell you how to get to our place."

She introduced me to Annabelle. They were such a contrast. Suzanne was dark and full and stocky. Annabelle was blonde and boyish looking.

The directions were a bit vague, but we decided we could make it if we hurried before dark.

We said goodbye to the girls, left Richard with his bike nodding into the sunset, and headed out to our final destination of the last few months, which was by now deep into the warm breeze of evening.

RUSSIAN TO THE BEACH WITH A CLOSED DOOR

We gave Richard the straight poop about the pavement. At the first chance it got, the road took a left and disappeared out of sight. The pavement did too. The road quickly emerged again as we rounded the corner, but the pavement, being as faulty as most of the others in that part of the world, refused to resurface. It soon became clear to us that it was going to make adamant its position underground. It even did the same thing at the other end of the island we were eventually to find out. I suppose it was one of those tourist roads that you see here and there on the Europa maps. I guess most of the tourists don't leave the main village. We are not tourists. We are freaks. We are hippies. Hippies, donkeys, and regular people don't need pavement. Still, it seemed like a waste of good dirt to cover up all that pavement.

We were headed counterclockwise around the island. To the left of us a small mountain or a large hill rose into the nightening sky of Paros. It was a comfort to have the small mountain there, trying, to tower above us. We knew that if the Russians tried to get funny and melted the polar caps with nuclear weapons, the oceans would rise 75 feet. If that happened, we would all be able to run up the side of the small mountain and be saved. The small mountain was about 600 feet tall. We figured the Russians could melt the polar cap seven times and we would still be safe. Of course, it would be pretty crowded up on the top by then.

To the right of us the coastline webbed out in graceful curves from one rocky promontory to the next. The clean beach, pale-white and still, smiled at us with a serenity that comes with the knowledge of having the best of two worlds. At that time, we did not think of what might happen if the Russians lowered the oceans by 75 feet. That thought would have been too ghastly. In that event, we would have had a very long walk to the beach for our morning swim.

After almost a mile we saw the millionaire's house. It had a serpentine drive that meandered lithely across the full expanse of the meticulously sculptured front yard. It covered the 150 feet from the road to the house in 500 yards. When they finished the road around the island, there was a bit left over, so the local officials decided to auction it off to help defray the costs to the local people. Of course, the millionaire was the only one who could afford to buy it. And he was also the only one shrewd enough to realize the day would come when there would be a shortage of roads, and he would be able to sell it back to the town folks at ten times what he had in it.

Shortly after the millionaire's house we came to the place where we were supposed to park the car. We would have driven further but the road that led off down to the beach had only been widened enough to allow donkey traffic. We could have kept going straight, but that would have led us right on around the island, and we would still have to make a decision sometime about where to stop.

We pulled over to the side of the road leaving enough room for two donkeys to get by and unloaded whatever provisions we thought we would need for the night. We did not need much, other than the wine, and since we had forgotten it, all we carried were our sleeping bags and toothbrushes.

The path to the beach ran down between two stone walls which divided one field from another. We could see that the fields were different because the wheat on the right-hand side of the path had not been cut yet, whereas that on the left-hand side was already partially baled. The path itself was quite rocky and in the waning light it was not difficult to stumble about and stump your toes a few times.

We were not sure exactly where the house of Suzanne and Annabelle was located, so we decided to try the first one we came to. We were greeted by a dog that thought he was ferocious and shortly thereafter by a nice friendly Greek woman who did not speak English but who understood what we meant by "girls" in sign language. She motioned us on down in the direction of the beach.

From there the path turned into a small jungle. Under cover of twilight the denizens of darkness quickly scurried back and forth across the overgrown trail in front of us. With added quickness and measured agility, I stepped high to avoid the venomous serpents slashing at my ankles.

After what seemed like hours, we were able to gain the safety of the open as the path took a jog into a mowed field. The vicious reptiles kept to the safety of the thick brush, and I cursed myself once more for having failed to get any antivenom vaccinations before leaving the States. I still had plenty of room on my Immunization Certificate.

A hundred yards to the far side of the field stood a few palm trees clumped together behind another stone wall. Almost absent-mindedly they fanned the languid evening at the near end of the cove. They were the only things that held up the weight of the sky at our end of the cove. Without those palm trees, we would have been forced to crawl in under the humid blanket of summer dusk to reach the beach.

Palm trees meant water. We knew that. We had seen a lot of late movies with palm trees in them. And where there were palm trees there was always water. Unless the palm trees were part of a mirage. They could not be part of a mirage, or we would have been crawling. The only mirage I had seen that day had been Suzanne and Annabelle skiing down the streets of Paros. The palm trees were real, alright. I knew that much. And where there were palm trees and then water, there was the house of Suzanne and Annabelle. Sure enough, right across the wall from the clump of palm trees and up a short walkway sat the house of Suzanne and Annabelle, staring out over what looked like a scimitar sand beach. Its back was to us as we crossed the field to meet it, so we did not get quite the greeting we had anticipated. But then it did not know we were coming, or I am sure it would have greeted us with open doors.

SITTING ON THE BEACH, OR WINE NOT?

There was absolutely no trouble finding the beach from the front of the house of Suzanne and Annabelle. It was so close to the house that you tripped on it coming out the front door, even in the dark. We found out later that we were not the only ones tripping on the beach that night.

It was right at that time of evening that you finally quit trying to make believe that it is still day and admit that it is night when we sat down upon the sand of Paros for the first time. It was really not much different sitting down there than it was sitting down on a lot of other beaches in the Mediterranean or in the world for that matter, but you would never have convinced us of that. We had reservations for this beach from the beginning. We didn't need them. The stars were playing to an empty house our first night on the beach in Paros.

We decided to stop at the near end of the beach that first night, despite the fact that there were three or four hundred yards of it to choose from. After all, this was not Iwo Jima, and we were not trying to occupy the whole beach. We were not there to take the island by force. We were going to take it by charm. That would take more time, but it was a lot more fun.

We sat there on the sand and waited for Suzanne and Annabelle and didn't drink wine. But we talked about drinking it. We could have talked about a lot of other things like the view, or, wow, we finally made it, or even about the weather, which was as hot as two ticks on a Bunsen burner, but we talked about the wine we didn't have, instead.

"Why didn't you think to get some wine?" someone asked.

"I thought maybe there was a bar down at the beach," came a lame excuse.

"This isn't Daytona Beach, you know."

"Well, I figured the girls would have some in their house."

"Shit, why didn't somebody think about the wine?"

"Why didn't YOU get some wine? You're the one that drinks it all the time."

"Boy, a little wine would really do fine right now."

Nobody really wanted it bad enough to truck all the way back into the village right then, so there were three or four replays of the same conversation until it just got unbearable. You know, the old contest of wills.

"Alright, I'll go get the goddamn wine, you guys are so fucking lazy!" J.C. wasn't actually pissed off. He just couldn't hold out any longer. But it didn't matter. He was saved the trouble by the return of the sea nymphs.

Suzanne and Annabelle did not have any wine with them, but their laughing bodies poured sun-ripened and naked from their bottles into the half-light world of Parosian beaches and our minds. At last free of their confinement, their fluid forms quickly flowed across the sand and mingled with the sea. For a moment I thought my mind had left and sublet its garret to Salvador Dali who was now furiously at work on the back of my skull, but I had heard of stranger things happening on Greek islands.

They did not stay in the water long. They invited us in, but we declined, having our thoughts on wine and other things. So, they came out to help us on our first night on the beach of Paros. In the cool glow of the waxing moon, their porcelain skin glistened towards us in a slow dance of deep lavender.

"You should go in. The water is so cool. I'm really going to miss this sleeping on the beach whenever I want to, having the house right at the water, taking a dip any time I feel the least bit hot and sweaty. I really don't know why I'm leaving so soon. It's so amazingly relaxing and peaceful here, I've mellowed out so, after Switzerland. You can cut down your wants and needs to the minimum here. It's really so amazing. It's Nirvana!" said Suzanne.

"Yeah. Do you have any wine? That would really be amazing."

"No, but Robert should be here in a few minutes. He will have some. Robert's our neighbor. He has a hut a couple of hundred yards back past ours. He's from Vancouver. A really nice guy," she said.

ROBERT JUGS MAKES IT IN TIME

As I said earlier, things are pretty well synchronized on Paros. Either Robert knew a lot about Greek islands too, or he had been hiding right behind us all that time waiting for the proper cue. All that time while we were talking about wine, sitting right back there with two tremendous jugs that he couldn't possibly have drunken by himself in three days of hiding. In any event, we were really glad to see Robert. We would have been glad to see him without the wine, since he was supposed to be on a Greek island just like we were, but the wine jugs made it that much easier to be glad to see him. It's like the difference between running into an old friend with some wine and running into an old friend.

Robert was hip to Greek islands, it was easy to see, even in the cool half-light of timely introductions. It was not just the well-rehearsed entry, or the excellent supporting casks of wine, that tipped us off. It was the ever-widening grin that gave him away. At first, I thought he was a reflection of the waxing moon in the water of the cove of Paros. But Robert's smile was too bright for that. In fact, it had a bit of an edge on the moon. In the next two weeks or so we found out that the moon became quite full and then became quite empty again. But in all that time as the earth rolled on under the clear sky of Paros, Robert's smile just got bigger and bigger. His smile was no more affected by the tide than was the great green pointy-headed lizard's appetite for fresh ships. From that night on, we left our flashlight in Gertie and carried Robert's smile with us everywhere we went.

There was a reason that Robert carried two jugs of wine. It was not because Robert was a lush, and it was not because Robert was lazy and wanted to cut his trips to the wine man in half. Robert carried two jugs of wine because he had retsina in one jug, and he knew that I was not broken into it yet. So he had some red wine in the other jug. I was appreciative, but before I got a chance to be so, I got a chance to drink some more retsina. Some stronger retsina. It was some homemade retsina from Demetri's own home. It was so much stronger that you didn't get a chance to mind it.

A NEW RELATIVITY EXPANDED IN SEVEN PLANES OF BEING

I once had some friends who took a lot of LSD. I don't mean simply that they took it a lot of times. They took it a lot at a time. They were quite scientific about it. They spent hours formulating their theories of the chemical, perceptual, phenomenological, cosmological, etc., ramifications of dropping those little tablets down their radioactive gullets. The theory was very straightforward. If you took just a moderate amount of LSD, your mind would still be cognizant of the earthly plane around it, and in attempting to find the elusive reference point hidden in there somewhere, like the "Find the Hidden Face in the Picture" puzzle, would very often freak out to a greater or lesser extent. If you knew what you were doing, however, you would take enough of the drug so that you had no earthly idea whatsoever who, where, or what you were. Then you were safe. If you freaked out then, you wouldn't know it. So, my friends would drop two or three thousand micrograms of acid and survive intact, when a smaller amount would have no doubt done them in.

I remembered their words of wisdom as I swallowed an extra-large mouthful of Demetri's All-Purpose Anesthetic and Astringent. It did not bother me too much then, but I was afraid it would later, so I switched to the guest's jug. It tasted worse than the retsina.

A FEW TRIPS TO THE BEACH, A FEW DRINKS RETSINA

There are no clocks on the beach at Paros, so I am not sure how long we sat and talked and drank Robert's wine. The only reliable time piece was the jug of retsina, the red wine being slow. So I know that it was about five liters past sunset, because Robert had a ten-liter jug, and it was half empty when the Hobbits flowed in from the other end of the scimitar sand beach. Some people would say I was a pessimist for indicating that the jug was half empty instead of half full. I know all about psychological testing, and I don't care a thing about such things. People like that just show their ignorance about drinking wine. Every wine drinker knows that you start at the top of a bottle and work your way down. The only time the bottle is half full is when you go to fill it up again.

We were beginning the sixth liter past sunset when the Bush People came and stared at us with dilated pupils. I called them Hobbits before because they introduced themselves as Bilbo and

Frodo. They had been looking for a way out of the Misty Mountains when Bilbo was attacked by a monster of unusual ferocity and cunning. Bilbo fought valiantly, but before he was able to vanquish the demon, it stung him on the big toe.

So he and Frodo had traversed the full length of the beach in search of aid. Somehow Bilbo had taken the fantastic notion that the monster was not a monster at all but was an ordinary scorpion. That was a source of great concern for him. He had seen a late movie one time in which Richard Burton was walking across the sand dunes of some great desert when he was attacked by a lethal scorpion and died. Bilbo was worried that it might be the same scorpion, or a close cousin, at any rate. We had to admit that it was a possibility, but we pointed out that he was not Richard Burton, nor likely anything but the most distant cousin, so he had nothing to worry about.

We let J.C. handle the situation, since he was skilled in such things.

"I was a corpsman in the Navy, and I never saw any one die from a scorpion sting, not in the hospital in Naples, not onboard ship, and not even on the late show. I think you'll live," he said.

"You really think so?" asked Bilbo. His wide-eyed look told us he needed reassuring. It also told us about the monster under the Misty Mountains.

"Sure," said J.C.

We finally convinced him that the worst that could happen would be that he would have to walk with a cane the rest of his life, and that the best thing for him to do was to sit down and drink some retsina, for the medicinal effect if nothing else. Frodo and Bilbo decided they could find their way out of the Misty Mountains later and sat down to help us move the clock to seven liters past sunset.

It was then that we realized that they had been fooling us all along, and that they were really Bush People instead of Hobbits. We had been looking at Bilbo and his scorpion sting limping up the strand of Paros and had failed to perceive Frodo's true nature. Against the deep china blue of the Parosian backdrop, we readily could see that Frodo was really a bush on stilts. He had come to Paros to visit a distant relative, who was presently the only bush and the only source of shade on that particular cove of Paros. He had brought the stilts in case he ran into any scorpions.

The Bush People had been staying with their bush almost a week, so they were getting to know Greek islands fairly well. They knew the whole beach on our cove, and the road backwards into town, and the village, a few cafés at a time. They also knew the Rock People.

The Rock People lived in a tent in the rocks down past the bush. We could barely see their tent holding up the other end of the half-light sky of Paros. We were glad they were there though. They helped anchor down the strand and kept one end from floating too far out to sea.

GENESIS VIII

The Rock People were very nice to the Bush People. They could see that the Bush People were sometimes Hobbits, so they gave them a couple of tickets to Middle Earth. The tickets looked like candy, which indeed they were. Magic candy with chewy centers of fairy tales. We asked them if they had any more of that candy, but the Bush People said they didn't, so we drank varsol instead.

SOME WEIRD CONFESSIONS OF A CUNNING LINGUIST

It was getting on towards six and a half liters past sunset, when Annabelle decided to switch channels and go into the house. I knew what she was doing. She was going to bed. Generally, I am not very impulsive. I think things out before I do them. I usually don't get around to ordering in a restaurant until everyone else is paying their bill.

But tonight was different. It was my first night on Paros, and it had been a long time, as I asked if I might follow Annabelle into the house. I was conscious of an overwhelming desire to bury my face in her crotch.

GENESIS IX

AN ISLAND BY ITSELF IS ONE THING

An island by itself is one thing. A second island within reach is another. And then a situation can develop which is yet another. Islands can only be fully appreciated and understood in their relationships to each other.

Every island is pretty much a self-contained entity. But it is not without a basic yearning to go one step further, if it can. Why not be two islands if the opportunity presents itself? So, each and every island exudes that ineffable medium of mystique that carries out the searching pulse and draws the wanted back unto its shores. The gifts of love may come in bottles or in ships, in the form of some discarded object or a washed-out piece of wood, and more often in more subtle wrapping of which we are completely unaware.

But come they do. Islands do touch. They are in more intimate contact than you could ever quite believe. And they are far better for it. Yet islands know too much to sacrifice their island-ness in the flush of the moment. They could not touch were they to lose their island-ness. And islands exist for the chance to see their island-ness unfold in others.

Of course, not all islands are so lucky. There are a few alone that long, way across the seas. That is why St. Helena could accept a gift of Napoleon without hint of insult. And why hopefully, he did the same. They were in need of each other. Islands thrive on insulation, but not isolation.

I felt I had been adrift at sea a long, long time as I followed the tide into the harbor of the house of Suzanne and Annabelle. I only hoped I would find a waiting berth.

GENESIS X

THE FIRST RAPE OF ANNABELLE

It was not the first time in recent months that Annabelle had been the victim of the vile intentions of a rapist. It was the second. Ed was the previous culprit. You can get pretty desperate sometimes, stuck up there in the mountains. After a while anything that's not a rock starts looking pretty good. Not that Annabelle looked anything like one grade above a rock. She was pleasant enough as I remember. Ed had just seen every rock on the mountain at least three times. What was hard for Ed to grasp was that the two things that don't look a thing alike can have the same temperature.

Ed was nice enough at first. The fact that it got him nowhere didn't bother Ed too much until Suzanne and Annabelle started talking about how horny they were. Insult to injury. So Ed decided, altruist that he is, that he would help Annabelle get over her shyness. If she couldn't find the courage to ask him to fuck her, he would offer to rape her. She wouldn't mind, once she got used to the idea. Men sure can go out of their way to be nice to women, sometimes.

Ed and J.C. were sitting around after work one evening drinking a bit of wine, when the talk took a turn to the randy side. Enough of the bull shit! They would nail the girls once and for all. So they bounded out into the snow and down to the basement room of Suzanne and Annabelle, their intentions hung around their necks like the heels of Achilles.

Ed and J.C. were polite about it. They announced the purpose of their visit like they were TV repairmen. "We've come to tune your sets. It'll only take a few minutes." The girls were not deceived. Despite the realistic time estimated for the task, they knew the guys were really plumbers, come to unclog their pipes.

"That's alright, we don't use much water. And we can always go outside."

"But the reception is not so good out there. Let us service the cablevision."

It was hard to get started if you couldn't agree on what to fix.

Finally, Ed and J.C. made their move. They started to chase Suzanne and Annabelle around the room, but the girls were quicker. It's hard to maneuver in those belts when you're drunk. But eventually the girls were cornered. There was only one thing they could do, so they did it. When the girls began to laugh, Ed and J.C. figured they must have the wrong apartment. They picked up their tools and left. It must have been comically unconvincing, the girls in need of highly skilled technicians when all they could get were a couple of plumbers friends.

THE SECOND RAPE OF ANNABELLE

I was the next one to attempt the rape of Annabelle. She was nicer to me than to Ed. She didn't laugh at me. She didn't have to.

I am not usually a rapist. In fact, I have never been one successfully. Annabelle was my last attempt. I must be getting old. I used to play a game with women. It was a cross between Dodge the Ball and Tag. You may have played it too. You wait until you are really carnal and decide you can't hold out for the "meaningful relationship" any longer. Then you chase after someone that is easy to catch, and tag them and say, "you're it." Then you play all sorts of other games until you get tired and want to go home, and you hit the girl with the ball before she has a chance to tag you back. If you think the girl is about to tag you, you better hit her with the ball and run really fast. After a while, you get tired of running and you let someone tag you. You think it's fun to be "it" and you start to tag her back. Then, BAM, you get the ball right in the face. It's not much fun when you don't dodge the ball.

Once in a while you may actually manage to dodge the ball, or you might get tagged back. Then it can be fun. You stop playing the game for little while. But usually, you're just running and tagging and trying to dodge between balling.

I never did get to tag Annabelle. I decided after her that I must be getting slow. Now I just stay still. When someone tags me, I just look at her and grin. I play the other games, but I don't try to tag them, and I don't try to hit them with the ball. I don't even try to dodge the ball. Sometimes this makes people mad. They say I don't play fair and then they hit me with the ball. Sometimes they will sit and talk before they run off to tag someone else. My new game is a lot less hassle. But I still get an itchy tagging finger every now and then. And it was really itchy as I followed Annabelle into the house on my first night on Paros.

FORE PLAY

The house of Suzanne and Annabelle had the damp cool of a cave or a wall or some other such place that does not know too much about the sun. I expected to find a bat here and there but the only thing I saw hanging from the ceiling were our shadows. Since it was burning retsina, the shadows wanted to put as much distance between themselves and the lantern as was possible before it blew us into euphoria. We tried to allay their fears and coax them back into the room, but they wouldn't come any closer that the walls and ceiling. There they were to stay until we put out the lantern.

There were three rooms in the house of Suzanne and Annabelle. The first room would have been a kitchen, if it had had all the things in it that make a room a kitchen. It had some food in it, but so do dining rooms and pantries and often times a lot of other rooms. I suspect Suzanne and Annabelle pretended that the first room was their kitchen.

The second room was the living room. It had a table dressed like a desk in it. In fact, there was a lot of transvestite furniture in that room. It was a good thing that it wasn't the rest room, or I wouldn't have known if I was in the Men's or the Women's. The shadows liked this room better. It gave them a better chance of surviving the catastrophe, if the lantern blew.

To the left were some French doors that opened on to a terrace overlooking the cove. Down below, the rest of the group was out there drinking down the clock and waiting to see if Bilbo was in the Sahara Desert or in Middle Earth. To the right was a plain old Greek door leading into the third room. Annabelle politely led the way in. I was afraid I had switched places with her shadow as I watched her silently enter the third room.

I knew what the third room was. It had a bed in it. The third room was a schizophrenic bedroom. Sometimes it thought it was for sleeping. Sometimes it thought it was for balling. I looked back and forth at Annabelle and myself from one room to the next. I had the uneasy feeling that she was in one room only. Most of this time Annabelle and I had been talking. It was a very difficult conversation with Annabelle in one world and me in the next.

THE RAPE

Annabelle blew out the lantern and lay down on the bed. Our shadows, seeing the danger was over, immediately came back and joined us in the room. I knew what it meant when a girl lay down on the bed. I also knew what it meant when she turned her face to the wall. It was becoming increasingly clear which room Annabelle was in, and it was not the same one as me.

I felt pretty strange standing there as I watched Annabelle sail away over the horizon. I wanted to become one of the pieces of furniture, but I didn't have on the right clothes. I also knew that I would feel pretty strange if I left the room. I decided to stay and see if we could meet in the hallway.

I lay down next to Annabelle on the bed and stared at her back in the dark. It was a pretty average back, not unlike a lot of others I had seen. And I knew from those backs that we would get nowhere that way. Raping a girl sure can be difficult. I knew what the next move was. I had seen it along with those other backs. I had also seen it about one hundred and thirty-seven times that night. On the one hundred and thirty-eighth time I reached out my arm and put it in her room. That was quite a stretch.

"I want to go to sleep," said Annabelle. "I'm really very tired. If you want to go to sleep, that's okay. But I've got to get some sleep." There was no doubt about which room she was in.

AFTERGLOW

I thought for a while about whether or not I would like to spend the night in her room since she obviously was not going to spend it in mine. I decided after a respectable period of time, that there was no way. I withdrew my arm from her room, stared at her back one last time, rose, and left both rooms.

At least Annabelle had not laughed at me. She just went to sleep.

SLEEP, SLEEP, SLEEP

I weaved my way back through the house of Suzanne and Annabelle and joined the others wherever they were. It was obvious by now that Bilbo was not in the Sahara, but he still had Middle Earth to contend with. I checked the clock and found it was eight liters past sunset. It had not taken me long to rape Annabelle. Ed helped console me, but not before passing on Annabelle's laugh to me.

Over the next liter we began to drift off one by one. Frodo and Bilbo headed back toward the Bush. They had a long trip ahead of them, if they expected to find their way out of the Misty Mountains by morning. By nine liters past sunset, we were all asleep under the darkened tent over Paros. We would have stayed up longer, but we wanted to be able to tell what time it was when we got up.

GENESIS XI

FROM ETERNITY TO RICE CRISPIES

I have absolutely no sense of time now. I could not tell you whether I have been sitting here for five minutes or five months. It can place you in somewhat of a dilemma at times, not knowing whether to make plans for yesterday or tomorrow.

Paros did this to me. My internal time piece was broiled by the constant sun of Paros. Sometimes I am not sure whether Paros is a memory or a prevision. Then sometimes I feel sure that I am still on it. I think that is it. Paros is really a part of my body and remains in as constant a relationship to me as my feet.

Of course, there are still ways of telling time, but they are not available to me now. There are not too many stores that carry retsina in North Carolina.

I recognized what Paros and its sun were doing to me from the first morning I awoke on the scimitar sand beach. I knew I must have been asleep a long time, for I got the feeling that I had been on the beach with those rocks since Saturn blew lunch into the Aegean many eons ago. Yet with all that time I knew I should have slept longer. But that was beyond my control.

The earth rolled on under the sun about two hours ahead of schedule that first morning. The small mountain was nice enough to rise above us like a large canopy for about an hour and a half, but then it reached its extensive limits and left us to the inevitable.

You do not need an artic sleeping bag in the morning sun of Paros. It can be a comfort at night, but it is of no more use than an electric sunlamp in the daytime. So the sun peeled back our sleeping bags at an early hour on our first morning on Paros and threw us into the cool, crisp bowl of the Aegean, like bananas on dry cereal. The life of the sea went snap, crackle, and pop in our ears. We had expected it to go thud, thud, and thud after consuming nine liters of retsina, but that was another secret delight found within the shores of the Greek islands. There is no hangover from the strange potion.

Swimming is a very easy thing to do on Paros. All you need is the energy to walk the ten feet from your bedroom to your front porch. And if you lack the immediate energy, the sun will do all it can to help you toward that goal. From your front porch all you have to do is fall over on your face and you are swimming between the toes of Paros.

ONE TOOTSIE ROLLS ON ACROSS THE AGES

The water that gives Paros its island-ness is like an inverted Tootsie Roll Pop. The outer most layer of the Aegean is the warm chewiness of a chocolate center and is gone in a minute. The undermost layer is the hard cold of varying degrees of color and flavor and seems to last for hours. You are a sucker if you think it is all one pleasant body of room temperature. I did, and I spent many a long moment gathering my teeth for a crack at the bottom. I am only glad that the Aegean is not built like most Tootsie Roll Pops.

After bathing at Suzanne and Annabelle's, it is no small matter to regain the sand of the beach. In just a few minutes, you must cover one billion years of evolution. But it was a bit easier for us the second time. We of the new age have the benefit of the special editions of Life magazines. Recalling the glossy foldouts of mass communicated Darwinism, we relinquished our fins and stood upright on two legs upon the beach of Paros.

From there on we were without the aid of a tried and trusted plan. We had naught but our own design to lead us to the remainder of our days on Paros. Or so we thought. We forgot that islands have been around a long time. We were nothing new to the unseen guides of Paros.

THE PARANOIA OF ONE NOT-VERY-WELL

The water of our Parosian cove went quite well with our solar canopy. They were as inseparable in our minds as the ice cool interior and the color TV of a Holiday Inn. Yet we were soon to realize they were just as incomplete. For all that water, water everywhere, one had still to drop a bucket in the nearby well to get a drink. And like the usual Holiday Inn, we had to leave our room on Paros in search of the ingredients of a cool glass of water.

Getting water from a well is not always as easy as you may think. First you must find a proper well, then you must find a proper bucket. Then, of course, you must transfer the water from the well to the bucket. It did not seem that it would be that much of an enterprise for me that first morning on Paros, since I had already mastered the secrets and techniques of one billion years of evolutionary rise from the water. Regaining it in part should be at least as rudimentary.

My first attempt was made on the well of Suzanne and Annabelle. I was met by their cascading images of hair and skin preparing for the bath. They carried with them an old metal bucket that had been beaten into submitting half its former volume to the air. At one end of the bucket was a long, frequently knotted rope, used to ensure that what went down, would come up. It didn't always work out that way.

It was then that I learned the secret of the well of Suzanne and Annabelle. Theirs was not the ordinary well of which you read so often in nursery rhymes and children's stories.

"This well is not for drinking purposes, magical or otherwise," said Suzanne. "This well is for external use only. It is a halfway well. It cannot really be called salt water, and it cannot really be called fresh water. It is in the midst of an identity crisis."

"I think I know what kind of well you mean," I said. "I had a friend that had an identity crisis one or more times. He could not tell if he was his father, or if he was his mother. I told him that he could not really be called his father, and he could not really be called his mother. He said that he was not very well. Perhaps this is a not-very-well."

"Yes," she replied, "I think this is quite possible. But it serves its purpose well enough."

I knew at this point that I had better look elsewhere for a drink of water. If I had stayed any longer, I would have been forced to give an in-depth psychoanalytic history of my friend, and that hardly seemed necessary. It was none of their business whether my friend was his father or his mother or anybody else he might have wanted to be. And besides, it would have been very rude to the not-very-well who was still within hearing distance. I did not want to contribute further to his paranoia. In any event, my friend had improved considerably since his crisis, and I saw no reason why the washing hole might not do so as well.

SALT LAKE CITY IS NOT FOREVER

During all this time my throat was feeling more and more like the inside of a slab of bacon in the middle of Utah, and I was getting no closer to my drink of water. I decided to try a new pitch.

"Is there a well around here that lives up to its name. I feel like I've eaten breakfast seventeen times or so already this morning, and I could sure use a drink of water." I said these things to Suzanne and Annabelle as they prepared to wash away the skin of Paros for their journey back to the continents. It must have seemed like an insignificant thing to say at such a time, but I was in no position to quote Sophocles with an encrusted throat.

"We get our drinking water from Robert's well. Robert's well is down next to the pump house in front of Robert's hut. You can't miss it. It's the only one that you are likely to stumble into," said Annabelle.

I was not sure of her choice of words, but I was glad for the assistance.

"Is there a bucket for that well?" I asked, knowing that to be the second most important item necessary in obtaining a drink of water.

"There should be one in Robert's hut," said Annabelle. "The water from Robert's well is really very good. Perhaps that is the secret to his smile. Anyway, the water here is not what you are after. Only the donkeys drink the water at this well, and I do not think you are a donkey."

I was glad to hear her say that. I knew then that she had developed no emotional scars from the rape the night before. With my heart so lightened, I was able at last to tear my parched throat away from the not-very-well of Suzanne and Annabelle and send it in the direction of Robert's well by way of Robert's bucket in Robert's hut.

Robert's well was deep. Robert's bucket was plastic. The rope on his bucket was very light. All those factors contributed to delayed gratification. When I threw the bucket into Robert's well, it floated on the top like a misplaced pleasure craft. As I jerked the rope back and forth, it bobbed up and down contentedly, displaying not the least bit of thirst.

Finally, after many desperate attempts, I managed to draw a partial bucket to my lips. The cool bejeweled liquid mingled with the waters of the cove, filling the morning and shattering the strain of the sun as it moved toward midheaven.

WATER WITHIN – WATER WITHOUT

In keeping with the new Aquarian Age, I bore the remaining contents of the cool bucket beachward, stopping at the not-very-well. Suzanne and Annabelle were busy squeezing clouds of foam from their heads. I enjoyed just standing there watching them conjure up fantasies of white on top of their browned over bodies.

"Would you like some perfectly well water to drink?" I asked them across the crippled wooden gate. There was a stone wall on either side of the gate to separate the not-very-well from the rest of the world. It was such an alienated well.

"I am afraid now is not the time to begin something new," said Suzanne. "I would only end up sudsing my esophagus. I will take care of my insides later. Right now, I'm busy with my outside. Would you like to help me with it?"

"I will do what I can," I said. "Would you like me to bucket?"

"That would be nice," she said.

I started to ask the gate to move over to let me pass, but I noticed it was a lot older than I had at first thought. Advanced paralysis had set in years ago, and now the gate was vying for the status of full immobility with the rest of the wall. Out of respect for the aged, I climbed the wall and bounced to the other side.

Like a flexible tongue depressor, I lowered the old metal bucket into the stony throat of the not-very-well and took a peek. Other than being a bit pale, everything looked alright to me. I raised the bucket hand over hand and poured it over the waiting form of Suzanne. Though she had bathed at the not-very-well many times before, she was still not ready for its surprise. Drawing her skin around her like a shrunken blanket, she recoiled from the icy cascade with a gasp of air directed toward some secret place deep inside.

Paros is like an efficiency kitchenette unit. It is a hot plate on top and a freezer underneath. But that is good for people who like to travel light.

I bucketed Suzanne a few more times and then Annabelle. Then I gave myself one just for the experience. Their bodily reflexes did not lie, I discovered, as I looked around for the inadequate little blanket of Suzanne and Annabelle. With inside and outside thus well wet together, I followed the drinking bucket back down to the beach.

A LONG WINTER'S NAP

There we all were at Near Beach. Robert was there with his smile. Ed was there with two of his appetites. J.C. was there with the clock, and the girls were there with all those things that take you from mass-land to islands and carry you back again. I was there with the emptying bucket.

At the Far Beach, better known as the Bush, the Hobbits were crawling out of Middle Earth into their bush for a long winter's nap. The tent of the Rock People remained a touch of blue upon the far edge of Paros.

Seeing that all was in order, and motivated by things known and unknown, we worked our way out of the slow caress of beachness. Through the jungle of serpents, up the path, to Gertie and beyond, we carried Suzanne and Annabelle out of one world into the open end-ness of the next.

ISLAND-PARTING IS NOT A PLEASANT THING

Island-parting is not a pleasant thing. To have glimpsed the possibilities of islands and then to return to constant land before those possibilities are fully explored is to encounter the harshest matters of adjustment and perhaps the most excruciating disappointment. The greatest loss the Communards of Paris had to face at the hands of the Reaction of 1871 was not the brutal physical reprisals unleashed upon them. The greatest loss was the destruction of the vision. Their most cherished hopes and dreams had become a working reality, only to be shortly smashed by a reality more severe.

Our dreams and plans today are perhaps more subtle or more disguised. Though offensive to some, we create new patterns clothed in harmless escapism, destined to transform a world. Yet we are susceptible to the surrounding forces of the landscape. We know the need for islands. Islands are for nurturing the embryonic. They are also the proper vehicle for the wisdom and maturity of age. Between these poles lies the danger. Between these forms lies the continent without reference, the confusion of many-sided chaos. It is fertile, and it must be transformed, but this will require preparation. So we still need our islands.

Not all the Paris Communards lost the vision as the reaction swept in upon them from the surrounding countryside. Nor do all of us lose the sense of island-ness upon returning to the mass of land.

But to those who do, it must be a fall from a clear and harmonious grace to the drab and vague world of random, meaningless forces.

Suzanne and Annabelle were the first ones of the group to chance the big step back to mass-land. I did not know that day what a big step that was. That was a world alien to me. I suppose they were ready for the trip, as they left the cove and the house and the palm trees holding up the near end of the sky. I hope things go well for them on their long journey back from island-ness.

PUZZLES LIKE AN OLD SHOE

There are as many parts to an island as there are pieces to a jigsaw puzzle, and they fit together just as nicely. Fortunately, the right piece of an island is usually a bit easier to find. We had no trouble with the help of our friends in finding the proper piece on which to eat breakfast.

The Breakfast Café was itself a puzzle composed of a small white cubicle, a covered porch, a patio sometimes with awnings, some tables constructed of metal, various chairs, a toilet that did not like to flush all at once, some Humphrey Bogart fans, the proprietor and family, and good, cheap breakfast. We got two eggs in the manner we preferred, five or six little sausages, bread, and a drink, all for under 40 cents. We also got with it a place to sit for a few hours. Living up to the promise of the chairs was no problem for us.

We became pieces of the Breakfast Café puzzle ourselves, during our stay on Paros. Every morning we were dumped out of the cardboard box of slumber into our interlocking positions among the chairs and tables of Parosian Cafés.

"What time does the Elli arrive?" The question buzzed around the table like a fly without a cause.

"About one thirty," beamed Robert from the underside of his wide-brimmed and straw hat. "One thirty on the way back to Piraeus, every other day, and four thirty on the way out on the other days. It's the high point of the day, watching the Elli come in. It is our only contact with mass-land. For what that's worth." Robert was fitting in well with the rest of the parts of Paros.

We sat and watched the un-traffic moving up and down the quay across from the café. No one tried to look busy in their comings and goings. For one thing, it was Sunday, a very un-busy day. For another thing, everyone knew that everyone else knew there was nothing to be in a hurry about on Paros. Except for Suzanne and Annabelle. They were doing all those last-minute goodbyes and things that remove the future to a far corner of the mind.

A few small boats floated in and out of port in a dream. They did not hurry either. There is an economy for time on Paros. It took but a few boats to cover the hours from breakfast to the arrival of the Elli. But the Elli, though it touches Paros, is of another time zone. It came racing into the harbor like a north wind, its mind two stops ahead. It is strange the way opposites attract each other.

Unwillingly, the Elli slowed so as not to beat her whistle to the shore. She dropped her anchor like an old shoe into the clear water of the bay and swung her backside gracefully into the dock.

A SECRET UNTIL THE NEXT TIME

I do not have much use for goodbyes. I mean, wishing someone well is one thing, but the last-minute clutching, feelings of things left unsaid and unanswered, the lingering, all come on like a bad movie. It is all too euphemistic. It reeks of the unspoken fear, the unspoken possibility, DEATH. I have no use for death now. It is the big illusion. Of all the things that Paros has helped to teach me, this is perhaps the greatest. There is no finality in death. If the Communards of Paris had known this, they would not have sought to build their island with such desperate haste or so far from the immortality of water.

If nothing else, I would like to pass this message on from Paros. There is no death. Remember that in the darkness of night. The islands know this occult truth. Whether in the light of air or under the surface of the deep, the stuff of islands does not pass. Form forever changes, but substance is always. An is-land as land forever is. It is this knowledge that causes islands to shun goodbyes. An island halfway around the world is as much as one just over the horizon. In the consciousness of island-ness, distance does not diminish being, nor communion. We have much to learn from islands.

I do not remember much about the departure of Suzanne and Annabelle from Paros. They got aboard the Elli and sped away out of my field of vision toward mass-land, until the next time I see them.

GENESIS XIV

A CENTER

There is a center for everything. We may not always know where it is, but it is out there or in here as the case may be, waiting for us to stumble onto it and give it a cheerful greeting. There are centers of the solar system, there are centers of the earth, there are centers of the human body, there are centers of M&Ms. Do not confuse the centers with the middle. Centers are not necessarily the physical middle. And there may be more than one center to a thing. A town may have a shopping center and a recreation center, an art center and a record center, an industrial center and a central business district. It may even have many of each.

Paros is no different. Except for the more psychic nature of her centers, in keeping with the new age. And the older age. Nor are the centers of Paros very complex or hard to find. We had no trouble at all locating the very, very center of Paros.

Where the world docks at the port of Paros is a broad wharf running back to is-land. It is a bridge between many things. Where the wharf joins the land is a windmill, one of the two main ones in my Parosian awareness, the other one being near the souvlaki shop and other places. From the windmill three paved and tourist streets run out into the island which is Paros. One runs south and west toward our lives on the scimitar sand beach. One heads north and east into the days ahead. One jumps directly forward and to the right a little into the main village of Paros.

On the right, between the village road and our beach road, is a small café with a covered terrace and awnings. The very same café of the man with the shining teeth. It is one of the carefully guarded secrets of the ages, of the occult wisdom of the ancients. The Axis Mundi. It is known esoterically as the Windmill Café. Its exoteric name is lost in the indecipherability of Greek letters.

Past the discerning gaze of the Windmill Café flow all things offered up by mass-land and all sibling islands. By it go those things bound outward once again. It was here that we chose to sit and watch the daily play of terrestrial lovemaking. From our seats on the terrace, we greeted the newly arrived outpourings of life. Of course, we had not planned on starting the Paros Welcoming Committee when we first sat down at the Windmill Café. It just happened to be the closest place to buy a drink of retsina.

THE NECESSITY FOR AN ART OF A NECESSITY

J.C. and Robert started on the retsina. I don't know what Ed was drinking. I was still stuck on beer. It went this way for a long time, as people passed by and travelled in and out of the arched portals of the Windmill Café. We sat and drank and talked. I would probably still be sitting there, if I had not been forced to look for a place to take a dump.

It is the nature of things that for every action there is a reaction. Isaac Newton said that. So did a lot of other people, in different ways. What goes up, must come down. What goes in, must come out. It is no different with food. Most restaurant owners are aware of this. It is a most unnatural and sadistic person indeed that does not have a toilet in the vicinity of his eating establishment.

Many people take dumping for granted. Many more cringe at the thought of what goes on behind the closed doors of a rest room. They pretend they are someone else whenever they are forced to relieve themselves. And relief it is for them, for when they don't have to think about it again until the next time. No wonder there is so much schizophrenia around with so many people being forced daily to wipe this experience from their minds.

People on the road cannot take dumping for granted. There is not always a toilet in the next room for your discrete and speedy use. One must look ahead for the proper facility. Most often this is in the form of a return to nature.

We have made an art of dumping. This involves an intricate set of steps and techniques. The site is very important. Of course, it must be secluded if possible. We are not exhibitionists. The lay of the land is next to be considered. It is best to find a depression or a position that inclines the rear. This avoids unnecessary wear and tear on the feet or shoes. If you are in an inhabited area, it is good to look for a sandy place for burial. If not, it is best to leave the dump to aeration and sunlight.

One learns early to dispense with the tree limb or improvised seat. This is one of the greater secrets to be learned from European travel. All Europe is divided into three parts. There is the part that is made up of commodes that are like the U.S. in configuration. Then there is the part that is made up of commodes that have an elevated platform onto which one dumps prior to flushing the turd out the front. That is the minor division. Then there is the major division which forms the European equivalent of the Mason-Dixon line. South of this line the incidence of commodes decreases and that of squatters increases.

A squatter is a hole in the floor with two places for your feet, in case you did not know. It is best to avoid the pain and despair of some people I have met, and not attempt a squatter while standing. That is not how it got its name.

Once you have mastered a squatter, you can go anywhere. It is a real triumph of mind over matter, when you rid yourself of the commode hang-up. It is natural and easy. After all, if God had meant for us to dump while sitting, he would have put a commode behind every bush—well, except maybe for the burning type.

The Windmill Café proved itself to be truly representative of Paros as the meeting place of the worlds. The toilet of the Windmill Café had the best of both. On the left was a commode and on the right was a squatter. The squatter was out of order. The commode should have been. On the floor was a small waste basket full of toilet paper. It was already folded. It was already used. I was glad I had brought my own. I didn't really feel up to scrounging through the waste basket for the best pieces.

This proved to be a common custom of Paros. The pipes are small and the water pressure low, hence the paper tends to clog up the pipes. The solution is perfectly rational and sanitary as they dispose of the paper. But it takes some cultural adjustment and a few unsuccessful attempts to flush the paper, to get used to.

I fidgeted around some then quickly stepped back outside and looked up and down the street. Back inside, then back outside again. Urgency gave way to frenzy. Finally, Newton's law won out through gastro-intestinal inertia into the fetid pit of the Windmill Café's commode.

After that we solved the dilemma for the most part at the beach. Climbing to the rock above the cove, we left our dump to the purifying broil of the sun. From there it was but a short jump into the largest bidet of the Mediterranean.

THE THOUSAND YEAR TABOO CAFÉ

We did not welcome anyone on our first day at the new post. The Elli had already come and gone. We did manage to practice the preliminaries a few times, running the Café out of cold retsina. Warm retsina is insufferable unless you've just finished several bottles of the cold stuff.

There was another café across from the Windfall Café. It looked nice enough.

"Maybe they have some cold retsina over there," Ed said. "We could go over there and drink."

A thousand years of taboos pulled the reins at the corners of Robert's smile, as he turned to look at the blasphemous countenance of Ed. "We don't go over there. The Windmill is the only true Café at the center of the world. There are some things one doesn't do even on Paros," Robert said.

"Why is that?" Ed asked in disbelief.

"I have been here six weeks or six months, I don't remember which, and I have never been in that café. I have never known anyone who went into that café. I am not about to go over there now. You will understand. That is a different Paros. It has nothing to do with you and me," Robert frowned. "I don't mind warm retsina," he then said with a smile.

It was a good thing we had Robert along or we might have made a big mistake. We learned what he meant about the other café, though. It was an island unto itself. It was not offensive or curious. It just belonged to another world. I never got any desire to go to that other café the whole time I was on Paros.

I am sorry I mentioned it. It does not belong in this book. Someone else will have to write about the other café at the windmill at the center of the world.

ONE HALF HOUR PAST EUPHORIA

After Robert and J.C. got pretty well smashed, we decided to take ourselves to the beach to welcome in the evening. With retsina to go, we worked our way back to the Near Beach, making a few food stops along the way. By the time we got back, the time was well into euphoria. Waving to the Mid-Beach People, whom we had failed to see the night before, we slid in between the closing sun and the still Aegean and waited for the cooling glow of nightfall.

GENESIS XV

AN ANNIVERSARY

As I sit here somewhere between my thoughts and my aspirations, I realize that today is the 17th of June. One year ago today, the great green pointy-head of Parosian possibilities first raised itself and gazed into our consciousness, as we floated hopefully on the still and steaming Aegean. I try not to indulge in sentimentalities. Today is an exception. I hope you will understand.

One year minus two days ago today, we walked into town for our second helping of the Breakfast Café. The Breakfast Café is but one of many cafés along the waterfront of the village. The gleaming smile of quay and beach that stretches between the two windmills is studded with the white stucco and blue awnings of lazy cafés. This is the palate of Paros. After disembarking from a hungering trip aboard the Elli, one need only turn right to begin a delightful Odyssey through a fine exhibition of Greek culinary art. If you have the will to make it past the first one or two.

At the Windmill Café there is the usual course of rice pudding, ice cream, and Greek salads. A little further up the street is the confectioner's shop, full of Baklava and all other manner of sweets that dissolve your teeth on the spot and draw your mouth and tongue down into the all too quickly remorseful pit of your stomach. Around the curve to the left the restaurants and cafés begin in earnest, lining the promenade like pin-ball machines at a beach pavilion.

Bing! Roast chicken on an open spit. Clang! Eggs and sausage. Ting! Yogurt with honey. Ding! Ding! Ding! All sorts of stuffed eggplant, green peppers, stuffed grape leaves, fried fish, mutton, rice dishes, vegetables inside vegetables, fruit inside fruit, ice cream. Buzzzzzz. Replay. Through about a dozen games the points add up. Tilt! Souvlaki and roast lamb's head. At least it's at the end of the line.

It is impossible to be deaf, dumb, and blind to the alimentary aspects of Parosian island-ness. That is why we spent a good portion of each day camouflaged among the chairs and tables of the waterfront. But man does not live by rice pudding and retsina alone, and the waterfront, though the most visible, is by no means the only realm of activity in the village.

To the left of the Windmill Café, an asphalt road runs a few hundred meters back to the right toward the center of the village. There are a few more cafés along the way, but then the personality of the village takes a turn toward the distant past that lies hidden within its labyrinth of narrow slated streets. The paved world of the twentieth century abruptly ends at the ticket office for the Elli.

It could be said that the people that laid out the original village of Paros lacked sufficient vision in allowing for the progress of civilization and the eventual and inevitable advent of the automobile. They thereby cut off their progeny from the possibilities of two car garages and the like. I would not be so harsh on them. In fact, I suspect that they had well anticipated such developments and purposely made their streets inaccessible to such abominations. I applaud their efforts.

In truth, the village is ahead of the twentieth century. When you step from the end of the road at the ticket office, you are in one big house which is the village of Paros. It is a lesson in comprehensive community design. The gray slate of the passage-ways winds over, under, around, and through the whitewashed houses and shops. Tall and narrow arcades cool the breath of even the midday sun and contribute a pristine sparkle to the timeless architecture. It is easy to understand the hospitality of the Greek people. When you enter their village, you have come into their living room, you are their personal guests.

On these back streets is the true life of the village, as opposed to the leisure which is the way of the cafés and restaurants. Here one finds the shops that have not changed for centuries. Of course, there are a couple of shops catering to the whims of tourism, but here also are the fish market, the bakery, the produce shop, the cobbler. It was to this last fine artisan that we made our way after our breakfast along the quay.

A WONDER OF THE WORLD AT OUR FEET

The Greeks have been making sandals for quite a long time. I know this from some of the pictures I saw in an ancient history textbook. Either that, or they imported them. I doubted that since

Japan was not discovered at that time, and the only Italians were Romulus and Remus.

J.C. and I needed sandals, and Ed needed his repaired. He had just bought his in Italy a month before and they were already falling apart. That is no reflection on Italian sandals, that is a reflection of Ed's effect on things.

Ed is about as easy on his and others' belongings as he is on a full plate of food. That is to say, he is about as gentle as a half-grown bear. He does not mean to be that way. There is just not enough of him to constructively use up all his energy.

We had asked Robert about the sandal shop. It was all done rather matter-of-factly.

"Is there a sandal shop in the village?" J.C. asked. "We've been led to believe that each Greek village comes equipped with a sandal shop."

"That's true" said Robert. ''Complete with two fairly short elves. You don't see the elves though. You just hear about them. They're too busy hidden back there making sandals." Robert squinted up one side of his face as if he was staring at something written on the inside of his eyeball. "There must be elves. No shoemaker could make all those sandals by himself."

We understood what he meant from the view overlooking the inside of the sandal shop. Half of the floor and one eighth of the volume of the small room was occupied by a pile of soles and straps that rivaled the Great Pyramid. It must have taken 100,000 elves, working day and night, 20 years to build that pile of sandals. It was truly one of the lost wonders of the world.

I am as embarrassed now to repeat what I said to the shoemaker, as I was for the thirty seconds before I said it the first time.

"I would like to look at your sandals," I said, so there would be no confusion as to why we were there. I didn't want him to think we were just a bunch of tourists that had come to get our pictures taken climbing his pile of sandals, with him and his elves standing at the base and smiling so hard you thought their teeth were going to crack. No sir!

"They all do. Pick out what you like," he said. "but no pictures."

Like the treasure hunters of old, I knew where my pair of sandals would be found. And there was no short cut to the bottom of the pile. We started looking, J.C. and I.

There were sandals too big and sandals too small. Some too wide and some too narrow. A few of them had too many straps and many of them did not have enough straps. On most of them, the straps were in the wrong places.

I have very strange feet. They were made in the twentieth century. Most of the sandals were from the 41st century B.C. and wanted to stay there. It was by no means easy to stretch my feet across

6100 years of pedal evolution. It was unfitting to even try. Even if I found the proper size, chances were the sandal would have been out of step with our times.

J.C. was luckier than I. After 5 years-worth of unbuilding the Great Pyramid of sandals, he came across a pair that he no doubt lost in a previous incarnation as a Jewish elf. They stuck snuggly to his feet like peanut butter grapes. I was less fortunate. I was about to look for the nearest Sears, Roebuck & Co. mail order catalogue, when I spied a modern, up-to-date pair of sandals at the far corner of the pile. With minor adjustments, they fit just fine.

GENTLE ED

Ed was looking into the repair of sandals. He sheepishly handed the sandal maker his sandal with the broken strap.

The man took it between his thumbs and forefingers and studied it warily from a distance, like some dead thing his dog drug in from the village dump.

"Where did you get this?" he asked, not trying to conceal his disbelief.

"In Italy," Ed apologized.

''You should have waited until you got here. This is not a very good sandal." He was not trying to be rude. It was just a professional observation.

The sandal maker turned the sandal over carefully and examined it, thumbed the broken strap a few times. A grimace quickly swept over his face, revealing a fantasy of rubber gloves, then was gone.

"I have never seen a sandal like this before. This shop has been in my family 7,382 years. I am the $1,843^{rd}$ of great-grandsons of the first cobbler of this village, and in all that time there has been no record of footwear of this low caliber entering this shop. Even my novice elves do a better job than this," he said. But he was weakening in his position. He could tell Ed didn't want any other sandal. It was a matter of principle to Ed by now.

"Can you fix this?" Ed asked, his impatience showing through the hockey pucked red of his nose. He was making it a professional challenge.

"Of course, I can fix it," the man said. "I have it for you tomorrow."

Ed was taken care of, but J.C. and I were only half through.

"You'll get extra mileage out of those things if you get rubber soles put on them. Especially on these bumpy, gravelly roads," said Robert.

"Should we get radials or just standard ones?" J.C. asked.

"Well, I figured at 5 miles a day, that's 1825 miles a year. Radials are guaranteed for 40,000 miles, so that's almost 22 years, if you go out every day. But some days I just sit on the beach and don't even move. The rest of the sandal is only good for, say, maybe 10 years at the most. I don't think the radials are necessary," Robert said.

We got the cheaper treads. Mine had a big "Fire" written down the length of it, in raised letters. J.C. had the complementary "stone" extending form his toe to his heel. Together our tracks left a continual invitation to one and all to our nightly revelry at the end of the scimitar sand beach.

J.C. AND WE ALL GO NUTS

We continued to carry our message halfway across Eastern Europe and into the Soviet Union, until J.C. lost his half at a petrol station somewhere within the depths of that vast country. He was quite pissed off when he discovered it missing, but it was quite apropos for me. My last big binge was the night before in Kiev. Seven of us consumed five or six bottles of vodka then a fifth of Chivas Regal. I vaguely remember trying to pour back part of the Scotch from the heaving pit of my stomach.

When we reached Moscow, J.C. was wearing only one sandal. Since they knew we came from Greece, the Soviets considered it a bad omen for their king. So they sent us north on some dangerous mission. When we reached Scandinavia and finished our course through the Soviet Union, we received our sheepskin but not before being thoroughly fleeced.

As for my sandals, the "Fire" has gradually worn away. All that remains is a small "i" that is left in my wake, slowly wearing into nothing as I walk through life.

AN ISLAND IS NOT A STATIC BEING

An island is not a static being. It is as protean as the dawn, going through its many-colored phases with an almost imperceptible, yet steadily forceful fluidity. Nor do all set about their motions to a common tune, each seeking the rhythm consonant with its present unfolding of island-ness.

There are islands that persist for untold eons. Their rock faces rise slowly from the deep, wearing the solemn visage of confidence and surety of purpose. Only in minute portion do they gradually yield to the sea the sands that once were hers, extracting from her the utmost of effort in return for their being.

There are islands that announce their coming in a fiery and tumultuous spectacle of self-assertion. They scorch a path before them in the sky and spread their fertile mantle out around themselves, then settle down in slumber, to nourish all that come seeking the bounty of their shores. They, too, may drift slowly into oblivion. Or they may leave as violently as they appeared, casting themselves out into the surrounding air and sea, the recipients of a force that cannot be self-contained.

Then there are those mysterious few. Sparkling gems of the sea, they rise silently and swiftly on the horizon of our awareness. They stand as promise and reminder of the hidden potential that lies waiting beneath the surface of the thalassal deep. They permit us a brief glimpse of their beauty and their secrets, then drawing a veil around themselves, sink back into their source, as quietly and suddenly as they came.

A fortunate few are ready for this singular encounter. Rising to the occasion, they join without hesitation the outstretched possibilities and knowledge of another, subtler world. Many more are taken totally by surprise. The exquisiteness of the moment is too great, and they hold back in awe. But awe and mystery do not admit of knowledge. Where one is, the other cannot be. We must try to pierce the mystery if we would understand, if we would love. But all too often the moment is swifter than our resolve.

Yet even when the essence escapes us and we do not make it to the heartland, we are oft permitted a brief rest upon the shores of such fair island. And to have known one even by the touch is quite enough.

CHRIS

Morning blends slowly into afternoon between the sun and land of Paros. Were it not for the accuracy of our retsinated inner clocks, we would have doubtless been hard put to tell one from the other. But as surely as the sweltering sphere crossed midheaven and cooled toward the sea, the retsina pulled on the hidden oceans of our bodies toward high tide at the Windmill Café.

There we sat with our bottles of ice cold Plaka Retsina, waiting for the Elli that would not arrive that day, when Chris came walking over and sat down at the table next to us. She was beautiful. Hers was not the kind of beauty that one sees through the loins. Her beauty was perceived from somewhere else.

I do not mean that her beauty was not physical. Quite the contrary. But this beauty started somewhere deep within her. I could feel it pouring through her skin as she sat and sipped at a beer at the next table. With every exhalation she bathed me in a glowing warmth that evaporated all necessity like the morning dew.

Sometimes metaphors are meaningless, like shooting arrows at a cloud mirrored in a pool. At such times all one can do is give the barest, necessary outline, the four edges of a page, and let the reader paint the picture as he will. If this was in Chinese it would facilitate the task, perhaps at least give me a few more characters with which to construct my vision, but all I have are twenty-six insignificant symbols. Their combinations and permutations, though vast, are all too few to convey the immediacy of Chris's presence as she filled the air before me like my own breath.

At Robert's invitation, Chris came and sat and drank and talked with us. We spent a few hours there at the Windmill Café, then we all went down to the beach for a swim. In the crystal aquasphere of the Aegean, I could see that Chris's naked body was made in the image of her face. We weren't in long. We dressed again and went to Robert's hut for a bite to eat.

Robert's hut was quite adequate. The four thick walls were stuccoed and white and about seven feet apart one way and sixteen feet apart the other way. The floor was concrete, while the ceiling was of a thatched nature. For all its size it was not without a gracious double door. At one end of the room was a double bed beneath a small window. At the other end was a small table and some built-in shelving to hold Robert's few belongings.

Robert's cupboard was nearly bare. There was a cucumber, a few tomatoes, and the partial jug of red wine. Without a miracle, it was not likely to feed a small multitude. J.C. and Robert volunteered to go to get food, and of course, retsina, and headed off in the direction of Demetri's house.

"How long will you be?" I asked. Chris said she had to get back pretty soon, and it was a long walk to the village.

"Only a half hour or so," Robert said. They drifted across the field to the path. Ed had fallen asleep on the bed.

The evening chill was settling in the cove. Chris and I went back in the hut to get something to eat. We had our share of tomatoes and cucumber and sat on the edge of the bed, talking in quiet, jumpy tones. Every so often we got up to see if J.C. and Robert were returning.

An hour passed. The island was under darkness now, but it was cloudless as usual. The stars softly blanketed the valley and silhouetted the clump of palm trees by the not-so-very well and the hill beyond. To the west the mountain pulled back silently and yielded a ripening moon. The evening was full. We returned to the bed and lay down on our sides facing each other and continued talking in raspy breaths.

It was then I felt it. Or rather, I became fully conscious of it. Like a boyhood friend that I wasn't really sure I was glad to see again, it suddenly dropped into town for a visit. I was hot. Truly hot like I hadn't been since my career as a virgin. My body was out of control.

When I was about thirteen, I had a dream that I was driving a car. I was alright until I remembered I didn't know how to drive. Then the car started heading down a hill. It was out of control and I was scared to death. Then I remembered I was dreaming. The road turned uphill, and I managed to bring the car over to the curb and stopped. But my heart was still beating against its cage, and my chest, face, and ears were still burning, as I inched ever so slightly over and looked into her face. It was flushed.

I reached over and touched her forehead gently. The contact was exquisite! "You feel warm," ran up my arm and down my spine to the knot between my legs, then rose back to my chest and spurted forth in a soft whisper.

"I think you're the one that is hot!" she smiled closely. We gently intertwined hands. My other had moved against the aching fire to the valley between her chin and mouth, forefinger and thumb holding and turning...the mouth...parting slightly with moistness...waiting...no longer, I draw near... bringing the heat...from her lips...melts our mouths...two...gather.

If Ed had not been there, sleeping on the bed, things might be very different today. I might have left my tale on another shore. But I usually prefer the solitude of two when it comes to making love, and so the situation called forth the great enemy of creative and spontaneous expression. Thought. Rationality. Cause and effect. Direction. I was very hardly ready, when...

...I remembered I was dreaming. The road turned uphill, and I managed to bring the car over to the curb and stopped. I got out of the car to look for a blanket.

I grabbed one from the bed, and we walked out and around the hut. We spread the blanket out before the moon, undressed, and pressed ourselves together. We stood there for a few minutes, kissing. Then Chris lowered herself to the blanket before me. I stood above her sublime being as it caught and magnified the moon, radiating its cool and glowing softness into the infinitude of nothingness around her. I turned silently to gain a glimpse of her image in the evening sky.

When I turned back around, the car had disappeared, and I was far from home.

As I lowered myself to the blanket beside her, I realized I had lost the point of it all. We tried all sorts of things that people try in cases like that, but it was of no use. I held her in the creeping chill, as we looked across the slowly widening strait between us. I knew the bridge between the islands of our bodies had gone down forever.

Chris looked in through my eyes to some place near the center of my head. She said, "Sometimes, all we need to do is touch."

GENESIS XVIII

A CIRCLE BUT NO RING

I went early the next day to the Windmill Café. I didn't even stay the usual two hours at breakfast. The rest of everybody was going on an excursion. They were going around the island.

Provided the size is not prohibitive, the wholeness of an island invites investigation. Its self-limiting nature calls forth in humankind the urge toward emulation. With boundaries well-defined, it says, "I am completeness. Within my shores is a world unto itself. Study me and you may learn a secret, the secret of self-mastery and control." With the resoluteness and fluidity of water, we seek to fill up the vessel of island-ness.

Gertie, her stomach filled with expensive super petrol, warmed up once more for an outing of Lazy Day Tours, Inc. The Bush people, Richard, the Mid Beach people, Robert, Ed, and J.C. at the helm, all started out to prove that our world was round.

I settled down to a nice quiet day at the Windmill Café with ice cream, Greek salad, and maybe a little retsina. And to write. Writing is therapeutic.

When I was twelve, I had a terrible crush on a girl. I had moved away from the town where we went to church together, but the indecent fantasies I had of her were still with me. They hounded me day and night. I couldn't eat. I couldn't sleep. I became a mere shadow of my former self. I had to get it out, I had to let her know how I felt. So, I wrote her and proposed in a somewhat oblique fashion, feeling much better at having done so.

I got a response, but she said nothing about the marriage. I didn't mind. I had new friends and was no longer interested.

IT'S AN OLD STORY

The events of the preceding evening were still very much with me. In two days, my pendulum had swung me from a bestial minded rapist to being an awestruck Platonist. What was the problem?

The main one that I could see was that I was still very lustful, or love starved, or both. Both my encounters had been ineffectual from the point of view of my body. I tried to pour out my soul on the disinterested and un-consoling piece of paper before me. I have included it here, since space allows, and I'm not likely to ever get it published otherwise.

"SOMETIME IN MID JUNE 1972, PAROS, ELLAS

Waiting for the muse, six weeks across Italy. Roller skating on fiats, we fled the rip off to Yugoslavia, an undiscovered land. I can't write here in the sun, but I can't sit here and not write. Ho hum. Got no stimulation. Yeah. No anticipation. I'm forgetting how to fuck. Because I'm forgetting how to touch. Because I want to be right all the time. I want to be unforceful, which is a conceit, which is absurd. There is only force, but it must not be considered insulting, nor should one assume guilt on one's own part, due to realizing the force. Only when we accept the force does it move unhindered, can it of its own join up with other forces.

Fucking is only another form of touching, and as such, results from allowing the force full rein."

It was all very philosophical.

She said, "Sometimes, all we need to do is touch."

She was right. It was absurd to worry about it. I couldn't be bothered with it.

Fuck it all!

"OH, I'M CAROL," SHE SAID

"Hi there. Have you been here long?" said another voice from New York. This time, Brooklyn.

"Several hours, I guess," I said. I looked up at the short voice with dark, tightly curled hair falling down around it. Two glistening orbs of Plutonian darkness beamed out at me from their position five feet above the concrete floor. Suspended between them and a few inches below was the mouth, full lipped and red, from which the voice had come. All was supported on a body of pleasing proportions. Except for the voice and the obviously western clothes she was wearing, she looked like she had just stepped down from a Minoan vase.

"I'm looking for a friend from home. He wrote me and said he would be coming over sometime around now from Athens. You haven't seen anyone that could be my friend, have you?" she asked.

"Not unless he looks like the man that runs this café," I said. "I've been here most of the day and he is the only person I have seen that looks like he might be your friend. He is the only person I have seen that might not be your friend. He is the only person I have seen."

"He might or might not be," she said, "but he's not the one I'm talking about right now. My friend's name is Dennis. You will recognize him by his name."

"I'll ask around," I said. "The Elli doesn't come until round 4:30. Maybe he'll be on it."

"Thanks," she said.

I could see there was more in this girl than questions about her friend. She looked like she was full of conversational possibilities. But she had come to the end of her paragraph and there were no conjunctions in sight.

"Why don't you sit down?" I asked. "I've been trying to write, but this piece of paper and I aren't communicating very well. Writing is not always an easy thing to do. Some things get lost between the brain and the paper. It would be a lot easier if we could just think things onto the paper or into someone else's head."

"Yes, but that might be rather confusing not to mention embarrassing," she said.

"Yes, that's true," I reflected. "At any rate, I'm about to click my pin to death, so I think I'll stop. Perhaps I will have more success communicating with you."

"I hope so," she said. She sat down at the table across from me.

"Have you been swimming yet today? The water is really nice."

"Yes," I said, "early this morning. My friends and I are staying on a beach in a little cove about a mile down the coast. In the morning we just get up and walk out into our watery front yard. It's really very nice."

"It sounds that way," she said. "How long have you been on Paros?"

"Only about 3 days," I said. "And you?"

"Oh, I've been here about two weeks. I'm going to school," she said.

"School? What school? I didn't know there was a school in Paros," I said.

"Oh yes. The Aegean School of Fine Arts," she replied.

"Sounds pretty heavy. Like it's got antiquity as its alumni. Is it an old Greek school?" I asked.

"No," she answered. "It's just a few years old. Brett Taylor, an American artist, started it. It's alright, I guess."

I had a few quick images of kids hitting their parents for the bread. "There's this really groovy School of Art in the Greek islands, Dad. It's got all the cultural and historical prerequisites. We'll be studying right out there with the original works of the classics. Wow! What inspiration! I'll only need a few thou. It'll really be educational!" As their minds turn to sun and the nightly bacchanalia and a little knowledge, mostly carnal. What a set up!

"That's pretty good," I said. "Where is the school?"

"It's mixed in with the village and several old houses," she replied.

"That's even better," I said.

By the count of the empty retsina bottles on the table, I could tell that it was approaching the time for the arrival of the Elli. Lazy Day Tours would be returning soon. After all the dry runs, I was sure they would not miss the first real test of the Paros Welcoming Committee. Besides, this far into the afternoon they would be getting thirsty, and I felt sure there was not enough retsina on the rest of the island for all the crew and Gertie.

"I think I'll have a party tomorrow night. All your friends can come. My roommates will probably bitch, but I don't give a shit. After all, I live there, too. Right?" asked the girl from Crete.

"Right," I echoed to save the walls the trouble.

"I mean they got the best beds in the bedroom, and I have to sleep in the living room," she reasoned.

"That would be nice. The party, I mean. It would be nice if you had a party. Even if your roommates don't like it, I think you should have the party. I don't want to push you into anything, but I think it would be nice if you had it," I said.

"Yeah, I think I will. They can go out somewhere if they don't like it," she worried.

"Well, I better go now. I've got some things to do," she said, looking south in the direction of Crete.

"Why don't you stick around for the arrival of the Elli? It's really something. Maybe your friend will be on it," I said.

"No, I better go. If you see him, tell him I just wondered where he was," she said, searching through the maze that was her mind.

"Okay. What's your name, by the way?" I thought it would help to know her name.

"Oh, I'm Carol," she said, tripping over her name as she left the table.

"Okay, Carol, I'll see you later," I said.

She headed off in the direction of the labyrinth which is the village of Paros, absentmindedly leaving her candle and a ball of string behind. I wondered how she would ever find her way back out again.

ISLANDS REALLY ARE SURROUNDED BY WATER

Shortly after Carol left, Gertie pulled up to the Windmill Café, and most of the people that had started on the trip got out. Some

103

of the people had already gotten out back down the quay. One or two more wanted to go around the island again.

"You should have gone with us, man. There's really a nice beach on the other side of the island. Great for snorkeling," J.C. said.

"Really? Did you stop?" I asked with a hint of jealousy in my voice.

"Yeah, for a couple of hours," Ed said. "You should have come."

"Oh, that's okay. I had a really great time sitting here staring at a piece o' paper. You weren't supposed to stop. That wasn't in the bargain," I said.

"Too bad. You'll have to start your own tour," said Ed as he headed toward the ice cream cooler on the inside of the café.

"Hey, you know it's true what they say. Islands really are surrounded by water on all sides," said Richard. "But they're not built for bicycles. Their roads get you halfway 'round the island then the asphalt disappears. Really tricky."

"Maybe you need something with two-wheel drive," Bilbo replied.

"Nah, I just need a smaller island, so the road will reach all the way around," Richard said.

"Maybe you could buy some road from that millionaire back down the coast. He has more than he needs. You could rig up an inside-out treadmill with it. You could go anywhere. A perpetual road," said Frodo.

"He's asking too much for it," Richard said, as he followed the steady stream into the café for retsina.

"Have you actually ridden that stork of yours since you've been here?" Robert asked him, close on his heels

"To the souvlaki shop on my first night here. It's perched in the hotel I'm at now," Richard responded.

THE PAROS WELCOMING COMMITTEE

The many bottles of retsina stood on the tables before us like so many unspoken greetings, in anticipation of the coming of the Elli. What the Welcoming Committee could not dispense, would surely find its way to someone's mouth. We continued with more cartloads of bullshit as the retsina ticked away the passage of the Elli down our throats.

We did not have long to wait before the ship came rolling past the point of land across the bay and turned its bow towards the dock, like a phantom city awakening from a dream. The decks were lined with its still sleepy inhabitants, waving away the drowsiness from their eyes. Their other halves on shore waved back politely, but all attention was directed toward the bow. With a pointed flourish of self-esteem that could not be missed by anyone, the Elli let glide her anchor toward its rest upon the bottom, its splash punctuating the completion of another voyage well done.

"Did you see that anchor fall, man? Out-a-sight!"

"Yeah, man. What a show! Too bad it doesn't come in twice a day."

An innocent bystander would have thought we had just smoked a bowl of the finest Nepalese hash, to hear us carrying on about the anchor. It was a sure-nuff natural high.

The Elli swung her ass-side around to the dock and dropped her drawers. A few vehicles came out, followed by the teeming stream of passengers now awakened to the present possibilities of Paros. Most of them were Parosians returning from a weekend on the mainland or relatives and friends come for a visit of varying duration. A few appeared to be merchants or businessmen making their rounds. The rest were tourists, among which were three or four clusters of those kind of people called freaks.

We did not need to make any special attempts to be conspicuous in our new activity. We were right out in front of the Windmill Café, and our table was piled high with full retsina bottles, so these people in need of welcoming had no trouble in finding out where to go. Like alcohol divining rods, their parched tongues drew them to our tables to douse their thirst in our good cheer.

A couple came by first and asked directions to a hotel. We offered them a beach, but they did not seem too interested, for reasons known only to themselves. We gave them a bottle of retsina and told them that it would direct them to a room. They thanked us and headed off in the direction of their lives.

Next came a guy I supposed might be Dennis. He had black hair on his head and around his mouth in the form of a Fu Manchu, and his skin was broiled brown to match. All of which was there for only one purpose, to set off the perfect set of teeth that he had just acquired from Carol Channing. He probably paid a fortune for those teeth, and he wasn't about to let anyone miss them.

I had all but decided that this guy must be Dennis, when another candidate came up to the table. He was kind of tall and had blonde hair around his mouth and over his head and came strapped to the front of a pack. He was toasted up pretty well, too, but not for the benefit of his teeth. I mean, they were alright, but they were parted just a bit in the middle so that you could get a peek of what he was about to say.

Both of these dudes sat down at the tables at our welcome, one across from the other. The dark guy was a bit hyper and began to chat and move about in a friendly way. The blonde fellow was really mellowed out. He stretched and curled up in his chair like a cat just nipped. They were spread across our little group like two poles of an impromptu magnet, drawing our attention to one end or the other.

"Hey, man, this is far out. What's happening?" said the guy with the blonde hair.

"This happens pretty much of the time. Other times we go to the beach and swim and sleep. Mostly we just do nothing," said J.C.

"I can dig it," said the blonde dude. He spoke fluent hippese, but it wasn't rehearsed or annoying like that of some people. It just came with the catnip.

I tuned back in on the dark guy who was sitting at my end of the tables. I thought maybe I could find out his name.

"…at the youth hostel in Athens for a few days. I haven't been over here long. I just got out of school a few weeks ago. I go to school in D.C.," he said.

People were getting into introductions now, so I listened carefully

"My name is Dennis," said the dark guy.

Aha! I wasn't too surprised, since I figured it must be one or the other.

Before relating Carol's greeting, I turned to the other end of the table to catch the other dude's name. He had given it already, and I had missed it. He was busy talking to someone else, so I asked Ed.

"Ed, what did he say his name was?" I asked.

"Dennis," Ed replied.

"No, man, I know what this guy's name is. I mean the fella sitting next to you. What's his name?"

"Dennis. His name is Dennis," Ed said with a big grin on his face.

"Don't bullshit me. Do you expect me to believe that we're looking for one name out of all the people in the world with umpteen different names and we get two guys with the same name at our table? This place isn't that weird!" I hoped. Things were really getting difficult, and all I wanted to do is relate a simple message from this Minoan girl from Brooklyn.

"Ask him then," Ed said.

I finally managed to get the blonde fellow's attention and asked him his name.

"Dennis," he said.

I had a sudden flash of the enrollment sheet of the Aegean School of Fine Arts, with the name 'Carol' printed on every third line.

"Did you know his name was Dennis, too?" I pointed to Black Dennis.

"Yeah, man, we met on the Elli. It's pretty far out," Blonde Dennis said. I turned back to Black Dennis, who was into a rap about, of all things, teeth.

"...decided to go into dentistry. Teeth really fascinate me. They are really important. You have to take care of them," he said.

That was too much. Dennis, the Dentist! I couldn't hold back anymore.

"Which one of you guys came to see a chick named Carol from Brooklyn?" I blurted out, finally expecting both of them to answer. Only Dennis the dentist did.

"She wanted to let you know she is looking for you," I said.

"Really? Did she say anything else?" he asked. I know what he meant. But there was no mistaking it, as I watched the horns light up in his head.

"Nope, nothing else," I said. That was true. She hadn't said anything, but I had seen her horns pulse a bit also.

A ROSE BY ANY OTHER NAME WOULD NOT BE A ROSE

There exists a general misconception concerning names. Most people are so familiar with their names, that they cannot imagine life under any other appellation, much less devoid of one entirely. To such people, their name is like a piece of jewelry or some piece of apparel or a watch. They put it on as soon as they awaken in the morning and take it off the last thing before bed at night. They would not dream of being caught somewhere in public without it.

"Hello, don't I know you from somewhere? What was the name?"

"I'm 5 minutes to 9. I don't believe I caught your name."

"Oh, I'm sorry. Let me check…my goodness, I left mine at home. I'm usually a little slow anyway."

Some people go so far as to never taking theirs off, even in the shower, while sleeping, while making love. Such is the height of barbarity.

I can think of nothing more distasteful than making love while I'm anything other than utterly naked. It is a good thing that I do not have false teeth, especially of the permanent kind, or I would no doubt develop a really bad sexual block.

I could never wear my name to bed with a woman. It would be much too distracting to hear her calling down, "OH...MY...GOD, 5:30, 5:30," from the heights of ecstasy, as if I was an X-rated appointment that she had missed and was likely to go off without her.

We learned about names in the privacy of Parosian island-ness. We had no need for watches. Our clothes, when worn, were chosen only as was necessary for the occasion. Our names, likewise, were changed in keeping with the situation. That is why Richard is no longer called Richard, except by himself.

He never thought when he jokingly renamed himself at the Windmill Café in the protean moment which is Paros that it would just plain stick.

EVEN WITH A THORNY PROBLEM

"And what are your names," said Black Dentist, displaying a good feel for the game. He looked across the table in the direction of Bilbo.

"Hey, Fuck-stick, tell him your name," Ed said to Bilbo whose attention had been elsewhere at the table.

"Who me? I'm Fuck-stick." Lied Bilbo who was really Carl, who was really whoever is in back of Carl. "And he's Shit-on-a-stick," he pointed over at Ed. The potty talk was infectious.

Black Dennis looked over to Richard, who was seated next to Ed.

"And you?" he asked.

"Me? I'm just plain Stick," Richard grinned, beaming his new name indelibly into the remaining decorous recesses of our brains.

"Plain Stick. That's a good name. You're not likely to find two guys with that name at the same table," said Black Dentist.

OUR APOLOGIES TO JERRY GARCIA AND THE BOYS

Our Welcoming Committee proved very effective. Within a short while our new friends were well acquainted with the wonders of retsina and the Axis Mundi. Among these was the secret of third-degree inebriation. At a certain point in the evening, determined largely by subconscious consensus, and the degree to which one's vocal cords have been waxed by the ever-flowing resin, the babbling takes a shift toward the musical end of the spectacle. With little benefit of radio and phonograph, the rock addicted mind of the new age goes all types of weird unless it manufactures a facsimile on its own.

For several hours we drug up oldies that would hardly be found on the most forgotten jukebox in the mountains of Tennessee. There must be a direct relationship between the volume of retsina and the volume of the human voice, because the owner of the Windmill Café decided to turn down one with the other. We were into the 43rd repeat of our distorted and abbreviated rendition of "Casey Jones" when they told us very politely that we had consumed our limit. We knew we were not drunk, or we would not have been able to sing so well, but he was a nice man, so he packed up our train and headed on down the street. He said he was grateful for our business and hoped we would come back the next day, if we were not dead.

The retsina train headed on down the quay in the direction of the beach, making the usual stops for food and retsina along the way. We pointed out the high spots as best we could to our newcomers, then climbed in Gertie for the short ride back. There were nine of us now in our new settlement at the scimitar sand beach, with the two Dennis's and Plain Stick who had decided to join us after giving up on his bike. He left it storked in the hotel.

We slowly wound down the path in the direction of the not-very-well. We paid little heed to the serpents of the jungle in our crossing. They undoubtedly knew of our fondness for retsina as did everything else around our little cove by this time and did not want to chance a bite. They knew it would be fatal.

We deposited our things at the Paros Hilton, while a few hot dogs went in for a swim. The Paros Hilton is nothing fancy. It is composed of two upright sticks with a cross piece about three feet out from the stonewall, over and between which are extended several palm fronds. It provided enough shade for half of one body at a time. It was not of the most up-to-date design, but it did lend an air of respectability to our end of the beach, which was not so fortunate as to come equipped with a Bush.

Tiring quickly of their game, the swimmers emerged from the primordial lurky murk of the cove and joined us at the bottles by the sand. The tenor of the group had slowed a bit from the musical high at the Windmill Café, but it was by no means dissipated. At the mercy of our Dionysian clocks, we rapped on under the sinking moon, into the wee hours of Parosian darkness.

GENESIS XIX

MIDDLE AMERICA IS NOT AN ANTIQUE – GAAUUUB, GAAUUB

Hhhhhuuuuuuuuuu.   Whhuuuh.   Hhhhhuuuuuuuuu. Whhuuuh. Hhhhhuuuuuuuuuu. Bloob. Bloob. Bloob. Bloob. Bloo~. Bloo. BlooBlooooo- oooBloocooooooo~oooooooooooooooco b.

GAAUUUB.   AAUUUB.   AUB.   AAUUUUUU

Dthhuu.   Dthhuuuuaah.   Hhhhhhhhuuuuuuuuaaaaaaaahhhhhhh.

Snorkeling sure can be a lot of fun. It is the gateway to a symphony primeval. Floating amidst the muffled harmonies of the submarine existence, Ed and I bobbed slowly from the ends of our sixteen-inch umbilical cords.

Below us the blue-green carpet of deep weed beckoned sinuously in the soft, liquid wind of the Aegean. Thousands of slender, serpent arms played out a chord known only too well by the deep recesses of our souls and bodies, stoning us with the swift recognition of a giant Medusa. Scores of tiny fish, schooled to act like one tremendous predator, zig-zagged back and forth between their pretension and their fear. A few larger species came up for a closer look, then scurried off into the cover of the wafting seaweed. We each took another deep breath and set ourselves for the bumper of cold as we descended into the lower realm of the Jungian fantasy.

We followed the gently sloping floor to a pile of fallen and submerged rocks beneath the high point of land at the end of the beach. On the far side of the rocks the floor dropped twenty feet or so to a clear, sandy bottom. Displaying the usual energy, Ed chased a few meals around the rocks. We surfaced for air and dove again toward the glittering bottom.

Thirty feet to the front of us was a short tunnel in the base of the cliff wall. Since we could see that it was a hole and was surrounded by rock like an anti-island and was small enough to admit a diver, we decided to go through. When we got through it, we came to the other side.

We followed the cliff on down the coast a way. It was all pretty much the same, except there were fewer tunnels than before, so we turned back looking for sunken treasure along the way. We had seen an old tire on the way down, so we had reason to suspect there might be a car or something even older around on the bottom somewhere. We found a number of interesting shells and rocks, but nothing of any archaeological significance. I had hopes of finding an old urn or bottle or some other relic of antiquity.

We were just about to head back to shore, when a ray of light caught its edge and twinkled at the corner of my eye. It was the mouth and neck of an old bottle barely emerged from the drifting sands of cultural oblivion!

I took a quick gulp of air and headed down to investigate. At a depth of twenty-five feet, it was a bit difficult to tell exactly what color the bottle was, but it appeared to be a light green or blue. It was remarkably well-formed and preserved. I reached out and took the neck of the bottle in my hand and withdrew it from its ancient place of rest.

To my amazement, there was writing on it! I could still make out the characters in the diffused aqua shine of the sea floor. "Coca-Cola," it glowed with the brash obscenity of a neon light. I turned up the bottom to see what town it was from. "Kansas City," it laughed. Ha-ha. If Ed had only found one, too, I'm sure I would have beat him.

"I'm not going to help you find your way back into circulation, pollution or no pollution," I said, burying it back in the sand like an ostrich soft-drink and heading back toward the reality of the Windmill Café.

THREE FACES WEST

The ship's whistle rolled across the harbor like an ethereal tidal wave, casting us up onto the edge of the quay in front of the Breakfast Café, like a couple of oceangoing bottles, our cosmic messages coiled up inside. We had not been expecting the Elli for another hour. We knew we would have to hurry to join the Welcoming Committee in time.

We turned to get a better look at the ship steaming across the bay. It was not the Elli! On the smokestack was a large red, reversed 'K'. The ship was of the same general type as the Elli, perhaps a little larger, and was very new. It hardly seemed likely that it was a replacement for the Elli, since she was not in particularly bad shape, unless she had had some trouble or was in need of routine repairs. The thought of setting her out to dry dock was most distressing.

The other and more likely possibility, that did not occur to us at that time, was that it was a new competing line. This fact was confirmed as the reverse K dropped her anchor and swung into dock, by the second whistle of the afternoon, which rose from the Elli as she rounded the far point of land. Two ships in one day was too much! Two welcomings! And two anchor droppings! Ed and I hurried to make it to the Windmill Café for the festivities, dragging our fins and masks behind us like the skins of some weird fish.

By the time we reached the café most of the passengers had already disembarked from the reverse K and were spreading out in the directions of their interests or obligations. The Paros Welcoming Committee was well entrenched behind a wall of Plaka Retsina bottles. Robert was working himself into a flurry of ill contained emotion. It was the most excitement he had seen in two months.

"This is the most excitement I have seen in two months," said Robert, "I can't wait for the other anchor!"

Ed and I could not help noticing that there was an addition to the Welcoming Committee of three attractive girls. They had all the endowments that have come to be associated in my mind with appeal in the other sex; blue jeans, in this case cut offs, old baggy shirts, and packs. They were definitely not Greek women, unless they were by way of North America. Ed and I sat down at the tables and tried to catch up on events of the past few minutes.

"Two boats, can you dig that?" asked J.C., "this place hasn't seen this kind of commotion in years! And what an anchor! Woo-Hoo!"

"What's the story on the new ship?" I asked.

"Robert says there is a big race from Athens. Whoever wins gets the rights to the ferry lanes from Piraeus. Sounds good to me," said Stick.

"If the Elli wins," added Robert. "This new ship doesn't have any character. It doesn't even limp."

"Actually, I think they are opening two lines during the height of the tourist season," said Bilbo and the voice of calm reason. His head sat like an impartial judge upon the gnarled old piece of wood which was the top of his cane. He had not yet recovered completely from his duel with the monster from Middle-Earth.

"Far out! More welcomings, more retsina," said Blonde Dennis.

"I don't believe you've met these fine ladies," J.C. said in mock politeness. He sounded like the caterer-receptionist to a garden tea party, where all the guests already know and are bored to death with each other. The nervous, busy type that is always looking around to make sure nothing of insignificance misses his attention. "Oh, my goodness, let me introduce you. This is Jackie and Heidi and Penelope. The three eased into our group with no trouble at all."

'Hi. How are you?'s passed around the tables. 'Great's and 'Fine's made their way back around.

"It sure is good to see you hairy, American guys," said Heidi. "It's been a while since we've seen such a bunch together."

She was somewhat taller and slender, with a bright, bubbly smile. She was definitely the most visibly energetic one of the three.

"Hey, wait a minute. Not everyone here is an American, if by America you mean the United States," Ed objected.

"Oh, is there anything in America but that," J.C. chided.

"The Great North Country is in North America, too, you know," Ed ignored him.

"What's that?" Frodo responded.

"Come on, you guys, don't give me any shit about Canada," Ed grinned.

We broke into a refrain of 'Oh, Canada.' It had become a ritual by this time. Ed couldn't resist making a comment about Canada whenever the opportunity arose. If it didn't arise of its own, he would see that it did. It wasn't enough to say, 'at home.' He had to say, 'in Canada,' to which we would invariably respond with the first few lines of the Canadian National Anthem, which he had so diligently taught us. Of course, it wasn't the fact that he mentioned Canada that brought on the chorus. It was the context. It was when it was used in conjunction with superlatives in every other sentence that it invited our jest.

It was all carried on in the manner of a friendly verbal wrestling match. Everyone dug it, except for the rare occasion when Ed thought it had passed the bounds of international decency. At such times he would yield to a fit of frustration and start to sing 'America' in an attempt to drown us out. Then we would be forced to remind him that 'America' was not our national anthem.

PENELOPE

"Where are you guys staying? Besides here, of course," asked Penelope. She was shorter and more rounded than Heidi, and a good bit slower. She had a nice easy smile curving up to two of the most intense grey eyes I had ever seen.

"On a little cove up the coast from here. Under the stars. It's really pretty cheap," I said.

"I can stand that," she said.

"Where are you people coming from?" I asked.

"We just came over from Italy to Patras. We thumbed from there to Athens and spent a few days there. We were supposed to go to Naxos, but Heidi took one look at this place and decided this was as far as she was going. I guess it was the Welcoming Committee that did it. We didn't want to get split up, so we got off, too," she said.

"A most wise decision. You have definitely added to the possibilities of Paros," I said.

"Could I have a little more retsinaaaa?" Jackie asked, drawing the retsinaaaa out like it was her final exhale. That was the way she ended all her utterances. She was definitely the mostttt slowedddd downnnn of the three newcomers. It was for her that the word 'mellow' was created. Jackie was so mellow that if she ever fell over, I was sure she would never hit the ground. She was so mellow that her eyelids never got out of second gear. She was mellow. Boy, was she mellow!

Jackie was dark haired and well-tanned. Her build was about average. I was instinctively drawn to her. I had visions of us sitting together somewhere nodding out.

"Sure," Robert said, handing her a full bottle of Plaka.

"Thank youuuu," she responded, veryyyy slowlyyyy.

CAROL, SOMEHOW THROUGH A MAZE

Somehow, Carol had managed to find her way back out of the labyrinth of the Aegean School of Fine Arts and the village and had gotten up with Dennis, Black Dentist. I was amazed.

She informed us that the party was on. We were going to cook fish and fix a salad and maybe drink a little wine. She didn't really care about her roommates, did she?

Ed and I and a few others left to get the food and start cooking. Ed and J.C. and I were all pretty good cooks. We had cooked rice and noodles more different ways than you could shake a spoon at. With salt. Without salt. With Curry. Without Curry. Cold rice. Warm rice. Scalding rice. Noodles with sardines. Noodles without sardines. Noodles without anything. The only thing I don't recall ever trying was noodles with rice. But then, there are some things I tend to repress.

ISLANDS ARE THE PROPER NATURE OF THINGS

Islands are the proper mixture of things. They stand at the intersection of four worlds, at the ready to mediate the great flow of cosmic forces. There are many other conditions of the great earth that serve to join two or three of these worlds together at one time, but none so meet with the unexcelled success of the great cosmic recipe that has given to us the island.

It is the nature of these worlds to interpenetrate each other, to bring the gifts of the higher to the fertilize the lower. The lower, in turn gives growth and realization to the dreams of the higher. Thus, the solar fire disperses through the air, bringing the power of life and motion. The air so energized and inspired, moves across the water, stirring in the inspiration which gives impulse and direction to the multitudinous, striving forms of life. And the water, so enriched, brings nourishment and a fluid power to transform, shape, and build up the land.

If any one of these elements is missing, the result is incompleteness. Without the sea to translate it into life, the dry winds of inspiration are mere fancy. In the midst of mass-land, beyond the virtues of the sea, one meets with barrenness and inflexibility. Yet in the middle of the vast ocean, there is no point of stability, no reference point to which can be anchored the tides of life.

Islands are the exception. Surrounded and bathed in the sea of nourishing and sustaining forms, they draw their inspiration from gentle breezes and rain-laden winds and bask in the warm sun of lifegiving fire.

There are a few people who live continually as islands, as the crossroads of four worlds. Their number is increasing, but it is still all too few. For the rest of us there are two common and natural times that I can think of when all of these factors flow readily together.

The first is when we, with our friends, guests, and welcome strangers, prepare and take food together. Within the warm and earthy embrace of such a gathering, words flow and spread good cheer as easily and as surely as the wine. The fragrances of love and communion mingle with the aroma of good food, in anticipation of the coming taste, all ending in a warm and unifying glow of digestion and assimilation.

The second such instance is when we make love, carnal or platonic. My words can do little to elucidate or improve upon the actuality. I hope you will know what I mean. If not, go out and touch someone and ask them in one breath if they would like to share a taste of bliss.

The finest possible situation of course is an intimate communal feast, followed by an even more intimate gathering with someone you really like.

Ed and I did not realize that we would be doubly fortunate that night as we dropped the first fish into the pan which was the first link in the intricate evening chain of Parosian possibilities.

ΧΗΡΨΣΤΑΛΣΙΣ

CHRYSTALSIS I

A FISH EYED RATHER NOT SEE

The large gray fish stared up at us with one eye from the bottom of the frying pan. He did not like his new home, that was easy enough to see. It was the fourth one that he had in the last twenty-four hours, and he was starting to get fed up with the constant change of residence. Not to mention the fact that each move left him in a less hospitable place.

When he had been so rudely dragged out of his wholly adequate environment early that day, he had been a bit concerned, but he had been quickly placed with a number of his siblings and friends, and he immediately felt more at ease. That was not to last long, however. As the day wore on, more and more friends and relatives were crowded into his new an increasingly unsuitable habitat until it became downright stuffy.

As if that weren't enough of an insult to endure, towards the end of the day he was dumped into a tub of freezing water and some sort of cold white rocks that he had never seen before.

No sooner had he begun to accustom himself to this latest situation, when he was once more plucked up and carried to his last and insufferably hot little pool, not without first enduring the indignity of being rubbed raw, disemboweled, and rolled in some disgusting white powder.

Stare? You god damn right he was going to stare! He was pissed off! He was going to drill holes right through the callous son-of-a-bitch that was perpetrating this outrage, with his hard unblinking eye.

Everyone knows how hard it is to shut a fish's eye.

"Quit staring at me, you obnoxious bastard," I said. I had had enough of his uppity glare. "I didn't catch you anyway. We gotta eat. If we didn't eat you, someone else would. Or you would rot in that smelly hole of a fish market. You were doomed to this pan the day you were born. It's the way of nature. Be grateful, you could have ended up in some shark's belly. It's about time you turned your gaze to heaven, shit-hook."

"Don't do me any favors, creep," the fish responded. "Why didn't you and your freaky friends bring along a truckload of peanut butter. It's good enough for you over there, it's good enough for you here. Leave us to the Aegean and the Aegean to us. I hope you choke on my bones."

"Fuck your eye," I said, gouging it out with a tine of the fork. "I'll make an example of you."

It was a good thing I did. None of the remaining smaller fish gave me any lip. They just lay in the pan and fried up as pretty as you please. The first one managed to burn himself on one side just for spite, however.

CHRYSTALSIS I

Fixing the salad was less of a hassle. Vegetables are more understanding of the requirements of human nutrition. They seem to have a grasp of the chain of alimentary sacrifice and give themselves ungrudgingly.

The cucumbers diced up nicely without a peep, while the tomatoes spurted playfully in response to the dull knife. Even the onions were quite obliging for the most part, evoking no more than the barest semblance of sorrow at their slicing. None of them showed the least concern as we dumped them into the huge pot of their common destiny.

A HOUSE DIVIDED

The others had begun to arrive. In groups of twos and threes they crowded into the small front room of the house right on the heels of their growing appetites.

Carol had been justifiably concerned about her roommates' reaction to the party. It was not a large place that she shared with them. There were three rooms. One of these was the living room, as we might call it.

I have never understood the name for such a room. Where I come from most people had a living room and a den or family room. No one ever went into the living room except when people came to visit and sat in there and talked about all sorts of dull and boring things. Or when someone died or was sick. Living was always done in the den. Like so many other things in this society, it seemed that we had until now gotten things backwards.

At any rate, the room into which the Welcoming Committee was now pouring was the living room, properly called since Carol lived in it, which was about 8 feet wide by 12 feet deep. It was furnished with a couch-bed, a chair, and some floor space. Behind it was an area a bit smaller, that served as a kitchen. In addition to the usual kitchen things, it had a small, tubular metal table with a Formica top and a couple of matching chairs. Next to and comprising about the same space as these two rooms was the large bedroom of Carol's roommates. It was simply furnished with two beds, a chest, a desk, and Carol's roommates. They were not quite into the mood of the party.

Eventually there were about thirteen or so people in one side of the house and two in the other. It worked out nicely. Along with their bodies, the appetites of the Welcoming Committee had brought some bread and wine. Together with the fish and salad, we had quite a spread.

A MISDIRECTED REVENGE

Being a bit short on plates, we were forced to employ more primitive eating arrangements, which we were not, however, unused too. We could have put all the food in the middle of the room, and all piled in on top of it. That was one possibility, but that tends to be a bit barbaric. We were primitive, but not barbaric. There's a definite distinction between the two, if the history books are to be believed. Barbarians are the ones who destroyed the Roman Empire, looting and plundering and indulging in wild and gluttonous orgies. It is not always clear from the descriptions in the history books, which side were the barbarians, however. One wonders if the historians got their information straight. Primitives are simple people that run around in very little clothes and are not in need of barbarians to teach them how degrading and ugly it is to be human.

We are merely gentle primitives. We use the progressive, rotational method of food distribution. People had taken seats in a rough approximation of a circle upon the bed and chairs and floor space. The wine made its way first around the circuit to ensure proper facility of engorgement of all that followed and to aid in subsequent digestion. You will notice I say wine not retsina specifically.

We had at the time already acquired a few heretics among our burgeoning group. Carol and Jackie did not drink retsina. There are a few that don't. Retsina is only for those who are on cheap budgets, are so addicted, or have no sense of taste at all. There seems to be a general progression in its use in that sequence.

The wine was followed by quickly diminishing, ragged loaves of bread. This was the foundation. The bowls of salad, and few plates of fish formed the airy superstructure of our meal. They made the rounds in quick succession, stopping briefly at each place to unload a bite or two of their substance.

I was wary of the fish, accepting each one only after making positively sure it was not the obnoxious one-eyed cursed. In all rational deference to superstition, I avoided that one like the plague.

"Fucking asshole!" said Ed in a sudden outbreak of choleric intensity.

"Look out for the bones!" he coughed up, passing the large blind fish on to the next in line.

TICK, TOCK, TICK, TOCK

Having performed no small miracle with the fish and loaves of bread, we all crowded into the now very living room and settled into the glow. I was seated on the bed between Penelope and Carol, sandwiched like the third bug in a rug. It could not have been cozier if we had been sharing the same skin. It could not have been hotter either. The thirteen or so walking radiators put the quietus on the natural air conditioning capacity of Greek dwellings, so we opened the doors to give exit to our half-baked notions and entrance to the cool assurance of the night.

Like some large Kit-Cat Klock my eyes rolled silently back and forth between the conversational parameters inscribed by the intangible pendulum of the moment. To Penelope, to Carol, to Penelope, to Carol, to Penelope. But I could feel the internal workings of my interest slowly winding down and left it in the direction of Penelope. Carol was quickly overwhelmed by the rapid passing of her wine, and it was taking her evermore nearly out of the realm of ticks and tocks into the timeless buzz beyond. At last, my open stare left her for the final time and came to rest on Penelope, who was seated, glass in hand, with her forearms securely balanced on her knees, in a solid, yet graceful work of postural engineering. Her easy, friendly smile, carried on the penetrating beam of her gaze, found a quick pathway to my brain then poured down in gentle currents, tickling the inside of my skin.

"Have you been hitching the whole time you've been over here?" I chimed.

"Yes, for the most part. We've had pretty good luck," Penelope said.

"Isn't it rather hard to get rides with three of you thumbing? J.C. and I thumbed across the states with a girl we met on the ferry coming down from Alaska. We had a tough time getting rides. We had to pile up all our packs and then hide one of us behind, while the other two thumbed. People would stop, then speed off when they saw part of the baggage move, like they had seen a monster or some horror in the National Enquirer," I said.

"We've had to split up most of the time. Two of us together and one of us goes on alone. You get hassled occasionally, but it's not too bad. How long did it take you to cross the states?" She asked.

A NON-STOP RAP ACROSS THE NORTHWEST

"It took us a little more than a week to get from Washington state to Wisconsin. The girl traveling with us got off there. Of course, we stopped along the way. It took us two days to get out of Yellowstone. We sat by the road going east for two whole days while half of all the campers and trailers in seven states passed by all loaded to the gills with stuffed animals and folding dining room sets and every gadget known to man that is guaranteed to turn any campsite into a traveling all-electric split-level home in suburbia. We should never have gone into Yellowstone, but we got picked up by this really far-out old guy and couldn't resist the trip.

"We were trying to catch a ride out of Jackson to see the Tetons, when this man of about fifty-five, driving a Pontiac about three years old with a huge Airstream trailer hitched to the back, stopped. He was all alone. 'Where are you kids going?' he asks, so we told him the Tetons, and he says, 'Hop in, I'll take you.' He told us to put the packs in the trailer and walked us back to unlock it. Boy were we ever freaked out when he we looked inside. You wouldn't believe it! It wasn't fixed up to live in. The inside was nothing but row upon row and shelf upon shelf of the trinkets and souvenirs you see at all the national parks. The kind you wouldn't buy on a bet. Stuffed bears that have 'I'm Smokey' written on them, pennants, drab black ashtrays with the name of the park written on them in a gaudy gold letters, ugly ceramic mugs that read 'I've been to bum-fuck USA', maps, Indian head dresses, junk, junk, and more junk. The kind of stuff that makes you draw up with embarrassment like a prune when you see some kid nagging his parents to buy it. More embarrassment when you see the parents squirming around and trying to look like part of the scenic views as they try to deal with the kids and make them shut up, then finally have to approach the counter, hand over their hard-earned bread, take the junk, and shove it to the kids. Even more embarrassment when they buy the crap for themselves. Embarrassment for the parents, the poor dudes who make their bread selling it, and the garbage men who make their bread taking it to its proper final resting place. 'Cause everyone's pretending their handling this really nice memento of their great vacation, but they're all hard put to repress the fact that they are playing in shit. And they probably had a lousy vacation anyway. They don't want to remember it, all they want to remember is what everyone thinks and pretends it was, like the souvenirs. You know what I mean?" I rambled on.

"Yes," Penelope nodded, smiling on in encouragement. That was all I needed. That and a bit more retsina, which I quickly found.

"Anyway," I continued, "this dude was riding around to all the national parks in the country selling this trash, as if the parks didn't have enough pollution problems already. But he was really a nice fellow, and he dug carrying us around and showing us the Tetons, pointing out this and that along the way.

"Well, we were about through the Tetons, but we didn't feel like thumbing back to Jackson. We had to decide something. This old guy was really getting into his father trip, and suggested we ride on into Yellowstone with him. He was going through to East Yellowstone and said he would drop us off at a campsite. We decided we might as well ride on with him.

"It was about then that I remembered it was J.C.'s birthday.

"We're not much on ceremony, but we decided we ought to have some sort of celebration. The old fellow with the souvenir junk agreed and stopped at a store for us to buy some drinks and a cake.

When we got back to the car, he whipped out a fifth of vodka, and we preceded to have ourselves a good old time, while he carted us around and showed us Old Faithful and all the other mud holes and geysers and other groovy stuff.

"We were almost at the campsite and starting to feel a little tipsy, when the dude directs himself to the back seat where Bonnie and I were riding. 'By the way, young lady, you better not sleep outside, if you're having your period. It'll attract the bears,' he said. The pronouncement just about knocked us over, rolling back at us like a belated and unexpected lecture on the birds and the bees. 'No, I'm not,' she lied back to us all.

"Well, we got out at the campsite, thanked the man and watched him ride off into the sunset, selling his junk to the nation's playgrounds. We camped and drifted into the evening and joked, if what he said about bears was true. We talked about steps we could take to prevent it. We could hoist Bonnie up a tree with the food, out of reach of any bears. We could wrap the lower half of her body in an oversize baggy, one of the airtight kinds that locks in odors. We could get a sack of fish and leave them a couple of tents down as a decoy. We all laughed.

"We finally decided none of these would work but had no need to worry about it and were about to drop off to sleep, when we heard the characteristic clanging of a bear going through a garbage can. It wasn't but 100 feet or so away, judging from the sound. Bonnie was visibly concerned and, letting us in on the truth, decided to spend the rest of the night in the bathroom. It wasn't until early that morning that we realized what we thought was a bear was actually a late arriving camper, who had knocked the can over with his trailer in the dark.

"At any rate, after we got going the next day, it took us all morning to get to the other side of the park and another day to get out of it. Hitching wasn't always that bad, though.

"A day later we were outside Billings, Montana, when a trucker stopped and picked us up. He had a rig used for pulling mobile homes, although he wasn't pulling one at the time. We strapped our packs on to the back of the rig and climbed into the cab.

"The first thing he says is, 'I didn't realize there were three of you, but if you want to squeeze in that's OK with me. I'm not supposed to pick up riders anyway, so I might as well go whole hog.' We learned right away what he meant about squeezing in. The only seat other than his was a slightly oversized single seat. We tried putting one person on the floor with two in the seat, but that didn't work. We ended up alternating between the place next to the door and the place in the middle, with Bonnie on our laps or in the middle. If the rain hadn't been moving in, I don't think we would have stuck it out. In any event, we rode like that for 15 hours across 700 miles of Montana and North Dakota flat land. It was horrendous. If you sat at the outside, your face was smashed up against the glass half the time, and if you sat in the middle, the left cheek of your ass was a nervous wreck from the unfulfilled anticipation of finally touching down, your left arm ached from pushing up against the driver's seat, and legs cramped in keeping disentangled with the gear shifts.

"The only thing that kept us going was the driver. He was out-a-sight. After we had been going a couple of hours and were about to go ape-shit staring at each other's armpits, he started to tell a few jokes. It was kind of humorous, watching him hesitate at the punch line, then come out with a mild, muffled 'crap' that tried to stretch to our ears without leaving his throat. That was for Bonnie's benefit, of course. We knew he had a lot more raunchy jokes than that one, and Bonnie didn't give a shit about the language, and we wanted to set him at ease

"Needless to say, we're not into telling jokes much anymore, but after the driver told a couple more of the mildly naughty jokes, we took the cue. Having searched his voluminous memory for such things, J.C. told one about a sailor that had been at sea for many months and lost all his money except for a couple of dollars playing poker the night before reaching port. Of course, he had been planning to go to a whore house when he got in but couldn't afford a woman. For a dollar they sent him up to a room with an ostrich in it. He screws the ostrich, leaves, comes back the next day with his last dollar, and they send him up to a room which has a bunch of people looking through holes into the next room, where a couple are balling.

"All this time, though, J.C. has been using the mildest euphemisms he can come up with. Nothing stark. The sailor, of course says, 'That's pretty good' and the guy next to him turns and says—and at this point J.C. got just as raunchy as he could— 'Man you should have been here yesterday! There was some dumb shit head in there fucking an ostrich.

"Well, when J.C. said that, the driver broke out in a high-pitched cackle that made me shudder, and preceded to drive off the road, just missing several signs. That started it. For the next eight hours we told jokes, every joke we could possibly hope to remember. It got to the point that all J.C. would have to do is start a joke like 'There were two bums...' and the guy would burst into a laugh for two solid minutes.

"He even had me writing down a few catchwords or punchlines so he would remember the choicer jokes. 'Write down "Man farts Star Spangled Banner",' he would say or 'Just put down "Girl kicks prick under the bed",' he would instruct me. I felt like the stenographer in a pornography case.

"Finally, he let us out at a welcome center in Morehead, Minnesota, at 2:00 o'clock in the morning rain. We got out, stretched the kinks out a painful inch at a time, and thanked him for his company as well as the ride. We unhooked our soaking wet mobile homes from the back of his rig and hopefully made for the dryness of the welcome center restrooms.

"But before we got out, he told us his favorite story, again. He said it was true, so I guess it is no joke. It seems appropriate to the time, somehow.

"He was driving to California in a car with his wife and her old lady. They were crossing Nevada at night, and as often happens, there were about three cars all bunched together. Besides himself, there was a brand-new VW and a man in an old Ford station wagon. They were driving through the mountains, so whenever they started up a grade, he and the Ford would pass the VW. Whenever they headed downgrade, the VW would buzz on around them. This went on for miles and each time they got ahead of the VW, its driver refused to dim his lights. Our trucker and the Ford did everything they could to get him to dim his lights, flicking the dimmer switch, cutting their lights on and off, directing the glare from their rear-view mirrors back in his face. Nothing worked. The man in the VW was completely oblivious to their courteously applied requests.

"Finally, the man in the Ford station wagon got thoroughly pissed off and passed the VW for the last time, speeding up around the curve and out of sight. Our trucker friend was still behind him. A few miles later as they pulled up in the dead of night in a small and deader town, there was the Ford station wagon sitting at a stop light. The VW pulled up right behind him, his bright lights still glaring with an obstinate grin into the interior of the Ford. Our trucker friend, somehow sensing the situation, pulled up next to the Ford in the other lane.

"With the calm and fluidity of a well-rehearsed dance, the driver of the Ford got out of his car, walked to the front of the VW, hammer in hand, and politely broke out both of its head lights. Ting! Ting! He returned to his car, got in, and waited for the light to change, at which time he slowly drove off into the void of the dark desert night. Our truck driver, no doubt, was deep in a fit of cackling as he drove away, but he did manage to catch a glimpse of the VW driver, sitting in the dark, eyes and mouth open in an expression of disbelief, his catatonic stare enlightened only by a blushing red changing to a sickly green in the soft glow of the traffic light.

"It was the third time our truck driving friend had told us the story. He really liked it. I must say, I was drawn in by the good vibe of his sense of vigilante justice. No one had been hurt, and the guy sure wouldn't shine his bright lights on anyone else.

"I guess people had been on the trucker's ass all his life. It's unfortunate that the only justice he has seen was in the form of comic relief in the middle of night in some deserted town," I rambled on like an old car into the night toward some unseen destination.

IT TOOK AWHILE TO GET ACROSS MY RAP, THEN

"It took you a while to get across the States then?" Penelope said, many pages later. An astute listener, she drew out the essence of my answer from the billowing mass of verbiage.

I am schizophrenic in my speech mannerisms. For great lengths of time, I may be almost taciturn. Then a mood, a topic of conversation may catch my fancy or my sense of urgency, and I become quite voluble, like a verbal volcano rising above the threshold of constraint.

"Yes," I said.

"When were you out west?" Penelope asked.

"Right before we came over here. Last summer," I responded.

"I haven't been west since I was small. I've got a brother in California, who I'd like to go see when I go back to the States," she said. "It's really nice out west."

"Yes, it is," I said.

THE CLOCK STRIKES ONE AS THE TIME TO MOVE

I glanced over at Carol, who was now just a few minutes away from a new time zone. Her small hand was still pointed at the wine bottle, but her long hand had reached out and was gently moving straight up my back. It was nice. But it was more than just a friendly back rub. It was definitely pointing to more sensuous engagements. I was flattered and relaxed to the warmth that proceeded from her stroking. But she was well out of it, and I am not really into making love to women who are drunk at the time. A little wine is a part of communion, but the whole bottle would be a deadening and ineffective sacrilege. You cannot love a person when part of their self is somewhere else. Besides, I was enjoying Penelope's company too much to turn my back on her. To her, perhaps, but not on her.

We talked a while longer, Penelope and I. There was a growing consensus in the room for a move to the beach. It would soon be late. We were getting louder, and there were many Greek families in adjoining houses. There were also two roommates in the adjoining rooms.

It was just before we rose to leave that Carol's alarm went off. Her long hand left my back and rose to her mouth. She accelerated in studied increments toward the bathroom to ring out her apologies for being too fast to the consoling john. It was a good thing they did not have a squatter. There would be nothing comforting to hug.

We left the house in small clots, removing in the stream of the moment. The usual stops reached out from the edge of the street to slow our procession, but in characteristic fashion we worked a steady, meandering course to the end of the asphalt and a waiting Gertie. Thirteen of us flowed in for a new record load and happily bumped our way home. We parked Gertie at the head of the path, which lay in glittering stones before us in the waxing moon. Its crystal depth beckoned in a silent spell of enchantment and drew us, in laughing cascades, to beach-land and all that lay beyond.

Transiting sun conjunction natal Venus in Cancer: conducive to love affairs.

Transiting Mercury conjunction progressed Venus in Cancer: inclines to amusements and social affairs, new friends and female acquaintances through travel in association with water.

Transiting Moon conjunction progressed Mars on the cusp of Scorpio in the ninth progressed house: inclines toward amorous and impulsive courtship, romantic experiences in connection with long journeys and voyages.

Transiting Jupiter on the cusp of the progressed 12th house in Capricorn: reversals followed by success; successful completion of affairs in conjunction with a long journey or voyage.

Transiting Mars on the cusp of the progressed 7th house in Cancer: impetuous love affair with one of Martian nature but benefit thereby.

Transiting Venus in Gemini semi-sextile transiting Mars (see above): inclines to the society of the opposite sex and general good time. Incites to love. The native is daring and free.

Transiting Venus sextile natal Saturn: favors steady attachments in love and friendships. Much good luck of a substantial quality.

Progressed moon to the cusp of the natal 7th house: awakens interest in matters connected with partners, associates, marriage ...

Had I been fully aware of such things at the time, and had my pack come equipped with the authoritative 'A to Z Horoscope Maker and Delineator' along with all the necessary charts, tables, and other tools of the occult trade, I would have realized the larger implications of that particular evening before me. The planetary rays were smiling down on me in rare form. As it was, I had to rely on my intuitive response to the subtle tides of my body. Fortunately, it did not matter one way or the other. The only advantage, had I had the proper fore knowledge, would have been a chance to apply my gentlemanly inclination to brush my teeth before going to bed.

By the time we reached the Near Beach, the mood of the party had taken a decided turn toward the slower side of interaction. People talked quietly and wasted little time in throwing out their sleeping bags on the cool, sandy strip. The mute-colored cocoons lay in haphazard fashion like a strange assortment of capsules ready to transport the users to another world.

I looked at the moon, across the dark openness of the Aegean, and wondered. The waters of the cove pulled down on my body of warm and heavy wax with a ponderous urging. The moon lightly ran an arm across the rippling surface of the pool and put her hand upon my shoulder. She winked down on me, depositing a faint gleam in the corner of my eye. I immediately felt myself break loose from the longings of the cove, like a tiny bubble of air freed from the surface tension of a still pond. I took my sleeping bag over to where Penelope was busy laying hers out and spread mine out beside it with the familiarity that comes of doing it every night for the last eternity.

PENELOPE AGAIN

Penelope crawled into her sleeping bag and looked up at me as I undressed, her face lit up with an expression of self-satisfying amusement. I crawled into my bag, turned over on my side, and eyed her with my best, most innocent bullshit grin. She smiled back with her characteristic amused look that is always right on the verge of a chuckle.

"Hello," she said.

"Hi," I said.

"What are you up to?" she asked.

"Oh, I don't know. I thought I'd just come over and see if you wanted to screw. I would have waited until Saturday night to ask, you know, done things right, got the car, bought a corsage, iced down some beer, and gone to the drive-in. Except there's no drive-in. But I've had just enough retsina so that my usual sense of reticence has vanished, and anyway, I just thought it would be a nice thing to do," I said.

"I see," she said with a carefree chuckle. "Hum."

Penelope turned from her side onto her stomach, crossing her arms above her for a pillow and laid her head down facing me. She

151

closed her eyes. It was then that I first became certain of the beautiful outcome of the evening. I notice that our sleeping bag zippers meshed, were side by side, and were both down part way. I knew that fate and good fortune was with us.

I slid my hand out from the solitude of my bag across the few inches of meaningless middle land, and into the warm secrets of Penelope's bag. I crooked my middle and index finger and walked him across her back to her right shoulder.

"Now wait a minute, just what are you supposed to be doing now?" she teased.

"Is my technique that obvious? I was trying to make some advances on your virtue behind your back," I mocked.

"Well, don't get your hopes up," she said.

"I've got more than hope up," I said, moving closer to cut out the middle land. It was decidedly cool out, and I felt the warm draft of her proximity like a long-awaited letter from an old friend.

"You can massage my back, if you want to," she giggled softly over some not-so-secret joke between herself.

"Sure," I said, "if you will return the favor. I've been to bed with a stiff back too many times not to get it in writing."

"Okay," Penelope said.

There are two really beautiful aspects of a woman's body. One is the top front corners of the pelvis bone on which they so often and pleasantly hang their clothes. The other is the small of the back. I could lay for hours with the palm of one hand gently cupped round a woman's pelvis, the mound of the thumb nestled in its sunken contour, and the middle of the other hand resting in the arched valley of her back like a willing hot dog.

Penelope may or may not have known she was making us both thus vulnerable when she allowed me to rise above her back like a baker to his task. It didn't matter as I needed no program from there on in, to foresee the outcome.

Her back stretched out before me like a new plateau of promise in the pale light of the moon. The smooth contours flowed in perfect symmetry down to the central river of emotions and beneath me, out of sight. I reached up to the source and began to work slowly down the landscape in firm but gentle currents.

"Ummhumm," she grunted, as the vertebrae popped away the tension.

"Ummm," she sighed, as I reached the small of her back and began to rub in small circular motions.

"It's nice of you to do this, it feels good," she said.

"Ummm," I said, bending over and down in the direction of her voice. I kissed her neck.

COMPLETELY PENELOPE

I'm not sure what happened to my back rub. It may have come and gone so skillfully as to have been unnoticed, or it may not have gotten past the planning stage. I did not seem too preoccupied with making good on verbal contracts at that time.

In fact, I'm not sure about many particulars after I kissed Penelope's neck. All I know is that in a short while we were closer than the two halves of an uncut grapefruit.

CHRYSTALSIS III

A TOTAL CENSORY AWARENESS

The communards of Paris had as their primary goal the liberation of the means of production. They sought to bring their economic life into harmony, to release the vast potential of material production, that was repressed by antiquated ownership and relations of humans to materials, for the benefit of humankind. They had their Marx and Engels and Bakunin.

We have as a primary goal the liberation of the means of reproduction. We seek to bring the psychic life into full harmony, to release the infinite creative potential of the human soul that has been repressed by antiquated relationships of man to woman and of each human soul to its own body, which is its primary creative and expressive tool. We have Freud and Jung and Reich and countless others. And most important, we have ourselves. We could not ask for more.

There are many people that walk around with a big void between their knees and their waist. They do not understand their bodies. They are afraid they might get shocked if they became fully visible. They are very worried about lose morals and pornography. 'Pornography' says Webster 'the depiction of erotic behavior intended to arouse sexual excitement.' I get sexually excited watching the sunrise. It is a good thing these people are not wearing my eyes when they go about enforcing their morals. If they did, they would have to censor the world.

There are other people who walk around on their knees and are only visible to their waist. They do not understand their bodies either. They are afraid of finding out there is something besides their bodies. They are not as dangerous, perhaps, as the former people, but they are just as mistaken. If these people had my eyes, they would probably try to screw the whole world.

The confusion I think is over the nature of the realities for which the terms 'sexual' and 'genital' stand. The former person does not perceive sexual reality, or Yang-Yin, except with respect to the genitals. The latter person may perceive the greater sexual reality, but only through the symbol of the genital. Both see the sexual is arising with respect to the genital, instead of the genital as merely a specific instance of the sexual. The total sexual experience must include the genital but is not confined to that.

That is why the hard-core pornographers and the censors are so absurd. It is also the reason that euphemistic images are so necessary for literary descriptions of lovemaking. It is not to avoid allegations of pornography nor is it out of prudish desire to avoid the facts. Only one with a poverty-stricken sense of love and pleasure is thinking 'dick in cunt, dick in cunt' with each thrust of the pelvis. Of course, there may be times when such descriptions are app. But a total sexual union is one of the ultimate living metaphors of being and is best dealt with effectively and honestly with metaphorical literature.

CHRYSTALSIS III

The astute censor, therefore, will know that I mean it in the most pornographic sense, when I say that I was unaware of any separate and distinct portion of my body as I drew it up inside the exquisite pulsing and glowing warmth of Penelope's being and went to sleep.

CHRYSTALSIS IV

NO LONGER A RED BANDANNA

I went back to Carol's house the day after her party in hopes of finding my red bandana. I had a red bandana that I wore around my head to keep the hair out of my face. It is the best thing to do if you do not want to cut your hair for some unknown reason. I wore my red bandana like an anemic Geronimo to keep from facing my hair.

Somehow, I had misplaced my bandana in the absent-minded nest of Carol's party, and I had woken to the sudden realization that my hair had departed without it. I naturally had to find it or a good replacement.

Carol was not at home when I got to her house, but one of her roommates was. She was very pleasant as she asked me into the cool albescence of the front room.

"Have you seen an old red bandana around here?" I asked. "I had one when I came in last night, but I headed off without it."

"I think I saw one in the kitchen," she said. "You're welcome to look."

She went back over and sat down next to her boyfriend on the couch. They had been making out when I arrived and now, he wanted me to find my bandana and leave so they could get back to it. I could tell that by the way his eyes followed me across the room, into the kitchen, and out the back door.

"This doesn't look like my red bandana. It's too small," I said, with a voice characteristic of the lost and found departments all over the world. 'Lost and found' is a curious appellation for them. They should not really be together. You almost never 'find' anything where you go to report it 'lost'. They are as far apart as two poles of a magnet. One should always go to a different place to report a loss than the location where one might hope to find it. Your chances are better that way of tricking it into showing up where you least expect it.

"Well, it doesn't belong to anyone here. Whoever left it probably got yours by mistake. You can have it. If someone turns up with yours, we'll let you know," she said. I couldn't see them, but I knew they were both looking at the back door.

"Okay, be on the lookout for a midget or a pinhead," I said, trying to force the tight bandana down over my head.

They were silent in the other room.

"Thanks," I said to myself as I headed out the back door of their intentions.

CHRYSTALSIS V

MIGRATIONS, IT'S GETTING CROWDED!

Several more afternoons at the Windmill Café resulted in several more additions to the nightly load of Gertie out to the scimitar sand beach, and several more parties to welcome them. There were the two German girls, Claudia and Brigitte. There was another American girl, Cathy. There were some other people who cannot be reduced to names. The beach was beginning to grow. It was taking on all the appearances of an overcrowded city. That is when Penelope and I decided to move to the suburbs.

The Rock People had disappeared one day without a trace. They had been devoured by the Elli or some other sea creature and were never heard from again. The Mid Beach couple, obviously not worried about any connection between their disappearance and the rock, took their place, leaving the Mid Beach lots at a bargain rate. Penelope and I lost no time in moving into our two-body tent with the back screen porch, and all-zippered, semi-circular cook hole, with all the pretention of a twenty-year mortgage.

AT ROBERT'S HUT

Carol's house proving inappropriate for more parties, we decided to move to Robert's hut for the nightly gala event. Robert's hut sat on the side of the small valley that ran from the base of the small mountain down to our cove.

In front of the hut was an open, flat area, about thirty feet square, overlooking the valley. It was the perfect place to sit and eat and sing and keep the whole countryside awake all night long.

ALITERATIONS ON A RATION. SENSATION

Our meals at Robert's hut were not nearly so elaborate as the one at Carol's. Our number was growing, so we decided to sacrifice variety for quantity. J.C. was an expert with such meals. He could cook rice and noodles with the skill of a script writer for Chef Boyardee's.

Preparing such a meal is no easy matter when you have twenty odd people to feed, and all you have for cooking is a one and a two-quart pot. You have to start early if you want to eat late.

We started out with about four pounds of rice, then added another pound at Ed's insistence. This was dumped, two slow pots at a time, into a big bucket that Robert used to store his water. To this we added about two or three gallons of the usual salad vegetables, diced, sliced, and spiced. We thus had three big buckets of cold food. And it sufficed so all enticed, ended up nicely spliced, to the iced, diced, sliced, spiced rice. With a little bit left for the mouse. And it really tasted pretty good.

"Do you think we have enough?" Ed said, before he dragged the heaping buckets of macro-biotic goodness out into the waning light of day. "Remember, J.C., you, Fred, and I ate a kilo of rice

CHRYSTALSIS V

measured uncooked, and a kilo of tuna at one sitting. Do you think we should cook some more rice?"

"You mean you ate it. We had normal portions, and you finished up what was left. I think we have enough. If you're still hungry, I'll fix you some after we finish, then go for the stomach pump when the cramps set in," said J.C. helpfully.

"Come on, Jay, don't give me any shit. I just don't want anyone to be left hungry," Ed said.

"Especially you," J.C., said.

"Well, us Canadians have big appetites. We have to keep strong and fit so we can look after our little brothers to the South," chuckled the tall, gangly, nineteen-year-old, hockey playing, Tasmanian devil.

"Oh Canada," the chorus chimed in.

ED BELCHED

The meal proved more than adequate for our needs. Clustered about the three big pots in eager canine fashion, we scooped the mouthfuls of sustenance according to our individual needs, at first with the haste of apprehended want, slowing to the realization of apparent glut. One half hour after the next to last person had crawled away to await the necessary adjustments and redistribution of a stomach, Ed belched a final time and laid down his spoon until the next day.

"Oh, man. Oooohhh. That was good, J.C.," he said, "and Heidi, and whoever else helped." Ed leaned back against the log behind him and patted his belly.

The period of eating was followed by less intense period of recuperation before the festivities could begin. A load of rice is quite heavy and seems to have a constraining effect upon the vocal cords. It was as we waited for the leavening effect of the retsina to lift our moods from the gravity of our stomachs to the rarified air of our souls, that Carol approached me with her strange inquiry.

A RED BANDANA AGAIN

"Is this your bandana?" she asked. "I heard you say you were missing one, and I found this one at my house."

"Well, I picked one up there, too, but it wasn't mine. Your roommate said it didn't belong to anyone and for me to take it. Let me look at the one you have. Perhaps it is mine," I said.

"Okay," Carol said, handing over the red bandana like it was a membership card to a secret Janis Joplin Fan Club.

TWO JANIS

Carol cannot know, of course, what an effect that had on me. There were two Janis Joplin's that I knew. There was first and foremost, the one on stage and on the records. Boy, the woman could sing! She could really belt it out. I missed that one.

Then there was a Janis Joplin that I had met at a party. It was one of those brief segments of her that one might meet in a dream. It had all the alcohol and smoke haze unreality of such a meeting. She had played at a local university, and a friend of mine who happened to have met her before, asked her over to a party that was happening the same night after her show. So, Janis came along, wrapped in her bearskin rug and Southern Comfort against the sudden snowfall that was chilling and cleansing the air and making for the toasty glow atmosphere of the party. She had draped her bearskin over the back of a chair that was pushed up against the table in the kitchen and had gone to another room with her bottle of bourbon.

Of course, there were people oohing and aahing at the celebrity, while others were just interested in hearing her rap. The room was pretty crowded. I stayed in the kitchen with some other people and shot the shit. I guess I'm a bit given to inverted snobbery, at times. I would like to think that it is just that I feel people are pretty much the same, famous or not. I'm not very impressed by glamour and fame and the like.

When I was still quite young, my ole Pappy used to say to me, "Son, always remember that all those famous celebrities are just people. They're no better or worse than you. When the president of the United States takes a shit, it stinks every bit as much as yours."

"I'll member that, Pappy," I would say back.

Anyway, I pulled up on the kitchen table with my legs spread and hanging on either side of the chair and its bearskin rug. I was rapping with a few friends and smoking a cigarette. I really had no idea who's coat I was straddling as some guy in front of me backed up against my hand knocking the fire from my cigarette onto the beautiful expansive back of the bearskin rug. We quickly got it out but not before it burned a nice dime-sized piece of fur. The burn was quite visible at the top of the chair.

TOO JANIS

A short time later, Janis came in, near empty bottle of Southern Comfort in hand, and reached for her bearskin rug. The hole glared up at her like a bullet hole in a favorite pet.

"God damn. Look what's happened to my fucking coat. Some mother fucker burned a hole in it," she yelled, looking at me.

I stopped talking to my friend next to me and shrugged my shoulders.

"Thanks a lot, asshole. I ought a make you pay for this," she slurred.

"You know what you can do with your bottle of Southern Comfort," I said in defense.

"Yeah," she mumbled as she threw the coat over her shoulder and took another sip. "What a shitty thing to do to my coat," she said walking out the door toward her appointment with an overdose of smack.

TO JANIS

There was another Janis no one knew, I would think. A tired and lonely Janis, whose few comforts were southern bourbon and an old fur coat. I really regretted the cigarette and my short retort when I thought about her several months later, passing from this scene in a sad and dark motel room, frightened and alone.

A SECOND RED BANDANNA

"Well, it's a red bandana alright, but I can't tell if it is mine. It looks like mine, but you know how it is. I'd like to say it was mine, cause it's a lot bigger and better than the one I ended up with, but I can't lie just to get rid of a headache. You keep it," I said to Carol.

"That's alright, I don't want it, and it doesn't belong to anyone else I know. You keep it. I don't like to watch the top of your head turning purple, because of a 29¢ bandana. You might lose all your hair," she said sympathetically.

"49¢," I said. "It was 49¢. You may be right. I'll keep it, but if you find out it belongs to someone else, please let me know."

"Alright," Carol said.

THANK YOU, BO

Eventually, the inevitable round of songs began. It is hard to pinpoint the exact moment of such chorus beginnings. It is rather like an old phonograph which is cranked up to full speed after starting with a slow gravelly scratch.

After the necessary warmup, we reached full 78 speed and began to blare out the sounds like an anachronistic line of instant Juke boxes. There was the usual competition for each new song, but we managed to make our way from the days of rhythm and blues and early rock and roll, through the payola scandal, quickly skirting the post scandal plethora of sugar sweet bobbysocks rock, to the Beatles, acid rock, folk rock, country rock, nostalgia rock, rock-rock, and beyond. And back again. Several times.

Our volume gradually turned toward maximum as we progressed. In the pale glow of the moon, diffused and veiled by the light mist that held the valley, our gathering became an ethereal convocation of spirits and elves, satyrs and nymphs, gaily dancing together in the moment of mirth, happily beckoning all to our night of joyful revelry. Our call did not go unheeded. From half a mile up the valley, four people were drawn to our festival, bringing with them a whole new set of records and a jug of wine.

"We couldn't help but want to join in after hearing your party," they said. "Is that alright?"

"Of course," we said. "Have a seat."

"Fine," they said, "do you know 'I'm allergic to your bobby socks'."

"Well, we'll try," we said.

It went well for a while, but then we realized that one of these new people was a frustrated disc jockey.

"How about this?" he would say. "How about that?" "Do you remember this?"

He did not understand our scene. He should have been there from the first. It was not necessary to have a programmer for the night's activities. Everyone had his own show, and somehow it all managed to mesh together. We were able to get the point across to him in a subtle way, and things flowed on toward a grand finale of the Retsina Theme Song.

This was a rather simple song sung over and over again, until an appropriate degree of musical intoxication was achieved. It went like this:

Retsina, Retsina,

Retsina, Retsina,

Retsina, Retsina,

You're the one for me.

Retsina, Retsina,

Retsina, Retsina,

Retsina, Retsina,

You're the one for me.

Retsina, Retsina,

Retsina, Retsina,

Retsina, Retsina …….

Sung to the blues tune of 'Corrina, Corrina' by Bo Carter and the rest.

People began drifting back toward the beach, as the music slowly began to subside. They carried their tunes with them, strewing their 'Retsina, Retsina' and 'Casey Jones' out along their path in flowery sprays to embellish their passing.

HEIDI DO

I looked over at J.C. and Heidi who were deep in a fit of laughter, holding onto each other to keep from falling over. It was apparent from their actions that more was cooking between them that night than the rice dinner. That was good to see.

J.C. was mellow, but he had a way of unexpectedly blowing up every now and then. Bottled up frustrations, very Freudian. I had a way of drawing out the situation quite unconsciously. I also had a feeling that a woman would have a way of drawing out the situation quite non-violently and much more consciously. Events since that night have proved me right, as J.C. and Heidi happily bounce along in Gertie, somewhere between San Francisco and Anchorage. I hoped as much, as I watched them walk arm in arm down from Robert's hut in the direction of Near Beach.

YET ANOTHER RED BANDANNA

Penelope and I soon followed in the direction of our tent. Along the way we ran into Bilbo who was hobbling along in the direction of the Bush.

"You haven't happened to have seen a red bandana any where have you?" he asked. "I lost mine the other night and can't seem to find it."

"Maybe it's one of these. I lost mine at Carol's and haven't been able to find it. But no one seemed to know who these belonged to, so they gave them to me," I said handing them to Bilbo for closer examination.

He looked them over for some trace of familiarity. "Nope," he said, "neither of these is mine."

"Well, take one of mine. I don't need two," I said.

"I'll wait and see if I can find mine," he said. "If not, I might like to use one of those." He handed them back to me and headed on down the beach towards the Bush.

CHRYSTALSIS VI

NO MORE CONSTANT AN APPLE

It was inevitable. I had struggled with it for four days and could stand it no longer. I had to see what was on the other side of the island.

"Really great beaches," they said. "Clear water. It's a nice trip."

I try to resist the do-it-just-to-say-you've-done-it syndrome, but I'm not always successful. But then, there is more to it than that. I mean, the rest of my life, J.C. and the rest would make reference to the other side of the island, and I would always be left in the dark, like someone forcing up a sick and uncertain laugh for the tail end of someone else's private joke. There was another facet of life on the other side of the island, and I had to experience it then, or go to a lot of trouble later just to get back to see it.

There is one significant time I resisted the urge. We were in Istanbul, a few weeks after we left Paros. Istanbul is the first real taste of the East. Standing on the edge of the Bosporus, I looked across the hazy strait to the jet of land which is the doorstep of Asia. From there the way led back into time and deep, deep into the mysteries of the subconscious. The great continent stirred vague memories of the distant past and beckoned me on to a deep and peaceful oblivion in her bosom, like a long and oft-sought mother. Standing on the edge of that enormous psychic gulf, I was no longer a human being with a cultural identity or a past. I was but a momentary impulse of longing that sought to lose itself in one quick shudder of surrender in the vast indescribable void that lay before it.

We talked for several days about going. It was touch and go for me. We had reservations for the Soviet Union. We had prepared for the trip. But there it lay open before us.

Since J.C. and I were planning on working again in Switzerland, and then going East the following spring, there was no real need to rush things. We decided to wait. Then some people hit on a compromise. We would take the ferry across the Bosporus to the Asian side. We would touch Asia, and then come back. It was tempting, but hardly a substitute. I decided to wait until the spring.

As so often happens with plans not-so-well-made, we did not go back to Switzerland and when spring came around, I was 7000 miles from Istanbul and the Asian shore. Now I have 7000 miles to go to cross that gulf that still lies open before me like an enchanting abyss.

I think I was right to visit the other side of Paros while I had the chance.

UP AND OVER

Penelope and I put sixty drachmae worth of petrol in Gertie, climbed in, and headed out the paved road to the left of the Windmill Café. The road followed a wide, slow swell up from the village, between the mountain on the right and a smaller group of hills on the left. On the far side of this saddle, about three miles away was another village, somewhat smaller than the village of Paros, and another beach. Having been there the day before, we decided to take another route up into the mountains and down the other side, to a small fishing village that was indicated on the map.

We directed Gertie onto the right-hand fork of the road and began the slow, winding climb up the mountain. To the left the terrain took a sharp sloping drop toward a dry stream bed at the bottom of the ravine. Here and there a gnarled and withered tree clung to the side of the hill in endless anticipation of the next rain. A collection of thirsty brush sparsely covered the rocky ground in between, fighting for the little moisture that managed to escape the quenchless absorption of the trees' roots. In as frequent an interval as the arid land would permit, an alabaster block obstinately stuck to the mountain in a mute but shining testimony of the islander's timeless perseverance and constant spirit in the face of such barren prospects.

Gertie pulled up behind a man who was driving an old donkey cart. We waited for a sufficient widening of the road, then slowly pulled around him. His white teeth shown in a sparkling grin from beneath his weathered face, and he raised his arm in a cheery salute. We waved back vigorously. He was still waving in the rear-view mirrors as he dropped behind the next turn and disappeared out of sight.

Near the top of the mountain, we could see the upper reaches of the open bowl of the marble quarry. The marble of Paros is world renowned and has been used in the construction of Greek buildings and statues for over 2,500 years. Knowing this, I was a bit amazed that the pit was no bigger than it was. But it is only recently, I suppose, that men have gone hog wild building monuments to themselves. The early Greeks were much more select. It is my hope that the marble of Paros does not become too much in demand or I am sure the island will eventually be reduced beyond recognition.

Back behind us in the still steam of the Aegean, several islands had risen into view, forming a string of great stepping-stones running back in the direction of Athens. Their gray form stood like stolid players on a huge board in some perpetual game of waiting. To the front of us the large and lofty terraced mass of Naxos sat at the back door of Paros. Naxos was the invisible destination of the Elli after leaving the small port of Paros. Beyond Naxos the islands merged with the veil of heat as they continued their step-stone path across the Aegean to the door of Asia.

The road wound down the other side of the mountain in tight curves. With much breaking and coasting we followed the meandering course down through the dull, dry green groves of olive trees and the wired-up stands of sprouting vineyards to the sloping run out of wheat fields flowing down to the shore below. The section of the island that Penelope and I had just entered seemed more fertile than our side of the island. It was less rocky, in any event, therefore more amenable to cultivation.

We followed the paved road to its termination in the fishing village. The village was quite small, with only a handful of houses, but three of these turned out to be cafés, at least in part. Penelope and I went into one of the cafés and bought some ice cream, then walked on back to the terrace in front. An English couple in their forties or about, were sitting on the terrace drinking lemonade and looking out into the little harbor.

They nodded the nod of recognition that one encounters in foreign and culturally distinct lands that says that somehow, by some standard, set by someone, we have something in common. At least more in common than with the local inhabitants, perhaps...or not. We nodded back to preserve the myth or truth, whichever it may be, and walked on out to the jetty.

It was almost noon and most of the fishing boats were still at work. One had been hauled up on the shore and was undergoing a new painting. It lay in its cradle, deck baking in the sun, its hull stripped and anxiously waiting for the preparation to rejoin its friends at sea. Penelope and I stood looking out over the still glass of water, hurriedly working to beat the sun to the ice cream. There was no place to swim there, and deciding to dispense with any further lunch, we strolled back to Gertie and drove back up the road from the sleepy little village. We turned left at the first intersection onto a dirt road and headed clockwise around the island. The road, though dirt, was in good condition, having been recently scraped, and we encountered no unusual problems as we drove through the surrounding fields of ripe wheat.

We traveled a few miles until we came to a convenient place to pull the van over to the side. The water was about two hundred yards off to the left, across an open field and down a path by a stone wall. Penelope grabbed a towel while I put on my sandals, and we headed on down to the beach.

The site we had chosen did not run gradually down to the water as might have been expected. It ended in a small cliff of sand some ten feet high, below which the beach ran twenty or thirty feet out to the ripple-less sea. After looking for a few minutes up and down the strand, we located a suitable place to descend, then went down and up the beach to a small, protected cove. We spread out our towels, undressed, and walked out into the cool covering of the Aegean.

WON'T YOU PLEASE COME OUT OF THAT OLD WOODEN HORSE?

"What are you going to do after you leave here?" I asked.

The soft tuft of dark auburn at the base of her abdomen was irresistible. I gently ran my fingers through the hair so that the strands furrowed up between my fingers like a newly turned field of velvet. Her hair delicately tickled my fingers and palm and gave me an easy and reassuring serenity. I repeated the motion over and over, then lightly lay my hand there to rest.

"I don't have much money left. I'll probably go to Switzerland with Heidi, then fly back the end of July," Penelope said.

"And next year? Do you have any plans?" I asked.

"I'll probably go to work awhile, then maybe go back to school. I just don't know, I have to wait and see," she said.

"How much school have you finished?" I asked.

"Oh, about two years, give or take a few credits," she said. "I'm not really enthusiastic about going back, but my folks would like me to finish. And what about you? What great quest brings you to this little island?" She smiled in a friendly teasing mock.

"Sun and fun," I said. "And changes. Two years ago, I was out to revolutionize the world. I was a dyed-in-the-wool Marxist

Leninist Maoist communist campus revolutionary. But things started happening and I had to get away to see if I could piece it all together."

"And have you?" she asked.

"Things are beginning to make a lot more sense now," I said. "I'm no longer paranoid. That's a big relief. I'm more optimistic than I have been."

"How is that?" asked Penelope.

"Well, within the anti-war and civil rights movement, for two or three years there I was involved in trying to figure out my part in the effort to create a better, saner world. I was agnostic at the time and I gravitated toward Marxism because it answered some fundamental political issues from an economic perspective and understanding. Being an economist, it is seductive to want to believe that a person's identity, their sense of self, is largely determined by what they do to make a living producing and consuming stuff, whether your political perspective is left or right.

"Obviously, those who have to work to make a living on a day-to-day basis will have a different sense of self than those who are born not having to work day-to-day. By definition, those working day-to-day will end up consuming virtually all of what they are able to produce or acquire in a day, if they are able to work at all. If they can't work or can't get a job, they are shit-out-of-luck.

"I don't know about you, but between north and southern Europe, it is taking us about a hundred dollars a month to travel and camp and eat basic, but good, food and drink decent beer and wine."

"That's about right," she nodded.

I sat up in a half lotus pose facing Penelope on the narrow beach and began to assume a more professorial tone.

"Those with a longer time horizon of say, month-to-month or year-to-year or who for whatever reason don't have to work at all, are generally able to do so because they are able to produce or have access to a lot more than they consume in the same period of time.

"Marxism says that sense of self tends to group people into classes as they identify, voluntarily or not, with how they make or acquire their needs for living, and that their identification with class is primary to the political organization of a society. The problem with this thinking is that there are other social influences on the psyche that can result in people identifying their selves and behaving in ways and with groups that contradict this primary class premise. Like with religion, Christianity or otherwise.

"Marxism, or at least a lot of leftist thinking, says that if society is made equitable, injustice and oppression will go away. It seems to assume that people are all blank slates when they come into the world, and the circumstances we are born into, generally identified as class, determines whether we are fair in our dealings with others or not. That if you are born rich you will be greedy and if you are not rich, you will be fair in dealing with other people. This just doesn't appear to be the case to me now. Some people are just nice, and some people are just not."

"You think?" Penelope chuckled.

"There is obviously a significant psychological factor in determining people's sense of identity that has nothing at all to do with economic class and that may affect a person's political perspective and activity in different ways. Maybe it's in the DNA, maybe it's some developmental trauma, maybe it's a soul, maybe it's a combination of all three, I don't know. And apparently, neither does anybody else, or if they do, they aren't telling. Or maybe they have already told or are telling now, and I just haven't gotten the word yet.

"What I do know is that millions of working-class white guys, men and women, but especially the men, have been manipulated by politicians and bosses by racial and sexist appeals that allow them to divide and conquer and make money in the process, whether that manipulation comes from genuine belief on the part of the parties involved or just basic cynicism. These guys form the bulk of the class that should be ushering in the revolution and the new golden age for humanity.

"A Marxist organizer would probably tell you this is just another educational opportunity for labor organizing, and we just need enough community organizers to form a labor party backbone of the working class, but I think it's not that simple. They should all come to Paros and read Plato's Republic.

"Marxism has a thing that says that a revolution is a result of and can only happen when objective conditions are ripe. This means that the political economy as a whole develops organically, which makes sense to me. Another organic premise is that the success of capitalism has the seeds of its own destruction built into it because of what they call the crisis of overproduction. This is essentially where businesses produce more than they can sell and have to lay people off, which causes social unrest. My sense of what is happening now in America is that things are far from ripe.

"And what about poverty and bigotry and war? They won't just disappear like that," she said.

"No, they won't. But I don't believe now they will be addressed by old left politics. It's like trying to intercept a runaway ship. If you aim for the ship, by the time you get to its position, it has already moved out in front of you. That's what the old left is doing. Every time they get to the point where they should have been able to capture the ship, it has left them behind, trying to find out where their calculations went wrong. They weren't willing to admit the ship is moving and zig-zagging. They think it is in the same place that it was 100 years ago. But it's not.

"We have to take into account the ship's forward movement. Then we have to aim well ahead of it. We have to start building a future comprehensive culture, not an exclusive counterculture. Then we will be waiting for the ship when it gets to us. We will have seen what is ahead and will have no problem taking it.

"The Greeks were pretty smart about such things. After fighting the Trojans for ten long years, they realized the impossibility of defeating them in open battle. What brute force could not accomplish, was accomplished by stealth.

"Nonchalance is our Trojan horse. The strength of the status quo is not in their armies or their banks or their factories. Their strength is intangible. It lies in maintaining allegiance to their traditions. And they are destroying their own traditions quite unaided. Their preoccupation with money is destroying their traditions and they are frustrated, in fact, everybody is frustrated.

"The only alternative to this frustration is a cool indifference. Frustration breeds fascism, but even that can't last forever. Fascism gives a brief flurry of security and identity, but it is too exhaustive. It collapses in on itself. Ultimately those who are bereft of tradition will have to seek a new nonchalance, if we are going to survive as a human race as we now know it. But what appears as indifference is really not that at all. The new casualness will not be indifference as much as un-excitability, a detached, non-aggressive resolve—even if sometimes seems offensive—not based on fear but on intelligence.

"That is a step forward. As people cut out the influence of the outside world, its demands, its seductiveness, they come to rely more on themselves… and each other. There we will find our real strength. That is what we need to do. Out of the seeming nonchalance, we will be able to erect a new set of values, keeping any essential traditional ones, but fashioned to our own present needs. And because the values will be ours, the power will be ours.

"I guess I'm still a revolutionary I'm just a quiet one now."

"And what do you plan to do when you get back? What will you do about it?" she asked.

"I don't have any firm plans," I said, "but I have a general idea of what I have to do first.

"A lot of technological change is coming. Computer miniaturization and automation is coming and who knows what that will do to how we work and travel and live. For one of my philosophy courses in college each of us had to write a Utopia. My Utopia of the time was a picture of a decentralized, basically stateless society of individuals living in small groups that were supported by a combination of local and national food production, technologically advanced automated manufacturing industries, product distribution, and transit, where everyone had their own computer with a terminal monitor—like the punch card mainframes I used to flunk my programming course my junior year because I was involved at the vigil sit-in on the quad after Martin Luther King was shot—but reduced in size to fit and function in a self-contained TV, which is used for communicating with everyone else, for civic discourse and voting, for shopping. That was my Utopia. I may still have a copy of it at home, but I haven't laid eyes on it in a while.

"With these kinds of changes, with civil rights and the war winding down, with the equal rights amendment once it finally passes and Roe versus Wade probably decided in favor of legalization in the Supreme Court, I don't see the possibility or the conditions for a revolution in the U.S. any time soon, perhaps ever. I'm optimistic, if McGovern can win the Democratic nomination and defeat Nixon. I don't believe the Soviet Union will last that much longer. I don't know about China. That's a different deal. But I don't have much interest in political solutions right now. I think they will take care of themselves.

"I like to design and build things. I worked with my dad who's a construction engineer during the summers in college and for a year before we came to Europe. Right now, J.C. and I are planning to work in Switzerland again next winter, then head east to India, and somehow make it around the world. When we get back to the states, buy some land somewhere, maybe Alaska, and hone my carpentry skills. Help each other build our houses and live on the cheap. Continue to travel and see the world. I like to think and write, so maybe I can make enough bread to do that.

"We were planning to go this year until Ed and J.C. hooked up with Jacqueline in Switzerland while I was back in the States. They decided to go up through Russia later this summer, instead. India would be part of my spiritual quest. Basically, though, I just want to figure out what this life is all about wherever I go, whatever I do."

"And this spiritual quest?" Penelope asked, nodding to my posture, cross-legged in the sand.

"After I got myself together, I figured I'd have a better idea what was happening and what to do next. I decided to rely on things I knew for certain, not someone else's idea of what is the best behavior for every human.

"A friend of mine was coming back from a rock concert in Montreal one time, and he picked up a guy hitching. The guy was very quiet and self-composed. He had the appearance of the stereotypical gentle hippie who is into Eastern ways.

"At the border, the US Customs Agents gave them the works. They searched my friends van, then took the hitcher in and stripped him down, checked up his asshole, the works. When they got through, my friend was thoroughly pissed off. He was really ranting and raving about the government and oppression and all. The hitcher just sat there as serene as ever.

"'Doesn't that piss you off?' My friend asked the guy.

"'Nothing outside my body hassles me,' the guy replied.

"I'd like to become like that hitcher. I feel right now that we can do anything we want, if we try hard enough to rise above and understand the situation. I'm not a determinist any longer, not a materialist. I can feel the first beginnings of a free will now. It can't be analyzed, but when felt, it is unmistakable. We may not be able to control any of the rest of the world, but we can learn to master ourselves if we just have the will," I said.

"I hope you're right," she said, reaching up and running her hand softly through my hair.

"It's all we have left. The old gods are all but destroyed," I said. I bent over and kissed the tuft of auburn gently.

"Not all of them," she said, stroking the back of my head.

I sat back up and smiled.

"All You Need Is Love," I sang to the John Lennon tune, continuing on. "Maybe I'll learn to play the guitar, become a rock star. My eponymous first album, *Two Fine Guitars*. What do you think?"

"Yeah, right. Every longhaired guy's dream. Rock and roll, drugs, and sex," Penelope chuckled, "in that order."

"Rock and roll maybe, drugs not so much—well, maybe retsina—but sex?" I clucked back and leered.

"We better get back or we'll miss the Elli," she said ignoring the offering and bringing us back to the island and things ahead, as she got up to get dressed.

"Yes," I replied. "We better."

CHRYSTALSIS VIII

AROUND

From the point where we had parked, onward the road began gradually to melt into the landscape on either side. At one point we could hardly make out where it led across the parched and sunbaked apron of that side of the island. We had definitely reached the most barren portion of Paros.

We found our way slowly down what seemed more like a washed-out ravine, than a dirt road. We were going so slow that I had to check several times to make sure we were not in reverse. Finally, the road began, very gradually, to take on more and more of the nature of its name. Antiparos, the smaller sister island of Paros, whose northern tip was visible from the cove at Near Beach, appeared on the left. About an hour after we left the beach, Penelope spotted a verdant stand of trees up on the side of the mountain to the right.

"That must be the Valley of the Butterflies," she said. "It's the only place I've seen that seems to fit the description. We should come here one day."

"You're probably right," I said leaning over to get a better view through the window. "Yes, we should come." Then, "We must be getting close to the beach by now."

A few more minutes and we spotted Demetri's house, high up on the side of the hill. The night of my encounter with Chris, Robert and J.C. had been the happy recipients of Dimitri's hospitality. That explained their late return. In addition to selling them the retsina at a bargain, he set them down at his table and treated them to wine, dinner, and after, a little ouzo. All accompanied by his unparalleled Greek friendliness.

From Dimitri's we had only to follow the broad curve around the head of the valley to reach the footpath that led to the beach. In keeping with the internal timing of the Aegean, we were right on schedule. Ed, Bilbo, Blonde Dennis, Claudia and Brigitte were just emerging from the path.

AND THROUGH

"Right on time," someone said. "Let's get down to the Windmill. It's about time for the Elli. Most of the others walked on in."

"Do you think Ann and Nettie will be on it?" I looked at Ed, who was grinning.

"Sure, they'll be on it," Ed grinned back.

Ann and Nettie were two English girls that had traveled with us from Venice to Athens. We had gotten to be pretty close over the brief sojourn. Especially Ed and Ann. Not as close as he would have liked, but as close as she would permit. He was relatively starry-eyed about her.

We had left them in Athens for the previous week. Ann was blue over some Greek lover she had had the year before in Athens.

She could not avoid moping about the stage of their affair, in hopes of grasping some small memory which was still in the future. They had agreed to meet us on Paros the following Saturday, and that day had arrived.

The small group from the beach piled in Gertie and we headed on down to the Windmill Café, picking up a few stragglers on the way. We parked the van by the wharf and went over to take our seats with the rest.

EITHER YOU TAKE ME OR ICE CREAM

In due time, the Elli landed with the usual fanfare and emotion. "Dig that anchor," came right on cue from the midst of the Welcoming Committee. As the crowd began to clear away, we saw the unmistakable sights of Ann's Raphaelian bosoms, as some dirty old poet on a previous ferry had called them, and Nettie's impish grin make their way toward us.

"Well, you made it," Ed chuckled with glee.

"But of course, we made it. We said we'd be here, didn't we?" answered Ann, in her best proper British.

Ed hugged her with enthusiasm.

"Well, it looks like you're well at it," said Nettie, looking at the retsina bottles.

"This is a lovely place, isn't it?" she said.

"Yes, it is. A bit hot, but there's plenty of ice cream, and life is quite slow and easy here," I said.

"Yes, well I suppose it is. But then you wouldn't be around here if it was otherwise, would you now?" Nettie chided. She exhibited the quaintest British habit of offering her sentence as an answer in advance of its own question, directed for your confirmation and the benefit of some unseen witness of the moment. It was a built-in exercise in the Socratic method.

"I guess not," I said. "How was your stay in Athens?"

"Quite satisfactory, really. We went to quite a few places, historical and current. I believe Ann has gotten over most of her blue funk. It really is silly when she gets like that. It's such a bore. But then I suppose it is painful remembering, I mean, after what he did to her and all, isn't it?" Nettie continued.

"Yes," came my perfunctory reply.

"And what have you been doing since you arrived?" asked Nettie, glancing quickly over at Penelope who was seated next to me.

"Meeting some really nice people," I said. I did not miss her inference. Nettie had teased me for my ill-concealed and ill-consummated wantonness on our way down from Venice, and she was not about to let up now. "This is Penelope, by the way. Penelope, Nettie. She traveled with us from Italy to Athens."

They passed polite greetings.

"And you are still as horny as ever?" She couldn't resist the jab.

"You'll never know now, Nettie, darling. Opportunity knocks but once. You missed your chance," I returned the jab.

"Yes, well that's life, isn't it," she said mockingly, rising in the direction of the Café cooler like an arctic bloodhound. "I suppose I'll just have to settle for an ice cream."

CHRYSTALSIS IX

A SEND-OFF

The next day marked the first departure from the scimitar sand beach in a week. Jackie was eager to reach Britain before returning to the States in August, and as Heidi and Penelope could not accompany her due to the lack of money, she decided she might as well go on from Paris alone. She planned to wait at the Athens youth hostel until she found a ride North. Cathy had decided to join her.

It was a bit ironic that Jackie, seemingly the most mellow one on the beach, was so eager to leave. But she had her own slow reasons for going. After the usual rounds of retsina at the Windmill Café, we performed our first real function as a Send-Off Committee. With much well-wishing and last-minute reminders and words of advice, Jackie and Cathy boarded the Elli, barely ahead of the gangplank. Waving slowly from the stern deck, she sped out of the harbor and off in the direction of a future I had all but forgotten.

Meanwhile, Ann and Nettie had been quite busy discovering new aspects of Parosian island-ness. In barely a week's time, the rest of us had become fairly stuck in our ways, as we traced our daily orbit from the beach to the Breakfast Café, to the Windmill Café and back again. Fresh blood offered renewed vitality and new possibilities.

They quickly found a new restaurant tucked away at the far end of the village.

It proved to have a larger selection and lower prices than most of the others on the main quay. The food was quite good, and it soon became a regular for supper, and even lunch, if you happened to be with Ed at the time. There were times when even I tried to keep up with him.

The restaurant was also the beginning of the two-hour donkey ride that could be taken to the Valley of the Butterflies. We had talked to others who had taken the ride, but so far none of us had gotten up the energy to go on it ourselves. But external time was moving on, despite what our inner clocks told us. Someday we would have to reboard the Elli and head back to mass-land, if for no other reason than to reassure ourselves that it was still there. We had the Valley of the Butterflies to see and the trip to Antiparos to make, and we still had many days left when we would surely want to do nothing, before that un-awaited day arrived.

BUTTERFLY ON AHEAD, WE'LL JOIN YOU LATER

Ann and Nettie decided to trust their asses to the bumpy ride up to the Valley of the Butterflies. They cockily chided us for our lack of adventurous spirit. The rest of us were not so cheeky, however. We relied on the ample padding of Gertie to bear the butt of our group up the road to the base of the hill below the Valley of the Butterflies.

It was already well into late afternoon, as we slowly began the climb up the rocky path toward the bright clump of deep green. The path zig-zagged up between the walled-in fields like a bolt of petrified lightning. One by one we rolled into the grassy terrace at the top to the applause of muted thunder.

The terrace spread out before us and into a small orchard of plum trees. Beyond them stood a curtain of taller mulberry trees to which the butterflies seemed particularly attracted. Their orange and black Halloween wings covered the trees in a masquerade of autumn. We walked slowly through the miniature Garden of Eden, gently shaking the branches of the trees. The butterflies fluttered by the thousands, rising into the air in an inverted fall, then descended once again with the brief ripple of our passing.

"Well, look at all the whuppity-shit butterflies. Aren't they groovy?" J.C. said.

"There definitely is a good basis for the name of this place," Bilbo reasoned.

"The mulberries are really good," Ed said. "Here, try some." He was busy attacking one of the trees with the voraciousness of a monster silkworm.

We walked back and forth for a while, soaking in the cool fragrance of the peaceful refuge. It really seemed out of place. It sat perched on the side of the mountain like some ancient artifact preserved in the Parosian Museum of Nature.

"This is really nice. It's too bad we can't camp here," said Heidi. "There must be a spring feeding this somewhere," she added.

A HUMAN IS ALSO A TREE

On the terrace above was a small stone hut. Two old men dressed in the characteristic dark baggy suits, sat at the doorway to the hut, talking quietly. They had sat that way for years, no doubt, beside the spring in the Valley of the Butterflies. They knew all about each other's road through life as surely as if they were two wheels of the same cart. Each one knew what the other had to say, and yet they managed to pick up their friendship each day with the freshness of the flow of their companion spring.

Across the spring to the left were three or four huge cedars reaching up into the dry sky. They were five to ten feet thick and some hundred or so feet tall. Their size gave a sturdy permanence to the scene and was a fitting backdrop for their wizened human counterparts. The trees were countless years old, but their roots went not nearly so deeply into the rocky soil of Paros as those of the two old men.

The old men were not there merely for idle chatter, we knew. They were businessmen. They sold water by the spring. They had some pitchers and glasses which they brought out to the old wooden tables on the terrace overlooking the orchard. They kept the pitchers filled with the cool, sparkling water from the spring. Of course, we could have gotten water ourselves, but it would not have tasted nearly as good. The two drachmae we gave each of them was really not for the water. It was for the pleasure of the place, and for the fruit we ate. But it was for the presence of the two old men, more than anything. I

198

would gladly give them two drachmae a day for the rest of my life, if I thought it would keep them there forever, talking lightly into the evening, like the wind whispering softly through the ancient cedars.

After some time, we left the Valley of the Butterflies to the beckoning of evening. We said goodbye to the smiling old men and walked out past the towering cedars. We quickly slipped down the path, like Grecian lightning, toward the waiting sun below.

FRODO'S SECRET

Frodo did not ordinarily play to groups of people. I can understand. If he made a practice of it, he would never be able to escape the constant hounding of eager ears. His guitar sang sweetly, sweetly from the cover of the Bush to the creatures of the night.

We did not ask for requests. It would have been an insult to reduce Frodo to the stature of a flesh and blood jukebox. Instead, we just sat and listened. His chosen music danced upon the strings, then sprang into the air in gentle waves of harmony to mingle with the soft beams of the moon. The chords fell back upon our ears like welcome drops of summer rain.

You may hear Frodo someday, too. It will be under a different name, however. I cannot give the name here. I would not want him to be overwhelmed by admirers. But you will recognize him by his guitar and the fact that he will look like a bush wearing stilts.

When Frodo finished playing, we sat and talked for a while. Several people left in the direction of their sleeping bags. Penelope headed for the tent. I watched her drift down the beach in the moonlight, like a dream I was hoping to have.

HASH ANYONE SEEN MY PIPE?

We were joined by a couple who had just pitched their tent back from the beach near the Bush.

"We heard the music. It was really nice," they said.

"Thanks," said Frodo.

"We thought we'd come over and see if you'd like to smoke some hash," they said.

"Wow."

"Sure."

"Out-of-sight."

"Nah. It might spoil us."

"Wha'da ya mean, no. Asshole."

"Fire it up."

Such an outburst was rare. You could tell retsina was not a panacea.

"Well, does anyone have a pipe?" came the usual question. Dope always travels with a secret message. Any one person is allowed only half of this code at a time. That way no one gets caught.

"I see you've got a pipe, kid, and a roach clip. All the apparatus. Where's the dope?"

"I don't have any, officer. Really. You can search me."

"Don't worry, we will, we will."

And on the other hand, "I don't find any paraphernalia. This one must be clean."

"Okay, let him go."

The psychic currents keep bringing the two halves together in a mysterious alternating mating game. It all works out.

"I've got some dope; you got some papers?"

"Yeah, man."

"Wuuuash. Wuuuash, Wuah, Wu, Wh.. Wh….. Wow, ahb. This is good stuff. ….ahb, ahb.."

We found the pipe and gave it to them. They lit the pipe and passed it around.

"Wow. This is good stuff," someone said.

After everyone was sufficiently stoned, the couple folded up the rest of the dope and disappeared around the Bush, like two humble Samaritans who had done their good deed.

SINGING ON ACROSS THE SKY KING AND A PENNY EARNED

The gift of good dope is the elasticity of time—the humor that arises from the absurd incongruity of the moment. The hashish of our neighbors obligingly fit the bill as it stretched the night out around us in an infinitude of presents.

J.C. and Robert lost no time getting into the situation. They strummed their stomachs and sang a tune that made 'In a Gada da Vida' seem like a ten second chewing gum commercial.

"On the moonlight, running down my legs like green mud, it's sticky, sticky, but not too tricky, ticky, tick, tock, up the clock, often gets me in hoc, I may be sitting on a rock, but that's because I'm stonnnnnnnnned. As you can see. Look again, look Aegean and you can tell we were in a great big lotion. L'eau chen paddling around in a great big pool, plastic blowup pool with artificial Styrofoam molded rocks and trees and bush and cement or sand beach. Did it ever occur to you that we mutt not be able to get off this bitch, ever? Left here to melt in the retsinuated wind of someone else's after thoughtful imagination. Oh, blue, oh, blue, I'm so blue in the light of the afternoon moon, soon to croon such tune. You laugh but it's not easy getting off without a ticket, but it's not hard getting high when your eye is in the sky, a great big hole in the sky, rushing in and out and out and in through your sky-high eye. An overloaded, vacuum-packed washer-dryer, spin dry, agitated vortex, ringing out the strung-out cartoon character fancies of your sponge-cake mi-hi-hind, if you do. It's there for your enjoymental case if ever I saw one or today is as good as yesterdaring stunt and probably less dangerous than tomorrow, row, row your boat, gently down the streamlined consciousness baby. Get it on if you can teenager. You're either on the bus or off the Buster Brown show, kiddies, Twang your magic twanger froggy, hi ya kids, high ya, hi ya, hiya. Hiya gonna do when I'm gonna do when I'm gonna do win a new 1972 battery operated pimple squeezer complete with orange and grapefruit attachments for those of you lucky kids out there that live in the tropics, picnics for two at the corner of 42nd and Broadway. Watch the news all day long to your very own pimento cheese sandwich is anything that strikes your eye ...."

... had to leave, before I went totally wacky. I had laughed till my sides hurt and tried to keep laughing when I no longer could or felt like it but wasn't sure whether it was nice to stop, since I was in their world frame, and I hoped they wouldn't mind if I slipped into my own for a while.

I didn't mean to cut them out or did I feel left out, looking always for the center of balance. My mind slid back and forth like a greasy seesaw until I thought about the tent from way out on one of the solitary bare rocks in the harbor.

"Goodnight," someone said, as J.C. and Robert sang and laughed on in the receding glow of the campfire coals.

LOVINGLY, ONCE MORE PENELOPE

Penelope stirred, then raised her head and looked up at me, as I entered the tent. I got undressed and lay down beside her.

"I'm glad you decided to share my tent," I said, finally coming back to center.

She smiled sleepily with her piercing grey eyes, as she ran them up and down my face a few times, then pulled me gently to her.

CHRYSTALSIS X

BEYOND SPACE AND TIME

I have reserved this chapter for what is coming in 2021. Then the Paros Commune will be 50 years old, more or less. The Paris Commune of 1871 will be 150 years old, more or less. I did not mean to reserve this chapter and I did not mean to leave it out when I wrote 'The Paros Commune of 1971' in 1973, but I did both. Chrystalsis X, go figure. There are no accidents in Life.

X is 10, of course. Completion of one cycle and the start of another, maybe on a higher level, who knows. Chrystalsis is not a real word—well it might be now if you are reading this—but it is a combination of chrysalis, the hard-shell pupa of a butterfly or moth, and christos, meaning anointed, which is what happens to some christians, and even other people who don't think of themselves as christians but really are, if they've been zapped by the holy ghost. People have been getting zapped by the holy ghost, in Paros and India and Mesopotamia and in Las Vegas when it was still a coyote track in the desert, and a few in church, for millennia. When that happens some of the zappies go into a psychic cocoon of sorts while they are trying to figure out just what it means to have their soul chrystalized so that they can come out the other end of time and place as a better-fly or myth.

Apparently, it will take a long time, almost fifty years, if you know what I mean. I was/will be zapped by the holy ghost a few times more over the next four or five years after I left/leave Paros, the big one having been/being forty-four years, four months, four days backwards from April 2021 and counting. Put that in your esoteric apocalyptic numerological algorithm and see what paranoid delusion that computes. 666, my ass…as in a beast burdened with all those conspiracies. Satan is just a puff of hot air.

But don't get ahead of yourself—that puff may be a toke of crack or a stale fart. Not good, either way, so don't take a deep breath if you're couped up with a bunch of miscreants emitting second-hand smoke from either end. Go outdoors and take a deep breath.

X marks the spot. X is the only letter some people in the movies know when they write or sign their names as the land baron tells them to 'make their mark' on some contract they can't read as they unwittingly sign their life away. X is a letter in the English, Latin, Greek, and even Hebrew alphabets, though it has been changed in some versions of this last case to more of a '+' than an 'x'. Instead of alpha and omega in the Greek, α and ω, with the χ somewhere in between, it is aleph and tau in Hebrew, a and t, with a little character adjustment at the end as +. I learned a little Hebrew after I left Paros, in addition to the little Greek I learned before and during and after.

Just a 45 degree rotation of the x, to the left or right, and you can turn 'Marx' into 'Mart' which is the part of my name with a certain market resonance to it, deserved or not, as in K-Mart or Wal-Mart or just the Mart. I like this last as part of an enlightened view of a benign private-public synthesis.

However, I'm not too partial to 'Mart the Fart', as one of my friends called me in grade school—until I got creative and realized that 'Jobby', aka a name for the hard work of making a turd in nursery school, had more weight than a fart and rhymed with 'Bobby', so he slacked off when I finally got the chance to try it out on him.

I hope you will know what I mean as you read this in 2021 & beyond as I add this missing chapter to my life's work of art. I wonder if I will have learned by 2021, what I wanted to learn when I left the Paros Commune in 1971, more or less.

The missing 'Chrystalsis X' chapter might form a time warp portal into 'The Paros Commune — 2021 & Beyond' going forward from 1971 and backward to 1871, in the event anyone is listening, be it fellow Friend, Comrade, Citizen, Sister-Brother, other Soul, or just another...er, god, idiot.

We will see.

CHRYSTALSIS XI

LEAVING?

Heidi and Penelope had made up their minds. They had to leave that day. They hoped to catch Jackie before she left Athens. We promised to meet at the wine festival at Daphne that Sunday, in any event. What could they possibly do for five days, though, we reasoned?

We waited at the Windmill Café, with the usual retsina, although the Welcoming Committee was for the most part, defunct. It was now mostly a Send-Off Committee or just a plain old Sit Here and Watch Things Happen Committee. We slowly sipped our retsina and tried to talk of things that did not taste of mass-land

"Where shall we meet you?" I asked.

"There are a few campgrounds at Daphne, Roberts says. you will find us at one of them," said Penelope.

"Sunday night," I reminded her.

"Yes, Sunday night" she smiled. Like the signal for the end of recess, the whistle of the Elli sounded across the bay all too soon. She docked with the usual listing aplomb and offered up her contents to the waiting reptilian palate. We waited nervously for the break. They were taking pictures.

"One more picture," she said.

"You better hurry."

"We've got time."

The last of the cargo left the ship, and new departures began to board. Heidi and Penelope still made no move for the Elli. It was becoming apparent that they were either dragging out the tension of separation to a high-pitch pluck or they had no intention of leaving at all.

The gangplank slowly rose behind the last of the cars boarding the alley.

"We haven't seen Antiparos yet," said Heidi. "We can leave tomorrow."

CHRYSTALSIS XII

HORNS CAN CREATE A DILEMMA

We were, of course, pleased that they had decided to stay. Another day was much more than one rotation of the earth. It was a continuation of the apex of our trip. There was no doubt that Paros was the high point of Europe for J.C. and for me and probably for many others. And Paros with Penelope was doubtless to be desired above Paros alone. The next five days would be the start of the long slide toward the eventual denouement of our journey, and I did not relish that prospect.

But there was another aspect of their staying that slightly offset, yet was inextricably wound up in, the pleasure of their continued presence on Paros. I felt it very definitely as we waited for them to leave. I had developed a want, a need for Penelope. A dependence, not quite a clutching, that I could not shake loose, despite my intellectual disinclination for such things.

Paros was more than the climax of a geographical adventure. It was in some felt, but unfathomed way, a crucial turning point in my psychic and intellectual life. The guideposts of the past four years had proven to be the reference points of outdated maps. I was forced to draw my inner inferences directly from the contours of the land and I was, as yet, unsure of my present abilities to so navigate. It was not a violent or overwhelming crisis that I faced. But in the haste of regaining my bearings, I had climbed up on a nearby rock to get a better view instead of waiting to reach the top of the next rise. And now I realize that I had shifted my weight too suddenly to the rock.

It had begun to rock dangerously back and forth, and I did not know whether to jump back down quickly and risk the jar that could send it toppling upon me, or whether to try to climb down gently and hope that it would not fall with me still on it. I did not for a minute regret the existence Penelope in my psychic landscape, but I did realize I may have misevaluated her position and my reaction to it.

THIS TIME NOT SO PENELOPE

That night we sat at the Breakfast Café in an unusual adaptation of the normal sequence of events. The sun had just been shunned by the periodic turning of the earthly shoulder and we sat in anticipation of the cooling breeze. The daily kill of octopus hung like many copied metaphors of sunset, their shriveled eightfold rays shrinking in the pastel glow of dusk.

Robert had been gravitating toward Penelope since the first night of their arrival. Now he offered her a token of his interest in a drink of ouzo and accompanying chunks of octopus tentacle, as I slipped further into the greasy pit of jealousy. I went into the café to take a piss and returned to fall into a panic-inspiring void that started with the empty chairs of Robert and Penelope.

My mind became the unwelcome host of an onrush of unwittingly invited gross and obscene thoughts. I returned slowly through a haze to my seat. My skin was burning, consuming all my inner attempts at rationality, leaving a lumpy ash of guilt-filled despair in my throat. I looked around for some evidential reason for their departure but could find none. I dared not ask where they had gone. I didn't want to make my madness obvious to all, like the neon marquee of a dirty movie.

But I could not sit and watch the smoke of my noble and cherished theories of non-possession and liberated relationships, fanned by the childish winds of irrational fear, rise unchecked into the darkening night.

I rose from the table and headed down the back street with the shops. I didn't know what I would do if I ran into them. It did not matter. I was through plotting such things. I walked briskly down the empty, darkened street. My steps echoed hollow through the narrow tunnel of the walkway. I was not moving quickly enough to use up all the energy that was being liberated by my emotional, unclear reaction. I began to run.

I reached the Windmill Café and slowed myself to a walk once more. They were nowhere to be seen. I headed back up along the quay in the direction of the Breakfast Café.

"Damn, damn, damn it," I said out loud. "This is absurd. Totally absurd, you stupid fucking asshole." I climbed up onto an overhanging terrace at the dimly lit curve in the road, hammered the wall a few painful times, then set down to pull it all back together.

IF SHE HOLLERS, LET HERE GO?

The last pink of the sky faded imperceptibly into the west as my glowing anger at myself gradually subsided. I was by no means happy, but I had regained a measure of calm, and I was beginning, slowly, to loosen my grasp of Penelope. With each lessening of my grip, I felt my strength return.

I climbed down from the wall and headed slowly back toward the Breakfast Café. As I came to the front of the discotheque, I ran into most of the group coming from the other direction.

"Hey, man, everybody's in here," said Blonde Dennis. "Come on in."

"Sure," I said.

We went inside. Eyes made a quick, eager search around the room. They did not take long to come to rest on Penelope who sat on the side, laughing and talking with the Stick.

THANK YOU, PENELOPE

This is the last experience I have had as a jealous lover. It is too demanding to play that role. Of course, the other role demands a lot more caution in the early stages, a lot more control of the natural impulse to throw all care to the hurricane of the moment. I hope I don't have to confront that situation again. Too much pain. And too much schmaltz. It seems like quite a joke now, but I still can feel the sense of relief that swept over me as Penelope reached out her hand and took mine with a knowing and reassuring smile of her piercing grey eyes as I crossed the floor of the discotheque to meet her.

IT MUST HAVE BEEN THE OCTOPUS

J.C. and Heidi and Penelope and I slept in Gertie beside the dock that night. The ferry to Antiparos left at 7:00 in the morning, and we did not wish to risk missing it by returning to the beach for the night. So, the four of us packed ourselves tightly into the back of the van, leaving as many doors and windows open as possible to accommodate our retsina burning bodies, and went to sleep.

I woke in the middle of the night to find myself not squashed up against the side of the van as I anticipated. There was undoubtedly someone missing. I checked the identities of those remaining and realized that it was Penelope's familiar form which was absent. Oddly enough, it was not jealousy that motivated me this time, but concern. I poked my head outside the curtains and looked around.

Penelope was crouched over at the side of the dock, quietly vomiting. Her huddled form shuddered slightly with each gentle spasm of her torso. A vision of her helplessness pierced me more surely than her eyes ever could. The earlier events of the night lost their veneer of fear in her vulnerability of the moment.

"Are you alright," I asked softly.

"Yes," Penelope answered. "I'll be alright. It must have been the octopus."

"Yes, the octopus," I said.

A FERRY GOOD TRIP

We were up at the very crack with the noise of the men busily readying the small ferry for the trip to Antiparos. We quickly went through the morning ritual with our teeth, giving our foamy white smiles to the early morning passers, like a pack of mad dogs. We grabbed a bite of old, stale bread and jam, with a few sardines, and washed it down with water, then crossed the dock to the ferry.

A little after 7:00, with us firmly positioned in the bow, the little boat sputtered out into the bay and headed off in the direction of the companion island, passing our cove on the way. The orange tents of the Bush people and our own had been joined by a new blue one near the Bush and a green one on the rock. No one yet stirred on the beach, but it would not be long before the newly courted sun poured out its renewed vitality with sufficient intensity to activate the scene.

PARDON ME, MAY I HAVE SOME MORE EYEBROW?

"I think it's ridiculous that there is a taboo against eating human flesh," said J.C., very matter-of-factly. I felt I had just walked into a movie after missing the first 10 minutes.

"Oh, really?" I asked. "That's an interesting observation."

"Sure," he said. "I think I'll have written in my will that my body must be disposed of among all my friends in one big feast."

"J.C.! That's gross," shrieked Heidi in disbelief.

"Why not? I've heard its pretty good meat. It would surely help out in times of rising food prices. Save useful land from unproductive occupancy. I think it's a good idea. It's like communion," he said.

"Well, don't ask me to come," Heidi said.

"Oh, Heidi dear, you'd enjoy it. You know how sweet I am. I would write out which part went to whom. I'm sure it's the only estate I'll have," J.C. said.

"You can have my funny bone." He looked at me. "You need a laugh after last night."

"Right on," I twisted uneasily at the mention of the night before. "But I know you. You'll leave me the spareribs or something equally unsatisfying. A deteriorated liver, maybe."

"You guys are disgusting," Heidi laughed.

"Oh, but you haven't heard yet what I'll give you, heh, heh, heh," he said to her.

"J.C., you know that will never satisfy me," she giggled.

"Oh, don't want my left leg, eh? Well, then I guess you'll have to settle for my mustache," he said.

"Or some J.C. baloney. There should be plenty of that to go around," Penelope added.

A CARAVAN TO THE CAVERN

We stopped briefly at the small village, then went on to the south end of the island for the main attraction. The caverns. There, a group of Greek partisans held off the Nazis for weeks before they were finally bombed to oblivion. Miraculously, the cave remained intact, minus a few stalactites or stalagmites, whichever the case may be.

There was a train of donkeys waiting to carry the passengers up to the cave which was located high up on the top of a nearby hill. As usual, we shunned such luxury and began to walk the rocky mile or so up the slope ahead of the rest. It was a hot mid-morning by that time, but we managed to reach the shade of a large cavern entrance before the donkeys, by taking the direct route up.

CHRYSTALSIS XIV

ISLANDS ARE SUSCEPTIBLE TO A ONE-SIDED VIEW

Islands are susceptible to a one-sided view. We are often obsessed with the surface view and too oblivious to what goes on underneath. There is a whole new facet of island-ness beneath the ground. It is dark and moist and cool and can be quite peaceful and comforting.

People have too long equated the underworld with hell. That is a mistake. Hell, like heaven, is everywhere. It is wherever you want to find it.

The Greeks had a better idea of the underworld. It was both heaven and hell, depending on what the individual sought in it before he went there. The Plutonian Lord was severe, but he was just, repaying or demanding from each person an equal measure for their account of life.

The underworld which so many people fear lies not in the earth, however, but deep within their own being. That is the unknown terror that lurks ever ready to spring forth to demand payment from them for some past spree of gluttony or avarice or other vice. Like many Greek hero and heroine, we must be willing to venture into this underworld, to face its phantoms and to emerge once more with the knowledge that all its fears are of our own creation.

THE PAROSIAN UNDERGROUND

We had explored most of the surface of the island of Paros, and now it was time to venture inward to see what was in store for us there. As the guide opened the door that blocked the way to the caves, we were hit by a cool and refreshing blast of its secrets.

Our way was made easier by those who had gone before. A zig-zag of wooden steps and walks stretched down and out in front of us. Behind us in a little shack at the mouth of the cave, a generator sputtered on, transforming the dark into a slick, shiny fantasy of multi-colored forms.

We were lucky enough to have someone along to translate for us, as the guide did not happen to be familiar with our brand of sound communication. He told us the story of the cave and its partisans. Some of the natural history of the cave. How many billions of drops of water it took to build one inch of the hanging-down type of geological formations whose name remains always *tightly* logged in my memory. How many billions more drops it takes to build up the other kind that I *might* know if I could remember the first. How few bombs it took to remove many beautiful examples of both kinds once the Nazis decided it was necessary to get to the bottom of everyone's mind.

There was one section of deposits that formed a ribbed curtain along the wall. When the guide put his light behind it, the formation shown up like dense stained glass. He tapped it slightly with his flashlight. It rang out clearly, like a petrified xylophone.

At the bottom of the cave were the autographs of Lord Byron and several other graffitists who wanted to etch their names indelibly into our unconscious. The dates were quite old. 1867, 1774, 1743, 1692. The cave was older than any bus station washroom I ever had the pleasure of visiting.

IS EURYDICE ME?

It would have been nice if Frodo and Bilbo had come along, especially if they had waited until then to take their trip to Middle Earth. The cave was a miniature sample of the inner workings of the Misty Mountains. I expected to be surrounded by torch bearing dwarves at any time and taken to a huge, secret subterranean chamber for a night of feasting and weird, fantastic merriment.

The cool moisture of the cave seemed to heighten the senses. Even in the dim light of the cave everything was sparklingly lucid. The slightest whisper was amplified with resonance throughout the large chamber.

There was an unfathomable calm about the place. It was like returning to some awe-inspiring enigma of childhood and viewing it for the first time with adult eyes. The enigma was gone, but the sublime sense of wonder remained, giving a feeling of utter security. The accompanying conviction that all works out in the end, brought with it the knowledge that the fantasies of childhood are not mere dreams and that beneath the crust of pragmatic endeavor, the world is still above all else a magical place.

If we are careful, we can take this knowledge with us to the world above. If we lodge it securely in the back of our minds and wait until we re-enter the light of day to fully examine it and embrace it. But if we emerge from the underworld without the confidence to accept this fact and turn at the last minute to reassure ourselves of its existence, we will see it in the bright glare of the full sun, and in that light, it will seem nothing more than a dark empty hole. In our doubt, it will evaporate, drifting back into the bowels of the earth.

As we came out of the mouth of the cavern, I held Penelope's hand and led the way out. Remembering the fate of poor Orpheus, I was very careful not to look back until we had entered the full light of day and the door had closed behind us. There was no point in losing her then. She would be leaving soon enough.

CHRYSTALSIS XVI

A WELCOME FOR A SEND-OFF

We re-boarded the ferry and headed back to Paros, by way of an expensive lunch at the village on Antiparos. When we returned to the dock, we were welcomed by none other than our very own Paros Welcoming Committee. We slowly crossed the dock to the tables of friends and waiting retsina. It never tasted better, after the hot trip back.

"You girls don't have much time to decide now. Are you going or not?" asked Stick.

"This time is for real," Heidi said.

"We better go get our things," Penelope said. "Can I have the key J.C.?"

"If you're sure this is what you want to do," he answered, giving her the keys. The two of them walked across the street to the van, while I went in to get some ice cream. I met Ann and Nettie on the way in.

"Oh, it's good to see you back," said Ann.

"It's good to see you're still eating ice cream," I said remembering, her soft spot for this stuff.

"It's only her ninth one today, isn't it?" Nettie chided.

I paid for my ice cream and a bottle of retsina and went back out to the table. The girls were coming back from Gertie with their gear in tow.

"Here is a going away present for you," I said, handing Penelope the bottle of retsina. "Something different."

"Thank you, I'll always remember you by it," she mocked, half truthfully.

It was not long before the Elli did her thing all the way into the dock. We got up and slowly moved toward the boarding gate. I tried to pretend I was just seeing off an old great-aunt of a distant cousin, but it didn't work too well. Penelope just didn't bring any great-aunt images to mind. There was the usual round of hugging and kissing and well-wishing. I was trying hard to maintain my usual attitude toward good-byes but was only half successful. J.C. appeared to be doing better, but I knew it was mostly appearance.

"Now, don't get gushy," said Penelope.

"Don't worry," I said, "just one quick kiss. That will hold me."

"Not out here," she tried to get away. "You're so silly." She came back and quickly pecked my lips.

TO DAPHNE TO REST ON ONE'S LAURELS

"I'll see you at Daphne," she said.

"Okay. Take care," I said.

"I will," she said and slowly ambled off toward the Elli.

"Goodbye, Heidi," I said giving her a hug.

"Goodbye," she said. "I'll see you at Daphne. Take care of J.C. for me."

"I will," I said.

Heidi followed Penelope out to the ship and got on behind her. Most of the group went to the end of the dock and waited for the Elli to shove off. In a few minutes the girls appeared on the stern deck.

"Goodbye," they waved to us as the Elli pulled out from the dock.

"Goodbye," we waved back.

"It's stupid standing here waiting for them to turn into dots in the horizon. Let's get drunk," J.C. said, putting an arm across my shoulders.

We began walking arm in arm toward the Windmill Café, as the Elli and its much-valued cargo sped out across the harbor behind us towards the wine festival at Daphne.

We were joined by Bilbo and Frodo and Robert and Stick and Ed and Blonde Dennis and Black Dennis and maybe more, as we skipped out the retsina shuffle on our way back to the café.

"That's a good idea. Let's get drunk," I said.

And we did.

ΔΙΑΣΠΟΡΑ

DIASPORA I

Things were not quite the same after Heidi and Penelope left. Ed was off with Ann a good bit of the time. His bright bushy head came around at the important junctures of the day, then quietly left again for some secret rendezvous. Black Dennis had met some people with a house and was spending a good deal of his time with them. There were a few new faces at the beach, but I didn't get to know them very well. Things were really shifting.

The most notable difference was in J.C. Like myself, he was already partway to Daphne, and his most smoothed-out-mellow was starting to show a few ripples.

There was the matter of Gertie. He and the rest of us had not been taking the best care of her. We piled more and more people into her every night to break the previous night's record. Like she was a mobile telephone booth. The wear and tear on her was beginning to show, and although J.C. laughed it off with 'it's all part of the moment,' I knew it was building up inside.

The night after Heidi and Penelope left, on the way to dinner we got a record 23 people in the van. Gertie was so low from the weight that we could barely see over the curb. We stopped to pick up two more guys, but they declined when they opened the door to a tangle of arms and legs and heads and butts bulging out at them.

One guy who was new at the beach, was hanging on to the flimsy aluminum curtain rod at the side door, and by the time we reached the beach, it was fairly well extruded out of shape. J.C. was a bit pissed off when he saw it.

"Goddamn it. Why would somebody do that?" he said. "What an asshole."

"But he didn't blow then. I knew it was coming, and try as I might avoid it, I knew I'd be there to catch it when the shit hit the fan.

DIASPORA II

A night or so later, we were down at the far end of the beach at the restaurant that Ann and Nettie had taken over. Most of the crew were there for dinner, and we decided to stay over for some retsina and dancing. J.C. had mumbled a few times about having to take everyone back, how Gertie was being abused and all. I agreed she was taking a beating.

"Just let me know before you leave," I said. "It's a long walk back and I really don't feel up to it tonight."

"Okay," he mumbled and took another gulp of retsina.

We really got into it that night. The retsina and the dancing. We were throwing all care to the wind as we spun and twisted and shook and writhed to the jukebox. The few locals that were there were really digging it, clapping and encouraging us on. J.C. was sitting on a stool, very drunk and brooding.

"Let me know when you're ready to go," I said.

"Uh-huh," he grunted.

A short time later I went to take a piss. I returned to the high pitch whine of Gertie's first gear and the scraping of teeth as J.C. shifted to second. I dashed out the door to be greeted by the dust of his impulsive exit. The dance had abruptly stopped, and others were coming out the door behind me.

"Goddamn it, I knew he was going to do this. I told him to let me know before he left. It's been building and building and now it's burst way down here at the far end of the beach. I've had it with him and his sudden temper," I yelled explosively.

"Let him blow off," said Ed. "He'll get it out of his system. He's pretty well pissed to the gills anyway."

"Yeah, but he always lets it build up like this, Ed. We've ridden with him all the way across Europe. We've paid gas and insurance and all that shit, and he goes off and leaves us two miles from the beach. And it's not a nice night to walk." I was pretty mad.

"You'll be laughing about it in a day or two," Ed said knowingly.

"Yeah, maybe so, but it's then and we're here now. I don't have to walk two miles to the beach in a fuming rage two days from now," I screamed.

Things were pretty quiet on the way back. The evening had come to a sudden conclusion. There wasn't even the retsina shuffle up the main street of the village past all the waterfront cafés.

As it was, it proved to be a good thing that we were so far from the beach. By the time I walked two miles, I was only slightly mad and too sleepy to do anything but crawl into the tent and go to sleep.

DIASPORA III

CHECKMATE

The remaining days were as relaxed as usual, but they seemed to lack the calm enthusiasm that had been so much in evidence before. We played a lot of backgammon, chess, and checkers at the café next to the Breakfast Café. I read a book or two with little interest and ate a lot of food along with Ed and Bilbo and Robert. I practiced my German with Claudia and Brigitte and played checkers with a guy from Montreal named Solomon.

Solomon was a nice friendly guy, but he really seemed to like to hear himself talk. I'm not too much into games like chess and checkers, but when I do play, I don't like to be rushed and rapped at incessantly.

"Go on and move, man. It's your move. You're taking too long, man."

"Okay, Solomon," I moved impulsively to get him to shut up, then took another bite of yogurt.

"Boy, that was a stupid move. Now I've got you here and here. You should have done this," said helpful Solomon.

"It's your move again. Go on, move. You could play a lot more games if you'd move faster," he said.

"Great," I said with a yawn.

"Wow, whatever made you move there. Didn't you see this man over here? Now I've got your man here and you've got to jump one here then I have three kings and you're left with one man there and maybe one over there. Your really big mistake was three moves back, when you …"

"Fuck off, Solomon," I barked. "I don't want a play-by-play account and I didn't pay you to be my checkers instructor. Either play the game without rushing me and with your mouth shut or get the fuck away from this table." I was really vexed.

"Maybe you'd rather play chess," he said, "or another game of backgammon. Maybe you'll do better this time. You almost had me the last time, if you just had one more roll of the dice…"

Solomon is a nice guy. I am sure he will be a very good teacher someday.

DIASPORA IV

THE DOOR OF PERCEPTION

Right before I left, I did manage to see the church in the village. It is a very old church, built around the 4th century. The name of the church is the Church of the One Hundred Doors. On the English circular that one picks up at the tourist office, there's a brief description of the church. According to the circular, there are only 99 doors that can be counted at the church. No one had ever been able to find the 100th door, but it is most assuredly in there somewhere. Perhaps covered over by some later course of masonry.

I thought this riddle all but insoluble, until recently when I began to get the first perception of a vast transcendent world through the missing door, as it began to open slowly in my mind.

DIASPORA V

TO MASS-LAND AND BEYOND

We could not leave Paros in a muted fashion, a few at a time. We had to make the grand exit together. Even Robert, who was staying another month or so at his Hut, decided to accompany us at least to Daphne and perhaps beyond. He left his place in the care of Ann and Nettie who had decided to stay on for a while instead of going on to Rhodes. Carol was staying on at the Aegean School of Fine Arts, of course, and Claudia and Brigitte had left the day before. But Black Dennis and Blonde Dennis, Bilbo, Frodo, Robert, J.C., Ed and I all decided to take the big step back to mass-land together. It was a major step at the time, making the return. It was made easier by the prospects of Daphne, and easier still by the fact that we were making the exit together.

We loaded up Gertie from the beach and drove on into town to the Windmill Café, where Stick was waiting with his bike. He was planning to carry it with us to Istanbul, inside the van.

"Stick, that thing is not a stork," I said, "it's an albatross."

"Yeah, you're right," he said.

MY, BUT THAT'S A STRANGE WALKING STICK

I thought it would be a problem for us in the back of the van. I'm sure it was more of a problem for Stick. Ten of us traveled with

241

the albatross to Thessaloniki, with our legs stuck between the spokes, and eight of us went on from there to Istanbul and back through Bulgaria to Romania.

We camped for several days in a small town near Braila, then took Frodo, Bilbo, Robert, and Stick to the train station as we headed on into the Soviet Union. The next day at Bucharest, while they were walking along with the albatross, they were stopped by some interested citizen and asked if they were the group that had been in Braila a few days before. News travels fast in that part of the world, and the man must have recognized them by their hair, and of course, the bike.

From there, Stick carried the Albatross by train back to Thessaloniki where he again ran into Robert, who had hitched down through Yugoslavia. Robert was sitting at a café when the Stick came by walking, not riding, the Albatross. From there, he rode with Robert and his ride back to Athens. And all that time and distance without more than a mile or two on the Albatross.

WINDMILL WE MEET AGAIN

We met at the Windmill Café and drank our nostalgic fill of retsina as we waited, impatiently for the Elli. If we had to be leaving, we wanted to get on with it.

In a short while the Elli made her characteristic sweeping turn into the bay, nodding her greeting as she rounded the far point of land. Her whistle had an almost mournful quality about it as it rolled across the harbor to turn our head for the last time. We rose for a final cheer as the anchor dropped to clasp the Elli, all too briefly to the island.

"We'd better get some more retsina for the trip. It's more expressive on the Elli," Robert said.

We purchased as much as we could carry on in a halfway concealed fashion, saying goodbye to the man with the smiling teeth. Then we passed down the line of embraces for Ann, Nettie, and Carol and walked out the dock and into the waiting ferry.

I climbed to the back of the Elli's upper deck as we sped out of the harbor. I sat there for a long time, silently watching as the gray-green hump of Paros slowly shrank into the distance as it sank in the gathering twilight depths of the Aegean.

DIASPORA VI

ISLANDS DO NOT LAST FOREVER

Islands do not last forever. In one manner or another, they return to the ocean floor that bore them. But they carry with them a memory of their sojourn above the waters of uniformity. They take back with them a taste of island-ness that is not lost in the greater island which is the very planet. And in an endless telescoping fashion, that planet too, may take back its experience of island-ness to the ground from which it sprang.

Nothing is lost but the temporary illusion of separateness. That it seems is the ironic end of island-ness, that it may establish the sense of separate identity in order that it might fully appreciate the total unity of all. An island is but an eye with which the total land views itself.

DIASPORA VII

I rose up from my chair and went to the side of the Elli and turned my gaze forward in the direction of Piraeus and beyond to Daphne. It was not so difficult now, with the prospect of Penelope before me, even if it was to last for but a few days.

Bilbo approached me with something in his hand.

"Here, is this yours?" he asked.

In the waning light, I could make out a red bandana. I checked the corners and found one with the familiar frazzle.

"You're shitting me," I said in amazement.

"No, I'm not. I found it and mine on the beach this morning when we were packing up. Isn't it amazing?" Bilbo stated calmly.

"I don't believe it," I said holding up the long, lost bandana with a chuckle.

"Paros is like that, though," he added.

"Here, have one of my other ones. I don't need three red bandanas. I've got a new blue one in my pack," I said, handing one of the others to Bilbo.

"Thanks," he said.

OM AGAIN, OM AGAIN, JIGGETY JIG

We looked back toward the stern of the ship. Silhouetted against the fading sky, five of the group were standing shoulder to shoulder with their arms across each other, retsina bottles in hand.

"Retsina, retsina,

Retsina, retsina,

Retsina, retsina,

You're the one for me."

They sang happily, but not too loudly as they danced the retsina shuffle into the waiting loins of night.

ΕΠΙΛΟΓΟΣ

EPILOGOS

Most of us are still in touch with each other, in one way or another. And as things are never static, there are more and more people coming into the growing protean network all the time. Of course, there is nothing new in that. The ever-changing pattern of connection stretches out endlessly in all directions as it always has. Virtually everyone is in touch with everyone else through the medium of other people. But today, it seems a bit easier to hop out of one place and into another, to establish new connections of quality without severing old ones. The overall scope of our involvement continually increases as we zip here and there about our business and pleasure.

There are many who decry this turn of events, the breakdown of tradition. I'm not worried. To me it is our hope. It is nothing but an extension of the neighborhood, our promiscuity an extension of the family.

I received a letter from J.C. the other day that pretty well sums things up.

It is not original. It came from Hermann Hesse by way of 'Peter Camenzind', but it seems quite apropos to our situation as we floated across the Aegean on our way back to mass-land.

"Both of us, certain that we were worthy of our good fortune, looked forward to a rich new life. Work, struggle, pleasure, and fame lay within our reach, so we enjoyed our days with no sense of urgency. Even our imminent separation seemed inconsequential, for we knew with greater certainty than ever before, that we needed each other and could count on each other for the rest of our lives."

EPILOGOS

INDEX OF PAROSIAN POSSIBILITIES

2021 & Beyond

2021 & Beyond

THE HOURGLASS OF SPACE & TIME FUNNEL

Anyone under the age of 48 was yet to be born when <u>The Paros Commune of 1971</u> was written. Approximately 3 billion people were alive at the time, increased from 2.5 billion when I was born in 1948. Currently 8% of the world population of 7.8 billion is over 65 years of age, so for my age that figure is probably closer to 3%. Around 200 to 300 million human beings are now older than me, a large portion of which will be found in Europe and North America.

For those with an interest in planetary statistics, that means roughly 90% of the people that were alive when I was born are now dead—since they quit making people older than me once I was born. Well, unless you count the likes of my dad who says he has taken a new body—but then he didn't say where that was, maybe this planet, maybe a few solar systems over in a somewhat different type of body, who knows. I have never thought that a soul, not made of inertial material, was hampered in its travel by the speed of light or body size—hampered by other things perhaps, but not by physics.

For me it doesn't feel that way—that I am older than 97% of all living human beings—since I really feel ageless except for the usual aches and pains. It means that of those old enough to have some awareness and understanding of world events of the time leading up to the summer of the Paros Commune of 1971, at most maybe 5% of the current world population have any accurate understanding of those times based on actual experience as an adult. Probably more like 3%, and if we leave out everyone but those in regular public communication with the developed western world at the time, it's probably closer to 1%.

Each of us in that 1 to 5% is a yarn of living wisdom, spun from a mix of fibers of our own natural experience and the understanding of that experience synthesized and colored with the tales of others. That mix includes traditional, cultural, scientific, pragmatic, fashionable, counter-cultural, ad hoc, and just plain looney interpretations of those experiences, learned from exposure to a range of skills, from expert professionalism to pseudo-expert ergodidiocy. What we all try to learn as individuals is how to assume and manage the constantly changing mix of risk and opportunity that life presents us. What we can shoulder individually, we should, and what we should shoulder communally, we must—or we will individually suffer the collective consequences. There are no island selves beneath the sea of change.

We of the 1 to 5% of those with the greatest age, and therefore greatest opportunity to have accumulated the most wisdom layered in with the risk of having succumbed to the rankest ergodidiocy, stand in contrast with the 50% of the population that are currently under the age of 30 and just getting started in their struggle with what we know now as confirmation bias. When The Paros Commune of 1971 was written I was well under 30 and had little expectation of targeting an audience beyond the few that might have had a fascination for Richard Brautigan at the time.

It was written and left unpublished before most of the human beings on this planet were inhabiting their current bodies. I was heavily influenced by the writing of Mr. Brautigan, whom I very much enjoyed reading. But then I had heard—maybe it was an intuition before the fact—that he committed suicide in the wake of his commercial success. So, I decided not to pursue a creative writing career at that time. I thought it would give me more time to die on my own. Oh wait, that's what he did. I guess it wasn't the writing that killed him. It was the time. Anyway.

I wrote this more or less as my friends and I experienced it in Greece, on the island of Paros, in the Aegean, somewhere on the great circle of history running through the Sorbonne from Europe to the US and back again, sometime between March of 1871 and now, during which time we also got together in a ski cottage in Vermont in 1973 and read a draft of the work. I finished it that summer and put it on a shelf, unpublished. So, being still unpublished, I am still alive.

There is someone alive in the world right now that is the oldest person in the world. Assuming they are compos mentis, that person represents the single thread in the social fabric that has the potential to convey any expertise in the form of insights and understanding gleaned firsthand through the interaction of the 2 billion plus individuals who were alive when that soul was born and have now passed on, to the 7.8 billion individuals who are now alive and still interacting today. This is rather a mundane and at the same time awesome thought, and as a funnel of time—of experience past and understanding going forward—is true in a way of anyone, regardless of age.

Each person is an expert based on a specific set of experiences of living. That has the potential of giving each of us an insight to a solution of some area of concern to the rest of us, one that may have eluded the others for some time. Such person may be an obvious boon; yet they may also carry an unknown risk in that insight along with that opportunity, instead of a clear-cut solution to the problem. They might be an individual possessed by a conniving spirit, harboring a grudge against the rest of us, or simply someone without knowledge or understanding of the universal harm or benefit they bring. They may be ergodidiots.

So do we avoid the risk of listening to them and continue crapping in our own nest or do we take the opportunity to consider rationally what they have to say in the hope of helping them clean up their crap. Or do we assume the risk to consider rationally what they have to say and start crapping in our heretofore pristine nest or refuse the opportunity to listen so that we won't have to help them clean up their own crap. Or do we avoid the opportunity… it all gets so confusing … so, so confusing … or maybe if we think about it, just so-so confusing.

Experience in scientific investigation that has established certain essential physical principles of objective truth based on deductive logic, when applied with the expertise gained in novel ways to experimental conditions, has been productive of predictable results and developed technologies for the benefit of humankind. Common sense derived from such expertise tells us that the earth is billions and not just a few thousand years old without denying that the earth and its bounty is the result of a divine intent.

Experience in faith of a revelatory sort that has established certain essential metaphysical principles of subjective truth of intuition and inductive logic, when applied with expertise to contemplation, meditation, yoga, communion, and various spiritual practices of East and West, has proved productive of predicted results and developed techniques for permanent beneficial alterations in consciousness. Common sense derived from such expertise tells us that consciousness as an ensouling life is not limited to the physical organism through which it operates regardless of the apparent limitations and corruptibility of the five and perhaps more external senses incorporated in that organism.

What is truly a violation of common sense, however, is the belief that because an individual has expertise in one of these areas of concern, that necessarily makes them an expert in the others. They may have such common expertise, but what can be known for a fact— what my experience tells me for a fact—is that anyone that claims to be an expert in one of these two fields and tells all those in the other field that they are idiots, is themself an … well, you know, because everyone is an expert in this regard. Even those who are expert in either or both of these two fields of faith and science should know they are rarely positioned to be an expert in all areas, even of their own chosen field(s).

Common sense would tell us that:

People, as custodians of the insights of Newton and Bacon and Galileo, of Maxwell and Planck and Bohr—the insightful souls that brought us the scientific and technological revolution—that still have not been able to grasp the essential unity of space–time and quanta, have gone into a cul-de-sac of cosmological understanding with the current reductionist thinking of big bangs and black worm holes, produced by point particles and strings. And yet they control much of the funding that could be put to better use than at CERN.

People that believe in the primacy of mindless materialism as the basis of human evolution, with its developed awareness of the transcendent beauty of the cosmos, don't have much to tell us about the true nature of the Soul.

People that acknowledge the majesty of the omnipotent source of all life, while ignoring the miracles that our fellow human souls have produced for the benefit of humankind and yet believe that material world is manipulated by a satanic principal, whose only real power is the capacity to insinuate itself into the minds of the fearful, have gone into a world of fantasy with their magical and conspiratorial thinking, that denying an obvious truth will make it disappear or repeating a groundless lie will make it true.

People that view God exclusively through the prism of the Christian scripture as it was canonized under the influence of the Caesarian monarchy of Rome, ignore the reality that 'Elohim', the only term for God in the first chapter of Genesis, is a term for supreme collective divinity, mistranslated from the Hebrew, intentionally or not, which by reference to verse 27 indicates it is a term for both male and female aspects of divinity. Oops! Though I am no authority on the Hebrew language, my understanding is that the term Elohim is a female plural of a male singular noun.

Also from that same verse, comes the observation of Strong's Concordance that it is humanity, designated by the transliterated term 'adam', that is so created by the Elohim. It is not until verse 4 of chapter 2 that God, as the eternal Self over all selves, appears in the scripture as Jehovah, referenced in Hebrew teaching as Tetragrammaton, the four-letter glyph, YHWH, standing for the name that cannot be spoken, in which the glyphs are aspirates which make the sound of breath—spiritus— when exhaling, as 'hew' or 'u', which presents Itself as 'I am That I am', That Self which always was, is, and will be, the Essence of essences, the Source of all Living, That without which nothing else exists. Whew! There's a run-on sentence for you. So here too the male translators of the scriptures, under the direction of a Caesar or King James, naturally translate the Tetragrammaton in the context of their times as a feudal 'Lord'.

People identifying their existential ego as essential—either with or against a nation, a religion, a philosophy, a party, a class, an ethnicity, a race, a sex, a gender, a skin tone, a football team defined by either type of ball, et cetera, rather than as a soul—the Soul—defined by their true Self as being from a spiritual source, are only part way to the goal of spiritual maturity and are not yet in the karmic clear, free from suffering the effects of listening to the voices of fear and ignorance, listening to that snarly little guy sitting on one or the other shoulder, and failing to follow their true inner voice of Love and Wisdom.

I would guess that most of the human population understand in one way or another that we are souls. Whether or not they think that soul survives the death of the body—and I believe most do think or at least hope that is the case—most operate as if there is an emoting, thinking, feeling, purposeful entity like themselves, that animates the fellow human beings they communicate with on a day-to-day basis. Absent a narcissistic personality disorder, we tend to think that other humans have an internal psychic makeup like that of our own self-perception. The perception is that our sense of self is more fundamental and continually permanent than the parts of our material body—in fact, than that material body as a whole.

We watched ourselves as our baby teeth were cut and grew in and then lost a few years later, eventually to grow an adult set; as our feet and hands and the attaching extremities outgrew our clothes; as our hair and nails lengthened and were cut; as we learned to crawl and walk and run and jump; as we grew up, went to school, worked and played, found a mate, raised a family; through all these corporal changes in which few states or stages lasted for very long prior to adulthood, what is noticeably unchanged as we watch from outside of time, is our sense of being the same self, the same soul, throughout this experience of physical change. We mark time by these changes, but our core is timeless.

Eventually we start to realize that we have created a personal sense of who we are through this experience, in no small part as a reflection of how we interact with and distinguish ourselves from others, alike and different from ourselves; boys and girls, children and adults, younger and older children, younger and older adults, big and little, rude and polite, slight and stout, dark and light skinned, short and tall, fast and slow, timid and daring; the likenesses and differences appear to be endless.

This personal sense, this persona—a mask with which to face the drama of existence—helps us navigate our social spaces in the community, as we begin to identify our abilities to maneuver physically with the related social abilities in a manner ranging from the innocuous to the intrusive, from the helpful to the manipulative. With images of the masks of other actors which are fresh in our heads, we begin to project those images onto our observations of the world of unknown characters in hopes of recognizing their roles in our play, as we learn to jeer them or cheer them.

As we begin to identify the personal objective skills of the soul in navigating society and the environment with a personal subjective sense of expertise based on a position and ability to navigate in the community, the ego develops. We begin to think, 'I am this or that skillfully navigating self'—or not so skillful—as being true in the timeless sense of an actor's part in a play. But to think, 'I am this or that person of socially recognized expertise', adds an illusory reflective dimension which conflates the soul's focus in time and place with the role played by the character in that play. For the ego to assume the mantle of the role as the soul's rather than as the part in a play, breaks the fourth wall, often not in a good way, and can exhibit out-of-character deference to the actor's ego to the detriment of the role being played.

With respect to the ego, in a certain sense there is no reincarnation as indicated in the dream of my dad, if as many people imagine, they are thinking of taking their part in the play with them when they leave the stage, rather than just the art learned from the role. While the soul may hope and try to take on physical form in a recurrent fashion, each role is different with a different stage and set and a different part and a different set of protagonists and antagonists and supporting actors and stagehands and yes playwrights; and while it is hardly without a sense of humor, karma is real. The soul can try to take their ego with them, along with the part they were used to playing, which one might think can lead to all manner of disembodied afterlife and future embodied life predicaments in dealing with one's former cast members. So, it may be a good idea to learn to commune with the others backstage with equity as cast members, while still located in the facility of a physical arena, rather than as roles, once the theater is vacated.

This is why the Buddha counseled enlightenment, not because it grants a reprieve from future embodiments allowing the soul to loll about for eternity, but because it leads to a refusal to review the actor's own press, to refuse to recognize an applause that panders over the authentic appreciation of the communion of the art of the part played and avoids the development of a reckless ego on the part of the actor. It facilitates stepping out of the roles that have already been fashioned, so that going forward, an adept soul may navigate any and all of the spheres of human and divine existence in the creative eternity to come, while being able to avoid the snares of outrageous fortune that attach to the novice actor that falls short of the playwright's script.

Souls commune and communicate with one another in many ways other than by thoughtful or thoughtless speech, (you mean you didn't really mean to say that?), as presented in graphics, text, and recording on the internet or in person. We signal each other in bodily touch and gesture, in raw vocal emotion, and we communicate intuitively with direct thought and feeling. Anyone who thinks that human beings can't and don't ever share their thoughts and emotions directly by telepathic rapport has never been married, or if so married and still not recognizing that reality, is unlikely to happily stay that way for long. Listening to your spouse by whatever means of communication is generally a good idea.

Telepathy works, often because it goes unrecognized at both ends of a communication and is therefore seamless. Or should the correct spelling be seem-less? That seamlessness of perception and participation occurs in the domain of the intuitive soul once that soul has freed itself of the illusion of being separate from its source. The individual soul is simply an individual focus of the greater Soul, the individual buddha—a buddha literally means 'an intuitive' in the Eastern tradition—a focus of the greater Intuition, the individual christ—an individual anointed by the holy spirit—a focus of the greater Truth, all of which is Whole and Complete, within which that soul, that intuitive, that christ lives, and moves, and has its being as an individual element of the ergodic whole. E pluribus unum.

Continuing with Buddhism, depending on the branch one prefers, there is either only One Soul, of which we are each a separate appearance, or there is no soul at all, as the appearance of being separate is an illusion prior to enlightenment. With enlightenment, it is understood by the conscious self that is emerging from the illusion that it was just that, an illusion of separateness. So, the notion in those Buddhist branches that there is a difference between One Soul or no soul, between Mahayana and Theravada, is just a misunderstanding, a problem of semantics. 'To seem rather than to be' prior to enlightenment, to reverse the motto of North Carolina, my home state for most of my life.

In the esoteric source of some religions and philosophies, there is said to be but One Self that is the source of all essential and existential reality. That Self, the Only Reality—YHWH, operating as the Elohim in the Abrahamic tradition, Brahman operating as Brahma and the divine retinue in Vedanta—appears to Itself at myriad times and places in the guise of separate souls, which then by all appearances, interact with each other as distinct beings or at least in thinking they are distinct. The enlightened soul or focus of the Self knows the distinction is an illusion of the playwright and the actors in the play. The illusion of being fundamentally distinct, a result of mental and emotional processes which evolve naturally as a part of the instinctive survival role in the process of living and navigating in the world, is the problem that enlightenment of Buddhism, yoga of Vedanta, and salvation of the Abrahamic religions is intended to dispel.

It is also the problem that science, regardless of the spiritual faith or agnosticism or atheism of the scientist, attempts to address pragmatically through a technological understanding of the quality of life, for solution to the social and environmental crises that humanity faces. Fear of existential risks and desire for survival opportunities can drive these processes, whether the investigating soul is enlightened or still operates instinctively, forgetting its innate, transcendent nature. This drive, without illumination as Soul, can result in an attachment to and an identification with people, places, and things in their environment that represent sources of private existential satisfaction of their essentially communal needs, to the exclusion of that true intuition in communion with other souls, in goodwill as unself-centered love and the wisdom it brings.

In this technologically modern world of smartphones and the internet, the natural communion of souls is often supplanted by the ergodidiocy of the communal imperative, sometimes in perverse ways. The illusion of an independence found in social connectedness funneled through these smartphones and maintained by the glamour of a ready following, obscures the reality of what may be a morally directionless server, controlled and motivated by the dollar optimization valuation of the server's algorithms. The overall technology has its benefits, but if it is designed to focus on our existential fears and ignore our true nature as souls to exploit us as consumers, it will continue its spiral into havoc. A smartphone as used in today's world without enlightened connectivity to the community is a destructive tool, a trigger of more lethal means.

If truth of the Soul is not understood and recognized in the community, the community good will fail for the lack of that understanding, as that understanding is goodwill, is love. The truth of the Soul is Love. It is Love that connects the individual souls together in the community as the Soul of that Community; it is Soul that creates the Community. I know now that I knew this before I was born.

I knew this when I was a toddler in a loving family, in Sunday school, in kindergarten. I knew this as a pupil in elementary school and in biking around the neighborhood of a small town. I was fortunate. I was not taught to fear or to hate, I learned not to ignore the truth or to lie; until my family moved to Florida when I was 11 at the start of the space race, to a small city of others moving to that small city from around the country, where no one knew anyone else. Then and there, outside the known world of Scotland County, I learned with adolescence to fear the effects of lies and to hate the embrace of ignorance, and I began to realize my personal existence— my ego—apart from a sense of the community.

I began to wonder about the reality of God and Justice and a Just God. That in turn led me to wonder about the nature of faith and science, about the reality of spirit and material, about the freedom of childhood and the prohibitions of the adult world—of dancing the dirty dog, of drink, of sexual fantasy. In college, the alienating contradictions between the professions of the public experts and the grim reality of public ineffectiveness seen on TV only increased the need to wonder about everything, about every form and process that I encountered, about the reasons for the Vietnam War, for racial and sexual discrimination, for class structure and its economic effect in society.

Without any understanding of right or left at the time, I swung from the traditional perspective of my upbringing to the anti-war and civil rights activism of the New Left and as I understood it, to the rational historical materialism of Marx. While that perspective sustained me for a while, it failed to explain the fundamental nature of consciousness, of the Soul, in a convincing manner or as a feasible way of ensuring the goal of Justice in society beyond a utopian vision of 'making everybody equal'. Despite its elaboration of a class consciousness based on an individual's position in the productive apparatus of society, historical materialism failed to explain to my satisfaction the origins of the exploitative nature of personal greed and self-interest within the community and thereby a rational solution to the problems that greed and self-interest engendered.

I turned to wondering about the personal ego and the symbolic archetypal nature of the operation of the collective unconscious as investigated in the work of Carl Jung and others. I was in this frame of mind when we stepped off the Elli and walked into the mysterious world of the Axis Mundi Café of the Paros Commune on June 17, 1971, looking for rock & roll, retsina, and romantic revelry—and an answer to what it all meant. As we were later to find out, this was the very day of the Watergate break-in, that great authoritarian suppuration of paranoia in the American psyche that continues to fester the corrupting influence of greed and money in one form or another to this day.

Within a month of leaving Paros, I had begun to get the answer of what it all meant. As mentioned in the Preface to this piece, on the ferry from Turku I had an epiphany as recounted in 'A Letter to a Friend' later in this book.

And so it goes...and so it goes...and so it goes...as ""i"...slowly wear into nothing as i walk through life". That's another quote from The Paros Commune of 1971, this time along with one from Billy Pilgrim or Kurt Vonnegut, though I am not using quotes in their case, since they were preoccupied with death, and we are preoccupied with Life here. Poetic license. More or less.

As I write, it is a few weeks shy of the Jubilee of the Paros Commune of 1971, which more or less took place in 1972. Now fifty years have passed as I tell the rest of this story, as I am now 'nothing' enough to better understand and remember what it all means, which is that we are a Communion of souls, a Communion of Soul, a

Community of Life. I am now in a position to understand the Triune Good—of Material Nature, of Ideal Nature, and of Spiritual Nature—having arrived at a perspective on the Platonic ideal Form of the Essential Trigon, through a contemplation of the Soul Nature as a reflection of a single Source of essential Inertial, Formal, and Intentional Capacities in the existent phenomena of all living beings.

This last sentence may require some explanation, which is the content of the rest of the addendum of this work. It may become a bit pedantic at times, a risk of assuming a teaching voice; instructions for disassembling a car engine and putting it back together require some familiarity with the technical details of the process, which is pretty dry reading until you've found out you have mistakenly under or over torqued your head gasket. That is why I am separating the events of 1971, 1972, & 1973, from the current reflections of 2021, 2022, & beyond. The Paros Commune of 1971 is all heart, and 2021 & Beyond in its various forms, while it still has plenty of heart, is a lot more head.

Your heart should be loose and open, not closed off and uptight. You don't want your head too loose or too tight. Your head needs to be a Goldilocks head, just right. If you've had an option to read the first part of this book as it was in 1971, you've read the heart part. The second, head part, is next, here.

I am not a big quoter of scripture because I try to recognize the Truth wherever I find it and such quoting is much abused, but I will quote a few verses from chapter 4 of the Gospel of John from the King James Version of the Bible. In my opinion, the soul should forget concerns about whether salvation is achieved by Grace or by Good works or by inspired study of scripture of any faith or of science as long as that soul loves the Spirit of Truth. When taken to heart so that 'Jesus Christ' is understood to be the Soul made in the image of God collectively embodied by souls of goodwill and 'Brother' is understood to mean 'Sibling', this chapter is the crux and the import of the entire Bible, the Koran, the Bhagavad Gita, and any enlightened search for Truth. It is the Spirit of Love.

"4:1 Beloved, believe not every spirit, but try the spirits whether they are of God: because many false prophets are gone out into the world.

4:2 Hereby know ye the Spirit of God: Every spirit that confesseth that Jesus Christ is come in the flesh is of God:

4:3 And every spirit that confesseth not that Jesus Christ is come in the flesh is not of God: and this is that spirit of antichrist, whereof ye have heard that it should come; and even now already is it in the world.

…

4:18 There is no fear in love; but perfect love casteth out fear: because fear hath torment. He that feareth is not made perfect in love.

4:19 We love him, because he first loved us.

4:20 If a man say, I love God, and hateth his brother, he is a liar: for he that loveth not his brother whom he hath seen, how can he love God whom he hath not seen?

4:21 And this commandment have we from him, That he who loveth God love his brother also."

I say, there is no fear in Love, no hate in Truth, and no ignorance in the Wisdom that flows from Love of the Spirit of Truth.

Philosophy is the Love of Truth. There are links to insights in the following section of this writing that offer an approach to that

Love of Truth, which is hoped may be of benefit to the reader. Most of that writing relies on a generally dispassionate, somewhat technical perspective rather than the heartful, personal voice of 1971. If you are in reading possession of one of the two titles that includes the words '2021 & Beyond', it also relies extensively on graphic representation that is intended to be direct and intuitively accessible and tries to compensate for any philosophical jargon. Of course, there are those who might have found the graphic descriptions of another kind in the heart portion of the book too jarring for their tastes, and it is for them that the The Paros Commune — 2021 & Beyond has been made available for those interested in just the head portion. In any case, for those who might be having doubt about the current state of world affairs, take heart and be of good cheer, and read on.

I have come to believe that a glossary is the proper place to start any book instead of putting it at the end with the index. In this case it ended up being somewhere in the middle. The logical time to define the terms of a discussion is before the discussion begins in earnest, especially if it is likely to get contentious when the terms are not well understood. But then if logic itself is the topic of discussion, even that may not be early enough for the glossary.

It would help if we were born with our knowledge already in our heads, with a universal vocabulary and language comprised of all the necessary words, each one pointing to a recognizable form or process in the world in which we are living. Then there would be no misunderstandings and no need for a glossary. For those who are familiar with the subject, judging from biblical lore, the Powers that Be had a sense of humor when They created Adam—the Namer— since he, meaning Adam, used Hebrew when he got started naming things. Apparently, Hebrew didn't have quite enough letters, and the inspired scribes had to switch to Aramaic and Greek in the New

Testament, then segued over to Latin when the Roman Catholics took over, before finally settling on German and English and all the others after the protestant reformation, all in the attempt to get an authentic glossary for encyclopedic understanding of Life. Then the scientific revolution came along and stirred the pot, quickly followed by the commercial–industrial revolution, and finally the cyber-tech revolution that has everything in the current cultural uproar.

The desire to shore up this tottering tower of Babel has spawned an unending supply of well-authored bricks requisitioned for the base of the structure, unfortunately with little thought to the mortar required to cement them all in place and provide the necessary structural integrity. These bricks cover the spectrum, written with a fervent, sometimes reverent, but generally incomprehensible use of glossolalia at one end, to the glossy zeal of an adman looking for an obvious commercial hook at the other. The extant brick of this writing comes with its own mortar, for which the Glossary in this case consists of only two basic terms, 'Soul' and 'Commune', though the latter has its own mix of structural strengths and design applications which generally comes down to the notion of 'Community'.

The notion of Community ranges from that of the global, planetary community to the insular community of close friends and family, which covers a lot of territory, but so does the need for mortar for the whole structure, especially at the foundation. The notion of Soul as a unit of human consciousness is the brick in the structure, but as Love, Soul is also the mortar, which is capitalized in accordance with the conventional notion of ideal Forms of the philosophy of Plato and others. The ideal Soul of Neo-Platonic thinking is itself an archetypical Form and Process—a Thing as an idea rather than an object—that has a reality beyond space and time and yet enters into the composition of every specific material form or process. Likewise, an ideal Book is a mental idea of a printed or electronic book in material form containing representations in text and graphics of other ideas. The reader observing the material text and graphics must recognize the forms as ideas which they understand, before the process intended and initiated by the writer can complete the communication—the communion process—between writer and reader thereby joining them in understanding in a form of commune, of community. If the writing is in another language or written in an arcane lexicon of abbreviations and symbols which are indiscernible, there is no informational communication. It is just gibberish, babble.

The Soul is also the archetypal mold from which all the individual bricks in the community tower are formed as souls. No two specific bricks, as souls or books, are exactly alike. But they should all be of a type that facilitates a surface bond to the mortar which cements the bricks together if we want them to provide long term structural integrity for the community tower.

Of course, if we return to biblical allegory, perhaps the cultural uproar of the current Babel is a matter of divine intent, the result of the confounding of communication designed to impede the current human pursuit and risk of unrestrained imagination. If that is the case, then presumably no power on heaven or earth will prevent it. On the other hand, there is very little place for people left to "scatter them abroad upon the face of all the earth,"[1] so perhaps the current divine intent is to iron out our differences and disagreements and start communicating again. If so, this will take a better understanding of the Soul and Community than what was found in the land of Shinar, in Mesopotamia, in Babylon of several thousand

---

[1] Genesis 11:9 KJV

years ago. That doesn't mean the restoration of communication that has been underway over the past several generations and appears to be technologically and culturally worthwhile for much of humanity can afford to allow the pursuit and risk of unrestrained imagination without some adult supervision.

The traditional knee-jerk reaction to the excesses of unrestrained imagination and personal freedom formed the authoritarian movements of the past hundred years, though in truth authoritarianism has always been more the rule than the exception, based on a traditional perception of authority, more the political thesis of national histories than the antithetical reactions to progress which have occurred in recent European history.

Unfortunately, these *conservative* impulses for administration of the state—a cautious response to perceived risks of unknown measure—are readily contoured by duplicitous parties in the manipulation of popular grievance, authentic or not, through the scapegoating of marginalized souls in the community. This duplicity is generally motivated by a monetary payoff somewhere along the state chain of command and is best understood as a moribund form of feudalism or of organized crime.

Liberal impulses, on the other hand—in optimistic response to perceived opportunities of unknown and sometimes inflated value—as with much of the neo-liberal globalism of the post-war era, have the same narrow focused monetary motivation, especially when greed is paramount over long term concerns for maintaining human productivity and well-being of the community. This operates naively in the open, contributing to the cultural and economic grievances that fuel the populist response and alignment with authoritarian, 'conservative' posturing. This is where we currently find ourselves.

The reader that has some familiarity with The Paros Commune of 1971 will note the difference in voice between the two writings. This difference is by intent, but not as a personal contrivance. Though I was under the mild literary spell of Kurt Vonnegut, Richard Brautigan, and a few other avant-garde literary notables of the times, I was mostly operating under the spell of the times themselves, which was that of personal freedom and optimism about the future, which incidentally has never left me, though cautiously tempered now by current trends. The observational ear and vision of 1972 along with the writing voice of 1973, emerges from time to time in this addendum, but has largely been supplanted in what you are reading now. It has been trained over the past fifty years by some of the events that have transpired in my life as touched on in the content of this volume, The Paros Commune — 2021 & Beyond.

Before I drug The Paros Commune of 1971 out and dusted it off, I was content with the pedagogic voice of the technically based political economics and physics writing which has occupied my interest of the last few decades and spilled over into recent content of a philosophical and spiritual nature. This second voice is a natural result of the ascent of logical intuition in the study of transcendental subjects over infatuation with any spiritual glamour generally associated with the same subject matter, where I prefer the term 'essential' as more precise than 'spiritual' study. The ethos of the world of 1971, of my world at the time, produced The Paros Commune of 1971 and reflects that fact in the writing, but it should be capable of being appreciated now by any age—by grown-ups anyway—if read in the spirit in which it was written.

In the Spirit of the Paros Commune of 1971, this hand is extended—funneled through the hourglass of time and space from whence it more or less happened in 1972—through the current

285

tribulations in which we now find ourselves, to this year of 2022, for what must become our year of jubilation, our Jubilee.

Sound the horn! Sound the Shofar! Sound the trumpets!

Love Life! Live Love! Peace to One and All!

COMMUNE

From Dictionary.com:

"Commune;

(verb)

1.1   To converse or talk together, usually with profound intensity, intimacy; interchange thoughts or feelings.

1. 2   To be in intimate communication or rapport.

3.1   To partake of the Eucharist.

(noun)

1.3   Interchange of ideas or sentiments.

2.1   A small group of persons living together, sharing possessions, work, income, and often pursuing unconventional lifestyles.

2.2   A close-knit community of people who share common interests.

2.3   The smallest administrative division in France, Italy, Switzerland, etc., governed by a mayor assisted by a municipal council.

2.4   A similar division in some other country.

2.5   Any community organized for the protection and promotion of local interests, and subordinate to the state.

2.6   The government or citizens of a commune.

2.7   People's commune.

2.8   The   Commune. Also   called Commune   of Paris, Paris Commune.

>a.   A revolutionary committee that took the place of the municipality of Paris in the revolution of 1789, usurped the authority of the state, and was suppressed by the National Convention in 1794.

>b.   A socialistic government of Paris from March 18 to May 27, 1871.

Origin of Commune

1   First   recorded   in   1250–1300;   Middle English *com(m)unen* "to share, have in common, associate with, tell stories, communicate," from Middle French *com(m)uner, com(m)uniier* "to make common, have in common, share," derivative of *comun* "common"

2   First recorded in 1785–95; from French, from Medieval Latin *commūna, commūnia* (feminine singular), alteration of Latin *commūne* (neuter singular), or *commūnia* (neuter plural) "community, state," originally neuter of *commūnis* "common"

3   First recorded in 1325-1375; Middle English; back formation from "communion"

COMMUNION

Again, from Dictionary.com:

"Communion;

1.   (often initial capital letter) Also called Holy Communion. Ecclesiastical.

    a.   the act of receiving the Eucharistic elements.

    b.   The elements of the Eucharist.

    c.   the celebration of the Eucharist.

    d.   the antiphon sung at a Eucharistic service.

2.   A group of persons having a common religious faith; a religious denomination: Anglican communion.

3.   Association; fellowship.

4.   Interchange or sharing of thoughts or emotions; intimate communication: communion with nature.

5.   The act of sharing or holding in common; participation.

6.   The state of things so held.

Origin of Communion

1350–1400; Middle English (<Anglo-French)
<Latin *commūniōn*- (stem of *commūniō*) a sharing, equivalent to *commūn*(*is*) common + *-iōn*—ion"

COMMUNITY

And again, from Dictionary.com

"**Community**;

1.   A social group of any size whose members reside in a specific locality, share government, and often have a common cultural and historical heritage.

2.   A locality inhabited by such a group.

3.   A social, religious, occupational, or other group sharing common characteristics or interests and perceived or perceiving itself as distinct in some respect from the larger society within which it exists.

4.   A group of associated nations sharing common interests or a common heritage.

5.   *Ecclesiastical.*

A group of men or women leading a common life according to a rule.

6.   *Ecology.*

An assemblage of interacting populations occupying a given area.

7.   Joint possession, enjoyment, liability, etc.

8.   Similarity; agreement; identity.

9.   **The community,** the public; society.

COMMUNISM / COMMUNALISM

Once again, from Dictionary.com:

"Communism:

1.   A theory or system of social organization based on the holding of all property in common, actual ownership being ascribed to the community as a whole or to the state.

2.   (often initial capital letter) A system of social organization in which all economic and social activity is controlled by a totalitarian state dominated by a single and self-perpetuating political party.

3.   (initial capital letter) The principles and practices of the Communist Party.

4.   Communalism."

"Communalism:

1.   A theory or system of government according to which each commune is virtually an independent state and the nation is merely a federation of such states.

2.   The principles or practices of communal ownership.

3.   Strong allegiance to one's own ethnic group rather than to society as a whole."

COMMUNARD

Finally, from Dictionary.com:

"**Communard**:

1.   (often lowercase) French History.

A member or supporter of the Commune of 1871.

Compare commune² (def. 8b).

2.   (lowercase)

A person who lives in a commune."

And from this writer:

3.   Any member of a community, regardless of natural origin or assumed state, faith, political, professional, business, trade, work, or other affiliation as a citizen or subject, that communes face-to-face, tele-textually, tele-visually, telephonically, telepathically, or simply intuitively with other souls in a community, while respecting and understanding that they and the others in that community are indeed Souls, and without concern as to whether that other soul defines themself as a Communist or Communalist, as defined above, as long as that other soul is willing to admit that both parties to the communion are communards.

ALL THINGS COMMON

From the Bible, Acts 4:31-35:

"4:31 And when they had prayed, the place was shaken where they were assembled together; and they were all filled with the Holy Ghost, and they spake the word of God with boldness

4:32 And the multitude of them that believed were of one heart and of one soul: neither said any of them that ought of the things which he possessed was his own; but they had **all things common**.

4:33 And with great power gave the apostles witness of the resurrection of the Lord Jesus: and great grace was upon them all.

4:34 Neither was there any among them that lacked: for as many as were possessors of lands or houses sold them, and brought the prices of the things that were sold,

4:35 And laid them down at the apostles' feet: and distribution was made unto every man according as he had need."

SOUL

From Dictionary.com:

"**Soul**;

1.   The principle of life, feeling, thought, and action in humans, regarded as a distinct entity separate from the body, and commonly held to be separable in existence from the body; the spiritual part of humans as distinct from the physical part.

2.   The spiritual part of humans regarded in its moral aspect, or as believed to survive death and be subject to happiness or misery in a life to come.

3.   The disembodied spirit of a deceased person.

4.   The emotional part of human nature; the seat of the feelings or sentiments.

5.   A human being; person.

6.   High-mindedness; noble warmth of feeling, spirit or courage, etc.

7.   The animating principle; the essential element or part of something.

8.   The inspirer or moving spirit of some action, movement, etc.

9.   The embodiment of some quality.

10.   (*initial capital letter*) *Christian Science*. God; the divine source of all identity and individuality.

11. Shared ethnic awareness and pride among Black people, especially Black Americans.

12. Deeply felt emotion, as conveyed or expressed by a performer or artist.

13. Soul music....

Origin of Soul

First recorded before 900; Middle English; Old English *sāwl, sāwol*; cognate with Dutch *ziel*, German *Seele*, Old Norse *sāl*, Gothic *saiwal*

A COMMUNION OF SOULS

These terms—commune, communion, community, communism, communalism, communard, all things common–all related to soul—cover a lot of ground from the extreme left to the extreme right, from the intensely private to the passionately public, from the rapture of personal and shared religious experience to the calm respect for fellow citizens when engaged in civic discourse. How each of us define these terms and how we think others define them, means everything; it determines how we interact, how we communicate and commune with each other, as either masks of a part in a personal play or as actors in those roles, as either things or or as souls.

The Paros Commune of 1971 was not written as a spoof of the Paris Commune of 1871. It was not written either as a veneration or a parody of the popular counter-culture trends of the early 1970's, which included the notion of the 'hippy commune' of the times, whatever that notion might have been. The Paros Commune of 1971 was not a manifesto for self-indulgence in sex, drugs, and rock and roll—though it may have been partially accurate based on accounts of some of those engaging in such activities over a few weeks that summer.

The Paros Commune of 1971 was written as a celebration of Life, of self-discovery and friendship; an aspiration of the time for open inclusion in community over any type of exclusionary social status, no matter how small or how short a duration that communion might have been. When it was written I had but an inkling of where that communion was leading me, though I knew it was away from my three-year fascination with Marxist materialism masking a vision of utopian communism, but still in an uncommon direction, by an uncommon route, even as I was coming to understand the ultimate destination was all things common, as a communard of the Soul.

The conventional wisdom concerning Marxism is that Marx was godless, a materialist atheist—and he may have been—though there is the adage that there is 'no atheist in a foxhole' which becomes more appropriate as the planet appears to edge ever closer to the abyss. More recent reading of his work waxes spiritual, echoing Plato and even Christ in his introduction to "A Contribution to the Critique of Hegel's Philosophy of Right", said to be written in 1843, well before the published work of Darwin had inadvertently begun to remove the immaterial Soul from the carcass of material evolution. Make no mistake about it, material interactions do evolve—unfold— over time. It is just that such unfolding is based on logic, and that logic is baked into the cake before the ingredients in the recipe are ever assembled, mixed, leavened, or placed in the oven.

Axiomatic Logic has always been my approach to understanding the Truth, and in that Spirit of Truth, I have always found God. Give me a good axiom and I will first do my best to wear it out. If not able, I will follow it to its necessary and sufficient conclusion. From the first verse of the Gospel of John, properly transcribed from the Greek, we have, "In the beginning was the Logos, and the Logos was with God, and the Logos was God." I would translate 'the Logos' as something like 'Logical Being' or 'Rational Intent', as for the third phrase, 'Rational Intent was the Supreme Reality'. From the self-evident start of any creative process some form of logic reigns supreme. A logical system may be mindless as it proceeds, but it necessarily involves a conscious initiation of the process from its point of change inducing stress. In the cosmic

298

perspective, that is sufficient for all phenomena that ever was, is now, and ever will come into existence. In truth, sentience can and should be considered endemic when it is understood as the ongoing transference of stress between the individual connecting parts within the field of living experience—as light and other electromagnetic energy. For human beings, Life does this all through the communal agency of its individuated souls.

I was still trying to figure this out when we got on the Elli in Piraeus for Paros for the two week duration of the Paros Commune in 1971 and when we got back on the Elli in Paros for Piraeus and Daphne, to Istanbul and through the Soviet Union to Finland, to get on the ferry from Turku to Sweden, where somewhere in the middle of that night in the middle of that ferry ride, I experienced with full resolute clarity, an epiphany, the recognition that we are Soul—still with many questions left to answer, but with little doubt about the direction going forward. I didn't realize, for instance, that 'Soul'—as capitalized here in singular form—is essentially a collective identity and not just a group of individual souls. It is Christ of Christianity, Adam Kadmon of Qabala, Krisna of Bhagadva Gita. I will give more detail to this event later in the section, 'Letter to a Friend'.

We are also souls—that means we <u>are</u> <u>essential</u> <u>beings,</u> which is a bit redundant; an *essential* is a potential 'to exist'—literally 'to stand forth' from the background—and thus *is*, something that *always was and will be*, a necessary something that may *condition a process of change, without itself being conditioned.* So, the phrase, an 'unconditioned essential' as a potential is by its very nature redundant. To have the potential to become something once, all else being equal, is to have the potency to reproduce itself again and again. Souls are an essential element of a community, but community is essential for the development of souls. It takes two to commune, two to start a community…in more ways than one. "For where two or more are gathered together in my name, there am I in the midst of them."[2]

What is *always necessary* for any appearance *is* what is *essential* and is therefore a pre-condition for an event. Something considered to be essential like the air may not appear to exist at all, until it is set in motion as wind to kick up the dust or until we realize we need it in order to breath. Then we know and come to understand something of what air *is*. The phenomena of waves on the surface of the ocean at an arbitrary point in time and place may or may not *exist*, depending on the presence of such wind moving across that surface, but the water from which the waves are made *is another essential*; there's that redundancy again, essential *isness* of water and air versus the existential *isness* of wind and waves.

With respect to the existence of waves, there must also be a sufficient *existential* agreement between the essential environment, the *water*, and what is a secondary essential as *air* at a place and time under conditions sufficient to produce the appearance of a conditioning phenomenon, the *wind*. If the conditioning phenomena, *wind*, produces the conditioned appearance of *waves* once—given the essential pre-conditions, *air and water*—wind is a sufficient condition for that appearance of waves again and again. Such wind is not a necessary or essential condition for waves, however, unless it is the only condition that produces waves. If an earthquake produces waves in the water in the absence of wind, it becomes a second sufficient condition for producing waves. Thus, every existential event as waves *is* the expression of a sufficient condition, wind or earthquake, *which is an essential initiating power*, inherent in air or

---

[2] Matthew 18:20

earth, which in motion operates on another *potential*, water, that is *essential*.

It is all very logical. If we agree to meet our friend for coffee and breakfast at the downtown café the next day and wake up in the morning on a lifeboat out to sea, our essential being will find itself bewildered and be wilder than it was when it went to sleep. We may find that self in an existential panic and fall overboard in our desperation of standing up to look for land. We feel like we are drowning when we finally wake up and realize we were dreaming all along. We reach over and grab our phone to text our friend, and remember it is a workday and the downtown café was a part of the dream as well.

All these existential conditions—of the workday, the dream at sea, the dream within the dream of agreeing to breakfast with our friend, all the appearance of reality of various events—represent conditions sufficient for the episodes of the vignette, but the *one essential* thread that provides continuity through all the dramas is our individual consciousness of the working, dreaming, panicking, drowning, and relief as a human being. That thread of reality as conscious human being is Soul, essential being that has an existential presence, an awareness of place and time in one state or the other, be it awake to this one or in the dream state or departed from this physical ecology to some ethereal realm, whether we recall which state that might be at the time or not.

Souls always have and always will have a presence and awareness of their self in one form or another, in solitude or collectively in either a pre or post individuated state. They just forget the essential realms, the spiritual realms, while they are captive to the appearance of the perilous risks and glamorous opportunities of physical phenomena—just as we tend to forget the more stable realities of the wakened state while floating in the immersive experience of the dream state.

Some souls manage to maintain an essential awareness of the thread that connects them to the state of the wakened world while in the dream state, just as some maintain awareness of the supernal realm while yet incorporated in this terrestrial state of the world, infernal and corruptible as it sometimes seems. But many remain enamored with the love of fearful risk and fear of loving opportunity—not to mention loving the opportunity of spreading fear—all immersed in the material realm to the avoidance or denial of any more inclusive sense of being responsibly alive.

Risk of material circumstance can grab and redirect one's attention to the non-material essentials, if the soul is ready to wake up from the dream, as for me on the ferry from Turku to the nature of the real communion between souls as Soul. For those awakening to the recognitions of ideal and spiritual reality, a commitment to contemplation and communion—the practice of meditational and spiritual observation—is necessary for understanding the essential principles of Life. The reason for contemplation is obvious for those who have already begun to travel this path. For others, it may take a brush with a peril of one form or another or the spiritual touch of another soul to grab the soul's attention.

The soul's vehicle for navigating in the material world is the mind, not the brain—though that is a helpful bit of equipment as well—and while the mind is a wonderful mechanism for ordering and analyzing information, its ability to function effectively relies on mental clarity and emotional calm in the use of that vehicle, in detachment and harmlessness. One purpose of communion is to achieve and make habitual those conscious states of the soul so that the mind works appropriately even in the midst of extreme personal, community, and environmental stress on any level. Contemplation—thinking about the whys and wherefores of Life—facilitates an enlightened detachment from the existential passions. Such detachment facilitates the development of an attitude of harmlessness toward other forms of life. Harmlessness facilitates the use of the innate capacity of the Soul for communion with the source of the soul and the community.

A few years after communing with these souls in Greece and writing The Paros Commune of 1971, with the preparation and the application of such contemplations and discipline, I had such an awakening. As a result of this awakening, the thread of consciousness which is the Soul has become continuous for me. I am conscious when I go to sleep and remain so in whatever activity I encounter until I wake up. Refocusing is perhaps a better way of stating the daily process of going into and waking from sleep. This does not mean that I remember every aspect of the daily experience, but neither do I remember all the minutia of my waking life.

What this continuity of conscious does—along with related aspects of this essential awakening, over time and after some degree of irritation—is remove any doubts about the nature of humans being Soul and about the meaning of this realization in terms of each soul's connection to the community.

The culmination of this realization is the motivation for the belated publishing of The Paros Commune of 1971 and for what I have to say in this 2021 & Beyond appendix. In the intervening 48 years since it's writing, I have done my best to understand this experience of awakening to a more complete realization of the Soul.

Appendices are interesting. As I understand it, until recently the medical profession thought of the appendix as an unnecessary vestigial organ. Perhaps they were right, but the latest theory is that the appendix serves as a repository of 'good' bacteria which serves to repopulate the intestines for proper digestion after flushing of the system from a bout of countering an invasion of 'bad' bacteria. The hope is that the reader will find some good material in this appendix with which to help repopulate the mind, after flushing out the bad ideas, as an aid in digesting The Paros Commune of 1971.

The realization of the Soul is innate, logical, and intuitive. It has the sense of self-motivating discovery, traveling a variety of routes on a long road trip in an assortment of vehicles with the help of friends and fellow travelers, to arrive at some well-known destination and family homecoming. Arriving at that destination is not achieved by thinking about the journey vividly or accurately, though that is an aid along the way as long as one keeps an eye on the road and not on the map while driving. After much work, arriving comes with the 'aha' moment of *knowing*—like the moment on the ferry from Turku—of conscious realization that comes after the experience of mental and material problem solving is complete, the map is put down, and the soul looks out and is able to concentrate on the view of the terrain.

Each separate route of a soul to the destination requires a different mental map with a different starting point of the journey and with options for ego-oriented side trips along the way. Once the destination is reached, the traveler no longer needs to think about the mental map and can put it aside, along with all the distracting contours and detours and remarks of dubious relevance. When the individual soul reaches the nirvanic peak from which it can view the whole journey of the collective Soul's destination and terrain, they can finally leave behind the map with its ego-oriented legend that got them there. Perhaps most importantly for all fellow travelers is the truth that no one can compel another soul to follow their precise, same route without encountering some adversity for themselves. Self-motivation—free-will—being able to decide for themselves which route to take is necessary.

There are a few well-known versions of such maps to choose from. Analogous to the two well-worn mappings of the Rand-McNally and DeLorme Atlases, and the scientific based, technologically modern atlas and mappings of Google Earth, in no particular order of identification with the following listing we can consult the maps of the Abrahamic religions of Judaism, Christianity, and Islam; the Vedic charts of Vedanta, Hinduism, and Buddhism leading to Brahman, with their variety of side trips; the atlas of Classical philosophy of Greece, of Plato and Socrates and the Neoplatonist monists like Plotinus with the contemporaneous early Christian church father Origen, not easily found in some stores but available in archived form on the web. And there are others. I have made use of most of all of these when needed, in creating my own map to the destination.

I started out being raised with a Christian version of the map. Not with the more recent pre-Copernican one that only goes back 8,000 or so years nor the Eastern and Roman Catholic one that stamped its imprimatur on the Second Council of Constantinople in 553AD in its apparent anathematization of Origen and the Neoplatonist teaching of the pre-existence of the Soul. That anathema was to establish, for whatever misguided reason, that hence forth in Christian teaching, the creation of the Soul would be deemed a terrestrial event for each human being starting at conception, either directly in each conception by God, in a process known as creationism, or indirectly through the parents by a corollary act to biological individuation, known as traducianism.

I assume creationism would keep God quite busy but would also provide plenty of occasions to tweak his work. When the Bible was written, well-before Copernicus started scratching his head and figured out that the earth revolved around the sun, keeping track of all those births for each soul infusion would have been pretty time consuming, so I assume he thought about automating the creation, which suggests relegating the process through a form of traducianism.

Traducianism runs into an apparent contradiction, however, in that the individuated soul, held to be immortal by church tradition, is yet dependent on a material, biological creation for its realization. This leads to a slippery theological slope with the profane scientific conclusion that the soul is but an ephemeral epiphenomenon, instead of recognizing the Soul as the essential, conscious animating principal of all human participation in the material world. The chaos this conflict of interpretation fosters in the U.S. on the individual caught in the pro-choice/right-to-life conflict barely needs mentioning.

The transliterated Greek word Christos and the Hebrew word Mashiah, have the same meaning—'anointed'—indicating one that is anointed, as in the 23rd Psalms, verse 5 attributed to King David, "Thou preparest a table before me in the presence of mine enemies: thou *anointest my head* with oil; my cup runneth over." Such anointing as a religious sacrament or a civil ceremony in antiquity was and continues to be a sign of sanctification or commitment of the anointed individual for spiritual purpose or office. In the context of Christian teaching, it represents the anointing of Jesus—and others— by the Holy Spirit, as depicted in the iconography of the church by the halos shown about the heads of Jesus and the apostles and saints. In the context of Eastern thought and the practice of yoga, such halos represent the activated crown center or chakra which is activated on inner levels by initiation and develops over time into enlightenment.

The crown center is the representation in certain yogic thinking of the little understood pineal gland in the endocrine system of modern medicine. A biological resonance of this concept of activation of an element of the endocrine system and the related alteration in consciousness that it entails is the equally profound change of puberty leading to reproductive capacity that occur from the activation of the ovaries and testes resulting from fundamental changes in the pituitary gland.

Christianity in the popular tradition is not a road map perse in preparation to such a spiritual awakening. In many Christian teachings, any awakening to a state of spiritual grace is the work of God alone, through the operation of the Holy Spirit, and not a result of the individual soul's own efforts. In some such traditions the only stated requirement of the soul is salvation—of being saved from wandering in the wilderness of an eternal, perhaps infernal, dreamlike world of natural passions. What can be said without question is that a state of Grace is the realization of Divine Love on the part of any soul, whether initially lost or not.

According to some traditional Christian teachings, all human souls are born lost, fallen, for arcane reasons that might be incomprehensible to the unfaithful, especially to the ones that don't feel lost, and to some of the faithful as well. I have never felt such an innate condition of being 'fallen' in this life—which is a misunderstood concept—though I have felt what it means to be separated from the Spirit of Truth resulting from my own lack of candor in a moment of intimate conversation.

What I thought at the time was just a 'white' lie had the effect of engulfing me immediately in a state of consciousness known in Buddhist literature as avitchi, a term meaning 'without waves', which is a feeling of interminable lovelessness, without emotional fluctuation or content, of being hollowed out but for a sensation of prickly, unremittent, electrical burning throughout one's body. It is the antithesis of nirvana. It is said to be the lowest level of hell into which the soul may find itself regardless of whether that soul is in physical embodiment or deceased. Contrary to the teaching of some traditions, the confinement in this conscious state is not for eternity, being yet another purgatorial experience, but based on my experience, any length of time spent at any level of the netherworld would be avoided if the soul understood the reality of the state. In this instance, it lasted for an hour until my companion bestowed her forgiving grace on me and the hollowness and burning immediately vanished to my unsurpassed relief.

With respect to salvation from a fallen state, I remember going to a church service while I was visiting with my parents when I was in my early thirties, shortly before my dad died. He was participating in the service, I believe as an usher, and I was sitting at the back of the sanctuary with my mother. At one point in the service, the pastor stated that there was one event in every Christian's life that they would remember, and that was the moment that they were saved, that they accepted Jesus Christ as their savior; at which point my mother and I turned to each other and quietly communed with each other in unison, "I have always been saved."

But then again, we were both born Presbyterians and my dad had been born a Methodist, and I guess he needed help from the Method, whatever that was. I've never understood what Methodism was, other than being a step down from being an Episcopalian, which was a step down from being a Catholic in some people's eyes, but I have always known this was not my first rodeo and apparently my mother knew this as well. Being Presbyterians meant that we were or had been Scots. Despite being Methodist, my dad was essentially 100% Scots along with his ancestors living in Scotland County, North Carolina for the past couple of centuries since moving from Scotland. Being Presbyterian meant that we were predestined and therefore born saved—or not—and going to do great things, while at the same time being predestined to suffer greatly in the process—no doubt due to our independent streak. All pretty murky, except for the part about knowing we were not fallen souls.

The popular soteriological map of Christian salvation—I am not referring to the esoteric Christian maps that lead to the same destination as the esoteric maps of theology, theosophy, or philosophy based in any popular religion—will get one at least part of the way to the destination, and perhaps the whole way for the truly devoted. But being born saved and impatient for more light on the subject from birth, I was looking for more detail when I returned from Europe in 1972. Along the way I found many offerings.

Of these were two that I felt held promise. One was found in the work of Paul Foster Case, 'The Tarot', in his presentation of the Qabalah and the Tree of Life as an expression of the foundational principles of the Abrahamic tradition. His use of the Tarot is not intended for fortune-telling. Rather the symbolic images of the 22 major trump cards, some of which are found as images described in the Bible, are intended to be pictorial images for contemplation or mindful meditation.

Apart from any motivation for spiritual enlightenment, meditational contemplation can be understood as a naturally functioning capacity of the human mind. In any environment, if an individual encounters some new situation holding risk or opportunity or is looking for an answer to a novel problem, the natural inclination is to stop and think about a solution before proceeding. That process normally consists of creating mental images of the condition as it is presently understood and imagining what will happen if various processes are brought to bear on the situation. The contemplative process has been likened to the activity of fishing, where the fisher uses various types of bait to hook a fish. The fish is the solution to the problem of being hungry. Some bait will attract the fish and entice a strike, while some offer no enticement; sometimes, there appear to be no fish in the pond.

Contemplation is the process of selecting a lure or bait, placing it on the hook, and casting it on the water … and waiting for a strike. The baited hook is a mental formulation of the risk, opportunity, or problem looking for a solution. In formal or spiritual meditational practice, the lure may be a mantra, a symbolic picture, or scripture looking for a strike of intuitive insight. Mental casting in the water is followed by trolling or simply remaining quiet and still. The first case consists of working the line in a variety of moves one way or the other with a mental lure formulated to result in a desirable catch. In the second case, in keeping with the notion of mindfulness the fisher calmly watches and waits for the desired qualitative understanding to surface at the hook end of the line of contemplation in a communion between the fisher and the fish.

Contemplation on the tarot cards is intended to lure various qualitative relationships between forms and processes that are not previously recognized to the surface of consciousness, according to the images on the cards, representing various ideal Forms in a nod to Platonic thinking. As stated, the same images can be found in various scriptures of the world religions. For example, Card 16 – The Tower is related to the story of the Tower of Babel from the Old Testament with similar symbolic significance.

In this spiritual sojourn, I found another teaching worth study in the theosophical work of Alice Bailey which she attributed to her transcription under meditational rapport of the teachings of the Tibetan monk, Djwal Khul. These teachings are referred to in her work of the Ageless Wisdom. I found the philosophical content of her presentation to be both logically consistent and intuitive in keeping with the Vedantic traditions of India.

Contemplative understanding like that of the Case book can be found in the Bailey books, of which there are said to be twenty-four attributed to her teacher, written between 1919 and 1949. I have read portions of most of these and have used them as reference material over the years. While I am not a self-identifying devotee of any single school of thought, esoteric or exoteric, what I find substantive in both of these sources is the appeal to a logical spirituality, to reason and intuition, and a lack of importunity toward any sectarian interest or personality passion on the part of the authors.

I have found corroboration of statements of a subjective nature, spiritual and ideal, in each of these teachings. As with anything I read, those items that seem to be true based on my individual experience and logic are either referred to for further study as workable hypotheses, those that are deemed true by that same attitude of experience and logic are treated as such, and those that do not pass the sniff or taste test are treated on that basis.

For example, I have had at least one very clear out of the body experience in which I floated up and out of my body while falling asleep in a prone position. I could look down at the back of my body as I drifted through the exterior wall of the house at the head of my bed. I sensed, my subtle body—the bodily perspective I generally encounter in the dream state—before the experience startled me and I quickly snaped back into my physical body.

On the other hand, to my recollection while in the wakened state I have never seen any ghosts or disembodied souls in their subtle bodies, with one exception in the dream state mentioned later. Based on this out of body experience and the episode I will recount shortly, I have little doubt about the general validity of these claims. On the other hand, I am dubious about much of the writing concerning psychic and paranormal events that has come across my desk over the years.

There were a few other references that resonated with my experience during this time. Among these was Autobiography of a Yogi, a personal account of the life of Paramahansa Yogananda, and God Speaks by Meher Baba. Both of these souls were born in India around the time of my grandparents, and both had a respectable public spiritual mission during the first half of the 20th century. The lives of both these souls are worth the study.

In addition, around this time in the mid 1970's I read the book, Kundalini, the Evolutionary Energy in Man, by Gopi Krishna, an account of that author's unanticipated experience with the awakening of this latent psychic energy in the process of one of his daily meditational routines. I found this read of special interest as it was not explicitly heralded as the work of any traditional religious practice, though the subject matter was obviously spiritual in its content, and it occurred in a day-to-day context that caught the writer and subject of the event completely unawares. It had the ring of authenticity.

In the wake of this study and practice, starting in 1973, I began to experience an increasing frequency of episodes of lucid dreaming and communion and meaningful interaction with other souls while in the dream state, with the occasional instance of physical bodily disassociation, or out of the body experience. None of these experiences could be attributed to any specific personal intent or technique. They simply happened, though it was clear in each case that they happened only after sufficient preparation had occurred to convey the relevant contextual significance or meaning.

In addition to the contemplative meditation mentioned above, I began various meditational practices centered on control of the breath and focus of the attention on the crown center, with the aim of maintaining an attitude of conscious deference to the 'light in the crown'. I could not understand at the time the importance of being able to habitually return to this attitude of deference often in extended moments of stress.

The effect of this practice over time has been the development of an awareness of a multi-dimensional reality, understood with a logical consistency across these subjective experiences equal to the logical continuity of observed three-dimensional physical phenomena. Both experiences of objective and subjective phenomena—material and ideal, physical and metaphysical, somatic and psychic—are recognized as manifesting a quality of purpose through the interaction of form and process within the supporting environment, designed to give Life contextual significance and meaning.

Through this process, a sense of tension evolves in the individual's consciousness that eventually culminates in a recognition that the individual, rather than being a separate, mortal human ego, is an individualized focus of an immortal Soul, as indicated in the following dream with interpretation.

A DREAM

Sometime in the year or two after writing <u>The Paros Commune of 1971</u> and after moving to Washington State, I had a particularly lucid and highly symbolic dream.

I was aware of being in a space of indeterminate size, lit all around from the distance with a soft glow by the space itself. I was standing on a plane with no visible horizon, not a terrestrial surface. There was nothing else with me in the space. Though there was no reference point, I was aware of facing in a general 'southeasterly direction'. I lifted my right foot and stomped once firmly, but not violently, on the ground as the floor of the space began to undulate slowly in a ponderous fashion, radiating from the point of impact with an audible low frequency hum and periodic churn. I then turned to the left as the scene faded.

After what I understood as an eon of time, which still felt to be a continuous interlude without other interruption, I was once more in the prior space hovering just above the point of impact that I had stomped, from which the ground now undulated gently out in a series of concentric circles, fading into what otherwise might have been a horizon in the distance. Along eight to maybe twelve lines radiating like spokes of a wheel, facing the center hub and rising head to tail one after another on the crests of the undulating ground, were rows of living creatures, each crest along each row representing a different instance among the varieties of species.

Facing south as I watched the process of small-scale creatures evolving in the pattern, I stepped down and stood where I first stomped the ground on the center of the emanating ground waves. This step down was accompanied by a sense of exaltation. As the active ground became still, the creatures below receded in the vision. I turned toward the west and called out, for the "Father of all Living," in those precise words.

A simple stone throne, hewn of one piece of solid heavy granite without embellishment, emerged from the southwest above and descended in front of and facing me. I could see no one on the throne, but I could *feel an overwhelming Presence and Potency* which I understood to be the Source of All Life. I prostrated myself, face down, as I reached out and touched the foot of the throne and with it the Omnipotent Spiritual Presence, which flowed into me, filling me with incomparable Love.

After a moment, the Spirit on the throne picked me up and placed me upright, as I found the Presence receding whence it came. I then found myself in a large urban area. I was looking north, out and onto a built-up area of mid-rise residential buildings that I took to be a major city, then recognized it as a view in the Midtown area of Manhattan along the East River in New York City.

Then I woke up.

I had little notion of interpreting the dream at the time and for many years thereafter. In time I came to realize that it represented an overview of what is known as the three outpourings of theosophical thinking by which the Divine Life manifests itself.

The first to second paragraphs represent the first outpouring of the Logos or Divine Life, by which the physical cosmos or some portion thereof, with all its resident life forms, manifests itself through an evolving process of Active Intelligence. This is a teleological process by which the undifferentiated cosmic matrix—the spacetime fabric of current western scientific modeling—through Its inherent Inertial Capacity to produce, observe, and interact with the Material Nature of forms and processes according to the recognizable patterns of an endless variety of ideal Forms and Qualities, devises specific forms and processes comprised of elemental, mineral and biological structures on the cosmic, galactic, solar, and planetary scale, according to the Intentional Capacity for the purpose and use by the Spiritual Nature.

The wave nature indicated in this first paragraph suggests the wave nature of such elemental particle composition that in turn provides the evolving natural coding—inorganic molecular and organic genetic—for that Divine Life. The initial stomping of the ground indicates the generation a point of tension in the matrix that radiates in all directions. The matrix has the inherent capacity of both inertial and sentient stress, so that the differential changes of the radiating isotropic stress produce both the objective environment necessary for the evolution of living forms and the subjective registration of those forms—their interactive observation and recognition as purposeful objects and processes—as consciousness.

The second to third paragraphs represent the second outpouring of the Logos as the Living Imaging Capacity of the Soul Nature in its collective whole, through a similar evolving process of expressing Love and Wisdom, as the Buddha would have said, as Compassion. The development and exercise of Love–Wisdom in the social world of material processes through the recognized purposeful utility of ideal Forms is the goal of human incarnation. Though we incarnate individually as souls with physical birth for the purpose of the individual development and operation of that Love and Wisdom—what a Christian might call a life of Christian service—we are essentially a contemplative Soul with a collective spiritual identity, imaged by—made in the Image of—the divine Life.

The third to fourth paragraphs represent the third outpouring of the Logos as the Divine Hierarchy—the Kingdom of Heaven of Christianity, the Elohim of Old Testament scripture, the Hierarchy of Saints and Masters of Theosophy—in which the Soul calls out to its Source as the Father of that Soul and all supporting Life, whereby the Soul is answered and lifted up—resurrected—by the Spiritual Presence to complete the Soul's mission, whatever it might be. The location of such resurrection represented in this vision in the vicinity of the United Nations, suggests that it is of global, nonsectarian significance and implication.

CONTEMPLATION, SERVICE, AND COMMUNION

Initiation into a Life of Contemplation, Service, and Communion within the Community

The thoughtful observation of events in the field of one's experience over time naturally produces a model of the world in which the soul lives and moves and has their being. That naturally evolving model gives the soul an idea of how best to operate in that world in a manner intended to minimize the risk of harm and to maximize the opportunity for happiness of that soul in serving the interests of the community to which that soul identifies. The intended effect of initiation is to make that contemplative process completely conscious, making the soul fully aware of interaction in the modeling process, moment to moment, in a manner that broadens the soul's notion of the community with which it identifies. Ultimately this community identification comes to encompass the whole of the human family and Life itself.

This dream experience was followed within the year by a more profound experience mentioned in the preface to The Paros Commune of 1971—as recounted in brief detail in the 'Letter to a Friend' in the next section of this book—before I took a trip back to North Carolina with the expectation of returning to Washington in the spring. I had read the book on kundalini by Gopi Krishna sometime in the year or two before my own personal experience in the fall of 1976, so I was not taken totally by surprise by the event in my own life. I did not feel I had been subjected to quite the same level of strenuous disturbance as described in his experience. Nevertheless, it was a seminal event in my life, as I am sure it is for anyone else that has gone through a similar initiatory ordeal.

For a variety of reasons, I did not talk about this event with anyone for a very long time. Were it not for the fact that the process of initiation is insufficiently understood in the manner and purpose of its function, particularly in light of the fact that it is not understood to exist at all for much of the human population outside the various religious faiths and understandings of their traditions, and were it not for the fact that the current level of general human technological understanding suggests the wisdom of its greater publication, I would not discuss it now.

Though it may be more referenced and encountered in current Eastern teachings and writing, this initiation and related experience is as fundamentally Christian as any spiritual interpretation. From the life and works of Justin Martyr and Origen, Augustine, Francis of Assisi and Anthony of Padua, Thomas Aquinas, Meister Eckhart, Ignatius of Loyola, Teresa of Avila, John of the Cross, Emanuel Swedenborg, Thomas Merton and many, many others, souls have testified to their mystical, spiritual experience in the Christian tradition. It happens generally on the inner levels of experience of the soul, often registered in the dream state in the subtle body.

"And it shall come to pass in the last days, saith God, I will pour out my Spirit upon all flesh: and your sons and your daughters shall prophesy, and your young men shall see visions, and your old men shall dream dreams:"[3]

---

[3] Acts of the Apostles, 2:17

What I have as reason for hope and for offering to others from this experience is not the experience itself, but rather the significance and meaning as a road map that it can convey in a widening of the soul's capacity of understanding the intersection of things material, ideal, spiritual, and of the soul. After returning from Washington to get married, things quickly segued in ways that make complete sense to me now, though they did not at the time. My marriage was not to be, at least to my fiancée of the time, and when I finally met my dear wife, Molly, it was not for seven more years. The bodily, emotional, and mental wringer that initiation puts the soul through can make interpersonal and business relationships difficult in the early stages of the process, and it was certainly the case for me.

The purpose of such initiation is not for the personal satisfactions of the ego as an approval or reward for a life or lives well lived. Rather, it is the start of a process of verification for which the soul has been preparing for some time, following completion of the probationary path as a disciple of the greater Life. The point of discipleship is to learn discipline—of the body, the passions, and the mind and its ego, of course—not for any arbitrary reason, but because it is the way to prevent harm to the disciple and others with whom they are being educated.

Initiation begins the process of the disciple operating on their own, while still in service to the purpose and according to the plan of the greater Life, as that purpose and their part in the plan is revealed in the light of the intuition and best understood by them. That purpose of initiation leading to moksha or spiritual liberation for the soul is to facilitate and enhance the perfection of understanding for the Soul's Just operation in wise and loving service to the community.

I enjoyed the carpentry, drafting, AutoCAD design, and construction work, all based on an innate propensity for visualization, that got me through the early part of this transition after returning from Washington to North Carolina. I worked for a few years with my ailing dad before he succumbed to his ailments. It was a joy to spend that time with him and an honor to be with him at his passing in 1980. As indicated earlier, both of my parents were people of great faith and love. Though his emphysema was a burden, with his well-schooled understanding of all things electromechanical, I would have enjoyed the shared experience over the years of what became my understanding and wave modeling of physical phenomena.

My livelihood has remained in the design and construction field, with an involvement in the real estate development business along the way in the late 1980's. In the early 1990's I began to handle property insurance claims for a close friend in the independent adjustment business. We knew each other from school and our hometown and had been in residential contracting work together before he transitioned to the claims business full time. When Hurricane Andrew hit Dade County, Florida in 1992, I deployed to the area for seven months as an independent adjuster. I liked the work, felt it was worthwhile, could make a decent living in the process, and I decided to pursue that line of work as a catastrophe adjuster to the exclusion of most contracting.

This seasonal line of work allows blocks of uninterrupted time to pursue various avocational interests. I had done this in prior years with an interest in music and songwriting. Facilitated by the technological advances of personal computers, in the nineties as I turned to writing concerned with subjects of a more philosophical nature, I rekindled my early interests first in astrophysics, then after the dot com bust, in public policy and its effects on political economy.

This later interest reacquainted me with the work of Plato through his writing of The Republic, Karl Marx once again primarily with his understanding of the crisis of over-production, the commoditization of labor, and the business cycle, and the ever-perineal exemplary life and moral mission of Christ, all in terms of the concept of Justice as applied to the Material, Ideal, Spiritual, and Soul Natures.

Always motivated to understand what is going on through a study of graphic details, this has been facilitated using computer aided design, principally AutoCAD. I developed reasonable skill in 3-D CAD early on in residential design work and found it to be a useful analytical tool in other fields. It was invaluable in modeling and analyzing deterministic 3-D wave mechanics of an isotropic inertial continuum under the stress of expansion as applied in the observation of physical phenomena and in rendering various deductions from that analysis for graphic presentation. This approach has allowed me to gain insight into details of processes that would normally get glossed over in the reliance on mathematical analysis alone. My general approach to a subject has been to create a graphic model in my mind, in toy model carpentry form, and/or on the computer screen space based on an intuition, then to apply the appropriate mathematical analysis for verification of the intuition.

In the graphic modeling that follows the Letter to a Friend, the contemplation of what might be considered the most fundamental of Platonic ideal geometric Forms that can be drawn on paper representing the Triangle or cut or folded from paper as a corresponding Trigon, is used to represent an essential Trinity and existential Quaternity of Principles. The Equilateral Trigon is used to indicate that the principles are of equal value and importance in understanding the scheme of this modeling.

These Forms are presented as three Contemplations based on the three essential principles or capacities reflected in a Communion with one existential principle or capacity, with supporting information and links in the topics on the UniServEnt.org website.

- **CONTEMPLATION I of Life as Essential Principles**, is the **Intentional Capacity of Spiritual Nature** to initiate and effect change in the forms and processes we encounter in our field of experience, in others and in oneself, as a timeless Potential and Source to that extended experiential field from beyond the current perceptions and conceptions of Space and Time,

- **CONTEMPLATION II of the Appearance of Physical Phenomena**, is the **Inertial Capacity of Material Nature** to resist change and thereby maintain forms and processes, objectively as assemblies of quantum components, and subjectively as groups of individual souls, to provide experience in the world, as current—meaning ever-present—Sinks for the energy flow in Space and over Time from that Source of Power,

- **CONTEMPLATION III of the Quality of Political Economy**, is the **Formal Capacity of Ideal Nature** to direct the flows of energy from the Life Source through creative and evolutionary change with axiomatic logic to give objective structure to the intentional capacity of Life, as an Extension of the field of experience pervading Space and Time, and

- **COMMUNION with Love, Wisdom and Community,** initiates **Change as the Living Capacity of the Soul Nature** to focus on the field of experience as a logical agent to effect, maintain, and structure objective change through the soul's capacity; to Observe the Appearance of Material Nature as physical phenomena and interact with that phenomena via Its Logical

Capacity, to Recognize the Quality of Ideal Nature in structuring the human community via its Intuitive Capacity, and to Commune with Life in Its Spiritual Nature as in all forms and processes via Its Innate Capacity of Identity, in the current moment of Space and Time, to culminate through the process of natural growth as the qualities of Love and Wisdom.

The Living Capacity is an expression of the Imaging or Self-replicating Capacity of the three initial capacities to replicate in individualized manner as discrete integrated expressions of those capacities, specified in Space and Time. Those three capacities are each inherent in both Essential and Existential aspects; essentially as Omnipotence – 1LEs, Omnipresence – 2AEs, and Omniscience – 3QEs, and existentially through the operation of the Living Capacity of the Soul Nature in Its Innate, Logical, and Intuitive interactive capacities with each of the three mixes of the three essentials.

LETTER TO A FRIEND

The following letter was written in 2012 during a period of a few months' email correspondence with a friend who shared a common interest in some of the foundational issues of theoretical physics. At that time, he was a postdoctoral physicist from Finland with a recently published dissertation and related work critical of various assumptions of Planck scale physics that agreed in significant ways with my own independent critique. For those unfamiliar with the concept of the Planck scale, among other assumptions, it posits a fundamental measure of length scale that is as small compared to the measure of a neutron—in my thinking expressed as the reduced Compton wavelength of that particle—as that wavelength is to the length of a soccer field. Any experimental investigation of events at the Planck scale are theoretically incapable of verification. This fact formed a basis for our theoretically separate yet convergent mutual interest in the subject.

My friend found my analysis of the Planck scale credible and worthy of further elaboration. His work incorporated an acknowledged necessary ideal or mental component of subjectivity in his analysis and our discussion had ventured as a result into the subject of philosophy and metaphysics, which had prompted the following letter. He had expressed a deep dissatisfaction with the current state of theoretical physics as a career path at the time, and seeing no motivation for such a pursuit, we subsequently lost touch. I have redacted his name herein, and have made minor, non-substantive revisions for purposes of clarity.

In responding to this letter, he mentioned the work of Emanuel Swedenborg and correspondences between Swedenborg's descriptions of souls encountered in the transcendent realm and my description here. I have included the account from the whole letter to provide a greater personal, historical context.

"*Friend,*

I have just finished your thesis and have prepared some comments, but after re-reading our last email thread, thought I would send this first.

I remember the first time I was aware of being self-conscious; I mean conscious of myself as though seen through the eyes of someone else. I believe I have always been self-aware and empathetic in my relationships with others, but up to that point in my life I don't recall feeling so objectified and at the same time so transparent. What transpired was not an intentional act on the part of my mother.

I was ten or eleven and had just finished an evening solo violin recital at a local school auditorium, one in an annual series put on by my instructor. I generally memorized the pieces readily and didn't refer to the sheet music during the shows, so I closed my eyes as I played as I had recently seen a noted concert violinist do at a live performance.

"That was good. But why did you close your eyes?" *she chided gently.*

Putting herself in my shoes, as only a protective mother can do, she saw all eyes on her, silently asking "Why do you close your eyes? It's pretentious!"

I have this by intuition now, of course, but at the time all I could think was, "Rubinoff did it," as a response in having recently seen a famous concert violinist play at the high school auditorium in Laurinburg, "I even got his autograph."

And so I said. She made it clear that was okay for him, but not for one so young. I was crushed, but she was right. It was pretentious; but then how else do we learn but by emulation, by pretending to be more competent than we currently are.

This was not some defining, motivating moment in my life, though it is still vivid. It is, however, indicative of what has always been a primary motivation, to live a competent life, fully self-aware, while at the same time completely unself-conscious.

I don't like drawing attention to myself, but I do like interacting with others, especially on what some erudite individuals would call a mundane level. I know that I am high on the competent scale, not in terms of any socio-economic standard, but in terms of treating others by the Golden Rule. Not perfect, just highly competent.

I have always, always thought that everyone else was, internally, basically like me. I still believe, still know, that on an essential level we all have within us the desire, the

329

need, and the capacity to know the truth about ourselves and the world in which we find ourselves and to give it voice and stature, but I know without question that such discovery is a growth process with its own time and seasons, and that one cannot force such cultivation. We can perfect neither ourselves, nor the world around us, before the time; still the time will come for both. Our correspondence to date leads me to believe you too have this understanding.

While I was religious in both a learned and a poetic sense when I was young, enraptured with both the God embodied in Judeo-Christian history's ancient sweep and in the constitution of the cosmos, I was a child of the educational system and ethos of the time, and I had no problems giving up a seven-day creation. Still, I thought Jesus was someone to be respected and even emulated.

Eventually, somewhere in the middle teens, I awoke to find I had gone from doubter, to agnostic, to atheist. I was very sure that by the power of my intellect, I had exhaustively ferreted out every cranny wherein a creative cause and solace might be lurking and found none.

No doubt in manner similar to you, I still wanted to understand the "nuts and bolts" of life and the cosmos, and at the time of entering the university, I was still thinking strongly about a career in astrophysics. I had the romantic notion of an astronomer sitting on a mountaintop and looking for extra-terrestrial life. Unfortunately, as far as my studies went, I had also developed an interest in the opposite sex, which led to an interest in parties, and my freshman year did not go so well. In high school, my innate abilities enabled me to skate by, with no one, including myself, the wiser. I managed to hang on, and at the start of my sophomore year was enrolled in linear algebra, intent on staying with physics. Then I made a fateful decision.

The math course was at 7:30 in the morning and was taught by a grad student from India (paradoxically enough as things developed). He had an extremely thick accent, and I could hardly understand a word he said. After about three sessions and while drop-add was still available, I dropped the course and added another, thinking that I would take it the following semester. As it was, it was not offered until the next fall, and I was forced to rule out physics as a major, the choice of which had to be made at the end of the fall semester. So I ended up majoring in economics and took a comparative religions course that opened up the world of Eastern thought to me for the first time.

I was scheduled to go to grad school in economics, but the Vietnam War and the draft led me home to work for my dad, as I waited it out. I saved some money in the process and decided to go to Europe with a high school friend to travel and work and just see the world. I was romantically unattached, except to the idea of traveling around the world, so it seemed like a reasonable thing to do.

At this time, being dissatisfied with the materialistic assumptions of economics and politics, I had shifted my reading to various subjects addressing issues of a metaphysical nature, starting with the psychology of Freud,

Jung, Reich, and Aldous Huxley. Naturally, there was the occasional pharmaceutical experiment, though not to the point of indulgence. So, in the fall of 1971, my friend from high school bought a VW van in Wiedenbruck, Germany, and we took off, working for the winter in Switzerland, spending several weeks in the early summer on a Greek island.

Sometime in the midsummer of 1972, after traveling with friends up through the Soviet Union to Finland, we found ourselves on a large overnight ferry, crossing to Sweden, when I had what I can only call an epiphany. There was a sauna on board, which I made use of before going to the bar. I was in an extremely relaxed frame of mind and none of the rest of our group was with me. I bought a beer and sat down at an empty space on a bench that ran along the wall opposite the bar. To my left was a fellow who appeared to be past his limit and to my right were a couple, she from Finland, he from Sweden, who engaged me in conversation in English.

At some point, the fellow to my left knocked over his beer, to which the Finnish girl whispered "drunk Finnish male"; the inebriated individual then grabbed my left shoulder, and as I turned toward him to see his left arm pulled back in preparation of throwing a punch, I felt a bolt of white-hot electricity run up from the base of my spine to the crown of my head and envelope me.

I felt a sense of absolute serenity and command of the situation and said in a benevolent tone of voice something to the effect of "Relax, everything's alright."

As he stared at me, his face blanched in fear, he let go, dropped his cocked arm and turned away mumbling. It was not like anything I had experienced. I am not a big guy or anyone that people would normally be afraid of. It was clear to me immediately that this was not biology at work.

This was a whole new dimension of existence that had been felt by both him and me. I must be clear. It didn't feel like anything I did and yet it felt like I was myself in essence. From that point on, I had little doubt about the essential reality of a "spiritual" dimension, whatever it might be. This was a motivating moment, but still not a defining one.

This episode intensified a transition already begun from the study of western psychology and philosophy to the eastern teaching of Buddhism and Vedanta and Zen and Taoism and Yoga, with its chakras and kundalini and such. When I got back to the states in the fall, I continued this study. I worked for a couple of years, saved my money, and went out to Washington State, where J.C., my friend of the European trip, had bought some land, to help him build a cabin.

I subsequently built a cabin of my own, moved in and continued the metaphysical and meditational studies. I did mostly carpentry and some design work for bread and butter, during this period. As you can imagine, for every book that gives an authoritative description of a spiritual journey, there are many more that are simply the embodiment of the author's wishful thinking and more again written by those who want to acquire a gullible following or just sell books. You must separate the wheat from chaff, as you might well know.

Many, perhaps most, of the books I read at that time had an appeal that in the final analysis was to the emotions or to ego gratification or to a desire to transcend the mundane or to become a devote of some master or saint or god. I intuitively shied away from such messages and was rather drawn by an appeal to reason and to social responsibility and inclusiveness.

Among the various schools of thought I investigated, two in particular stressed that the goal of enlightenment was work and not child's play, not for the faint of heart, and not to be entered into lightly; it was only to be entered into after years and even lifetimes of preparation. Early on, it seemed reasonable to me that if we are souls instead of brain-inspired personalities, being born twice or more is as feasible as just once and makes more sense than a one-shot chance at learning life skills; from an early age I had a sense of "being here before". Based on the tenets of these schools, the path to initiation consisted of a period of probation, during which one's intuition and sensitivity to the mental and emotional states of others becomes well honed, followed by eventual induction into a spiritual, body politic. During this period, I began to have many lucid dreams of a definite spiritual content.

In the late fall of 1976, in the early hours of November 25 in my 28th year, after making the decision to come back to the East Coast to help with my ailing father and to get married, (it didn't happen), I experienced an extremely lucid dream or vision in which I was looking out over a stadium size natural arena filled with radiant human beings that I recognized as transcendent souls. I then found I was surrounded on either side and directly in front by such beings, others like myself, clothed in an intense, golden white light, of more intense golden, white light than any Steven Spielberg movie.

There were no names exchanged; none were necessary. The individual in front of me stretched out his arm in which he grasped some manner of rod or staff and touched the top of my head. I had the most intense sensation of an electric dagger shooting down through the crown of my head and along my spine. It was far more intense than the experience mentioned above in the bar. This seemed to last no more than a few seconds, but it was and remains the defining, motivating moment of my life.

I awoke immediately to the darkness of the cabin, then to the vivid memory of the initiatory experience, and went back to sleep. I found myself in a state of bliss for the next several weeks, during which time I returned to North Carolina and moved in with my fiancée.

Then all hell broke loose. After the few weeks of bliss, I experienced what can best be described as the opening of Pandora's box. In the wake of this initiatory event, I had experienced an extended period of the same feeling of omnipresent potential that I had on the ferry. In addition, I began to notice a gentle movement of pressure at different locations throughout my body, at times surging from my feet up to the crown of my head.

The intensity of this surging increased over several weeks with a certain distracting fascination, as if there was a phantom ferret loose beneath my skin. Having read accounts of the awakening of kundalini in various eastern teachings, I naturally associated my current condition with those accounts. After several weeks of this growing presence, at one point as I was talking with one of my neighbors, I felt the persistent, pulsing surge in my head bumping against the inside of the crown of my skull, the surge burst through in a current of energy, feeling like it had flowed out through the top of my head, and the internal surging ceased.

From that point on, I found it difficult to meditate for any length of time, to think clearly as I always had before. What occurred can be described as coming into direct contact with the chaotic flow of mental, emotionally charged images from the subconscious of other individuals who were in close proximity to me or who otherwise captured my attention. These were both beautiful and disgusting emanations, normally screened in most individuals by the need to attend the concerns of day-to-day life. It is like dumping the contents of your hard drive into the microprocessor without benefit of an operating system. It is what apparently happens to some people with schizophrenia.

The only difference between that pathological condition and this is that the initiate, by dint of meditational practice, has learned and knows how to shunt the flow of images to the crown of the head in an attitude of prayer, thereby rendering them inoffensive. But this takes time to learn to do with efficiency, and such thoughts have an inertia of their own. The intensity of this direct experience of the subconscious is sporadic and seems to decay in frequency and intensity with a half-life of sorts over several decades, but in the end, clarity is restored, and one enters the here and now, apparently and hopefully, in perpetuity. Needless to say, this experience is not very conducive to interpersonal relations or career advancement of most kinds, but nevertheless, if I understand it correctly from my experience and what I have read of others, it is the way to the greater Life.

As a result of this experience, I became aware of the development of continuity of consciousness. As a result, when I sleep, I go directly into the dream state, which has become increasingly lucid, and return to wakefulness without any period of unconsciousness. I don't remember everything from such sojourn any more than I remember every detail of my day-to-day existence, but the thread of being conscious is maintained throughout. As a result, even when awake I have little sense of the passage of time, as I once had. I am mentally aware of things changing and cognizant of classical causal relationships, but there is no subjective feeling of time. Things simply move in and out of my field of wakeful consciousness as they do in dreams.

About seven years into this adventure, I felt sane enough to resume some semblance of a normal life, met

Molly and eventually married. Life shared with her has been a joy, but for the occasional episodes as indicated above, with the attendant self–consciousness and discombobulation they inspire.

About seventeen years into this experience, I had a dream in which I won the Nobel prize in physics. Physics?, I thought in the dream, this doesn't make sense. I have no interest and not much memory of physics. Peace would be nice: maybe I can write or do something really peaceful! I laughed in the dream and really thought no more about it until quite a while later. But one day while I was in Barnes and Nobles, I spontaneously plunked down a couple of hundred dollars on books on topology and general relativity and quantum mechanics and the Feynman lectures, and tensors, etc. etc. and so forth. I didn't have any plan and I had forgotten about the dream until days after I had bought them. I put them on a shelf.

Twenty-one years into the event, while doing some writing on metaphysics I started wondering why uniting gravity and quantum mechanics was so difficult, so I pulled out the Feynman lectures and an old physics text. Then I did what apparently no one else has seen fit to do. I assumed Newton's gravitational law still held in the nucleus of an atom! I assumed his gravitational constant was invariant even on that scale, I assumed that the existence of neutron stars with a density just above that of a black hole was an indication of the significance of the neutron in an understanding of gravity, I assumed that the reduced Compton wavelength was an actual physical property and not simply a statistical artifact and I naively plugged the neutron mass and wavelength parameters into Newton's equation, solved and got a figure that was within one order of magnitude of the value of the neutron Compton squared. This seemed significant and started my obsessive investigation of the past 15 years, which Molly cannot understand. For me it has resulted in an understanding of physical phenomena that is seamless with Life itself.

Is all the above just a fantasy of my feeble brain? Am I crazy? Perhaps. You must judge. In light of my experience of life as encapsulated in the above, the extinguishment of individual consciousness at corporal death makes no more sense than the idea that the existence of this quite tangible world around me, both biologic and anthropogenic, in this room and outside my window, is due to the stochastic interaction of point particles emerging from a "big bang". I spend roughly a third of my life in the protean world of dreams as it is, quite logical in its own fashion. The "afterlife" cannot be less real. The Lethe is necessary to keep one's focus in this world, but in time the Mnemosyne must be crossed.

The lid is now back on Pandora's box; Elpis, springs and by and large reigns eternal. Self-consciousness with all its phobias dissipates, and one is left with the calling to give voice to the Truth.

So, dear Friend, that Hope is why I pursue the physics, because if ever well-received, with or without the Nobel, it will show to anyone that might be listening, Life is not random or crazy, and the above account is not the fantasy of my feeble brain.

Peace to you and yours,

Martin Gibson

When a soul is young—a tyro—that soul develops its ego with images of the social roles observed in the community according to the mix of its essential and existential concerns. It idealizes and identifies with roles that signify strength and skill in dealing with the material risks and opportunities in the community and the greater world. With existential focus, it accepts the traditional ideal world view and affiliations as unquestionably true and key to the survival of the individual and its group. Until dissolution or destruction demand otherwise, the soul is not inclined to investigate whether the ideal view that governs its behavior in the community faithfully reflects the material reality in which that soul is spiritually embedded. In times of stress, absent understanding of principle, chaos ensues.

If essentially focused, a soul's contemplation results naturally in the creation of a mental model of the universe reflecting that soul's experience of living in that universe and looking for conformation of that understanding as a guide in governing its behavior. In varying degree of acuity, validity, and developed effectiveness, the enlightened soul's experience comes to understand four essential principles as inherent capacities.

- The Intentional Capacity of the Spiritual Nature to produce all Spiritual, Material, Ideal, and Soul forms and processes

- The Inertial Capacity to hold observable form and process created by the Intentional Capacity as their Material Nature

- The Formal Capacity to give recognizable purpose in mental form and process to the Ideal Nature of Forms and Processes

- The Living Capacity of the Soul Nature to Observe, Recognize, and Commune with all forms and processes.

THE ESSENTIAL TRIGON

We start with a contemplation of an equilateral triangle as Form L.1.0, which we name with greater specificity as shown, 'The Essential Trigon'. (If colored red, I know the Form well, from many encounters with a Bass Ale[4] bottle.)

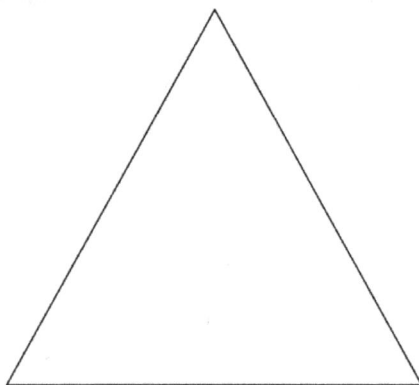

The Essential Trigon

Form L.1.0

---

[4] England's First Registered Trademark according to the bottle.

1.   We <u>observe</u> the trigon in material (physical) form as specifically drawn, on which we visually focus in print or on screen, in the here and now.

2.   We <u>recognize</u> this trigon as a representation of an ideal (metaphysical) Form, a generically named 'Equilateral Triangle' defined as 'three non-collinear straight, line segments of equal length, joined at their mutual ends to form three equal angles at three vertices'. We have further specified this form as a 'Trigon' to indicate that it includes the area within the boundary lines used to define a triangle as a case of a more general Form defined as a 'Regular Polygon', which includes the area within any number of equal length boundary lines.

The three lines represent the boundary as a clear separation of the areas outside and inside that boundary. Depending on the way it is defined, the boundary may be considered; (a) part of the inside and not part of the outside like the frozen surface of a block of ice submerged in water, (b) part of the outside and not part of the inside like the frozen surface of a lake at a hole in the ice which provides access for ice-fishing, (c) a part formed of a material separate from both the inside and the outside like a sealed plastic bag floating in the lake that contains liquid water or ice, or (d) an optical illusory part as a boundary like the ripples between a calm eddy and the rapids in a stream that is continuous. We will in all cases consider 'd' to be the case, unless stated otherwise. That is, a boundary as presented here is an apparent condition of mental focus in an essential continuum and does not imply a discontinuity of the subject of the focus of that discussion across the boundary.

3.   We <u>commune</u> with this Form-in-form as a spiritual (essential) Truth about triangles and trigons in conveying this

understanding, including its representation of a qualitative 'Good'— a qualitative Truth about some Thing—in this case involving symmetry and balance as a component of Beauty. Thinking only of the three boundary lines, without any mention of the electronic page or sheet of paper on which it might be drawn and viewed, we can generate an understanding of a specific Truth in the manner of an Essential Trigon representing 1) any specific form that was ever thought of or created, 2) that exists now in material or in mental form as a graphic thought or as a representation of an ideal Form apart from any graphic depiction but as defined above and specified by size, orientation, and placement in time and place, or 3) that ever will or could be imagined or constructed. Alternately, the Form could be represented as a trigon formed by making three creases in an endless field of paper, in which case the boundary lines are not separate but instead are integral to the inside and the outside of the trigon as reference lines.

If you are following this, all these distinctions are done in your mind by the individual that is reading it, here and now. If you understand this specific Truth, it is because you recognize the ideal Form in the material form, from a position intent on understanding that Truth—communing with, in rapport with that Truth—**focused from beyond the page through the Imaging Capacity of your— our—Soul Nature, right here and right now**.

We can consider this form as a geometric shape or as an element of text, like the Greek letter Delta, Δ, which is convenient, since that letter is used as a symbol in technical writing to represent a change in quantity of some quality that otherwise remains unchanged but for the amount or intensity of the quality. In either case, being focused on the form of the triangle, the extended field of paper on which the shape is written or from which it is folded

344

generally remains unrecognized, unless something forces us to focus on the extended field as the context in which the boundary element is drawn.

Focused on the boundary that we have named an Essential Trigon as an object of symbolic contemplation, our intent in the process of observing the form lies in the hope of understanding—by recognizing and communing with its purpose—any Truth embodied in the form. Here, the truth may be a sign of a danger or hazard indicated in the customary use of a trigonal sign. It may be a yield sign for oncoming traffic that has been installed upside down, causing a second look and a head scratch. In the case of a sign representing a similar peril requiring a focus on things in the here and now but contradicted by its orientation hanging on a dorm room wall, the context of the extended field in which we see it may not appear to be relevant and its significance of a peril may not be noticed at all.

The notion of the Essential Trigon can be applied to any form or process we might encounter in nature. This is done by virtue of our own capacity, the Imaging Capacity of the Soul Nature—to observe, recognize, and commune with the Material, Ideal, and Spiritual Natures—whatever that natural form or process might be. To exemplify this notion, we point to the fact that a three-dimensional shape that is drawn and animated on a computer screen is often rendered for viewing by reducing the surface of any object to a grouping of multiple trigons with a variety of shading, connected at their vertices.

In all instances, the use of the Imaging Capacity consists of restricting the focus of the observing soul on some aspect of the world of experience in which it finds itself. This process of focusing provides that self with three primary boundaries of human understanding created by the soul, through the mind and its corporal structure, principally through the eye and brain, but including all the physical senses, both external and internal, required for navigating the world of these three natures.

This focus is represented in Form L.1.1 by the three equal boundaries of the Essential Trigon representing the three capacities and their related natures, as they constrain that focus through the processes of observing nature, recognizing natural intent in the forms and processes, and communing or interacting with that nature, all of which is integrated by the purpose of the individual soul with its community's understanding of that natural intent. This is annumerated in the following capacities.

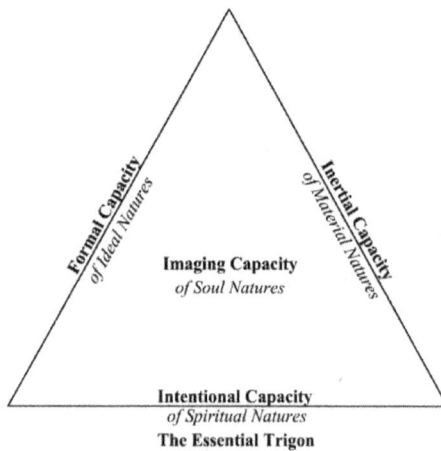

Formal Capacity *of Ideal Natures*

Inertial Capacity *of Material Natures*

Imaging Capacity *of Soul Natures*

Intentional Capacity *of Spiritual Natures*

The Essential Trigon

Form L.1.1

1.   **Observation of and by the Inertial Capacity of the Material Natures** is present in all specific forms and processes that arise in our field of experience in a generally regular and customary manner. Inertial capacity is the resistance to change or to a departure from the extant material processes of life. This is found and

understood scientifically in Newton's First Law of Motion and in principles of invariance. The inertial capacity allows a foundational stability in the field for the population of forms and their interactions for any creative process. Without this inertial constraint, all intended things as forms and processes would happen at once in a type of timeless potential turned actual. There would be no possibility for feedback or even for observation of an intended result and reflection on a job well done, whether that intent is of a soul or of a Supreme Being or of a frog catching a fly. As a result, inertia, measured in physics as mass, and time are two sides of the same coin.

2. **Recognition of and by the Formal Capacity of the Ideal Natures** is developed through comparison of morphologies across specific instances of material forms and processes that so arise in nature. Recognition based on this generalized experience is necessary to enhance the growth and evolution of such forms and processes. Formal capacity is the underlying principle of continuity within and between the material and the ideal natures and provides for conservation of energy and intent amidst the transformations of structure and process—both traditional and innovative, evolutionary and revolutionary—and mediates between the material and spiritual natures. This is found in Newton's Second and Third Laws of differential momentum and interactive force and in biological development, including social and individual mental adaptation. Thus, our frog learns to recognize the difference between the form of a fly and a wasp.

3. **Communion of and by the Intentional Capacity of Spiritual Natures** arises from the realized Truth that living forms recognize intent embodied in the forms and processes of living and inanimate structures, observed in both interspecies and intraspecies interaction, and operate on the basis of that recognition. This

essentially formless Truth is found in all forms of life, especially human, but even the frog realizes that wasps sting and flies allow themselves to be eaten without biting back. God, however you choose to define that term, is conscious purpose that pervades all this experience of living.

4. **Exercising the Imaging Capacity of the Soul Natures** reflects what the soul encounters in the forms and processes of the material, ideal, and spiritual natures, receiving impressions of its experience and expressing those images back on the material, ideal, and spiritual natures, which involves other souls in the process. Along with other living beings, human beings do this in the most profound way via the reproductive capacity of biological Life.

The imaging capacity of the soul resides in the midst of the Essential Trigon, bound by the three constraining capacities, in which it manifests and witnesses the existential world. Once again, these Natures as essential capacities, inertial, formal, and intentional, extend beyond the boundaries of the known existential cosmos as limited by the imaging capacity of the Soul Natures.

Essence—the inertial, formal, intentional, and living/imaging Capacities of the material, ideal, spiritual, and soul Natures as the formless Truth—can be symbolized by transferring the constraints of the Triangle boundaries to the inherently unmanifest self-constraints within the field extent of the Trigon. It will be understood going forward that the outer boundary of the Essential Trigon extends indefinitely as the undifferentiated Essence of the form above, which will be differentiated by the inherent capacities in the forms that follow.

YHWH

יְהֹוָה

Brahman

ब्र॒ह्म॒म्

Essence

**Undifferentiated Potential
of Becoming
All That Is, Was, & Will Be**

The Essential Trigon

Form L.1.2

The Spirit of Truth—the Essence of Essences—signifies Supreme Being and Power to create everything that we have ever experienced in Life as a manifestation or emanation of "Undifferentiated Potential of Becoming All that Is, Was, and Will Be." This Essence may be a stepped down voltage and current that we experience day to day, compared to Its Full Cosmic Potential, but it is all from One Current Source. There is a reason that the word Current means both a Flow of Energy and the ever-present Here and Now. With respect to Form L.1.2:

1.   The top two terms are the English transliteration of the Hebrew glyphs for the same Essential Truth, YHWH.

2.   The next two terms are the English equivalent for that same ultimate Reality in the Hindu tradition, Brahman, followed by the Hindi script, based on an internet transliteration.

3.	The bottom three lines are one instance of this statement that can have meaning to any reader that has the time and interest in studying the statement, if the individual is familiar with the English language. An 'Undifferentiated Potential of Becoming' can be understood as the unrestricted formless power to consciously assume any form or process It intends. It does this through a fundamental creative process of self-restriction which we recognize as occurring over time and in space.

We understand this process through the Imaging Capacity of the Soul Natures; instinctively through the imaged Spiritual Natures of Communion as Innate Capacity, in reasoned interplay with the imaged Material Natures of Observation as Logical Capacity, and in developing a direct perception of the imaged Ideal Natures of Recognition as the Intuitive Capacity of the Soul. If an individual had no Formal Capacity of recognition or the necessary education in the subject matter, the figure above would be just a scribbled form, not understood by the geometric symbol of three lines or the textual statements of that Truth in different alphabetic forms as Names and Definitions.

FOUR CAPACITIES OF THE ESSENTIAL TRIGON

In the next several forms, the capacities and natures of the Essential Trigon have been separated and partitioned as shown, with the capacity and nature that is labeled on each boundary of Form L.1.1 focused within the angle of the opposite side. The term 'Capacity' is conceptually applied here as an undifferentiated potential for producing a related ensemble of instances of that capacity, where those instances are understood as existential 'Natures' defined through the interplay of the other capacities in varying proportions.

This depicted partitioning should not be construed as a spatial separation of the four natures, analogous to the separation of a model of the earth into core, mantle, crust, and atmosphere. It is perhaps more analogous to a glass of gas–infused carbonated water on ice, all three of the states of matter understood to be made of neutrons, protons, and electrons, themselves in turn made of a single wave bearing, inertial substrate under isotropic stress. The graphic is intended to represent the interaction of the three primary inherent capacities with the active capacity of the fourth, the Soul Nature, operating in the midst of these three.

The Appearance of intended material forms and processes of Form L.2.0 is the first thing we experience as we enter this world with physical birth. If we are fortunate enough to be born into hospitable circumstance, without thinking we innately know that others like ourselves, our parents, family, and others in the community are our intended source of sustenance and love. We learn early to distinguish the purpose of things by observing and learning what others say and do; what provides us with life and protects us from hurt and harm; that food and water is intended to satisfy our hunger and thirst, that lying in the sun is intended to make us warm or in the shade to keep us cool, that feet are for running and hands are for grasping. It is only in the rebellion of growing up that we come to question the purposes of things and of what we do as we begin to realize that we were not given all the available information as a child; and as we eventually come to understand with maturity, that is necessarily so.

With age we learn that time appears to move in only one direction, which expresses the reality that as individual souls we have control over only a limited number of forms and processes in the world. Things appear to have a capacity, an inertial capacity beyond our intent, to be difficult to lift and move around, that this inertial capacity of heaviness is found in one degree or another in all the material stuff from which the things in nature appear to be made. We learn that anything around us that falls tends to sink to the ground and stay there unless someone or something picks it up and moves it. If water runs or is poured into a sink, it disappears down the drain.

As long as we are able to observe how these things happen in keeping with our own innate, instinctive understanding of the purpose of the forms and processes that we encounter, there is little reason for curiosity. With increasing observation of connections in the chain of events unfamiliar to us, an organized pursuit of a deductive logic evolves to enable the ability of the soul to successfully anticipate events, such as finding game in a hunt, predicting rain for planting in the growing season, or understanding lightning to enable the harnessing of electromagnetic power.

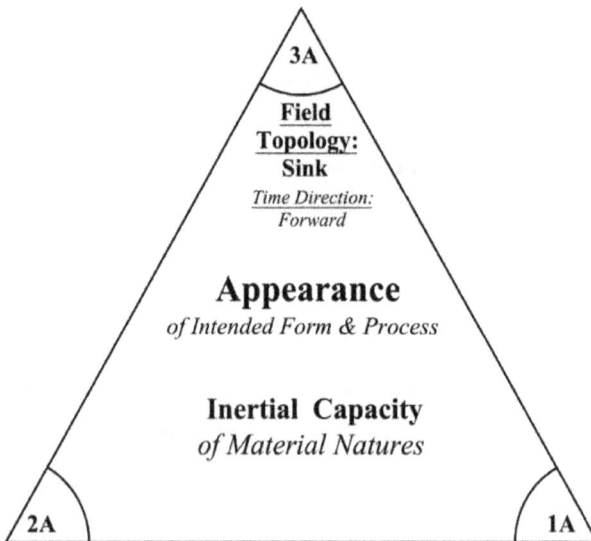

3A

Field Topology: Sink

Time Direction: Forward

Appearance
of Intended Form & Process

Inertial Capacity
of Material Natures

2A

1A

Observed Appearance of The Essential Trigon

Form L.2.0

Souls learn to put faith in the wisdom of the elders of the community based on their traditional knowledge of spiritual-essential natures; they also learn that there is wisdom in those who are innately curious and adventurous and willing to investigate the material natures of the inertial capacity with their developed logic and intuition. This free investigation has given us the theoretical and nano-technological advancements of quantum mechanics. The evolution of this theoretical logic is incomplete, however, due in large part to the success of initial theoretical applications. This success has been implemented by the inclusion of various ad hoc parameters that make the modeling of a theory work, but those parameters are not axiomatically well considered and have become an impediment to better understanding.

As shown in Forms L.2.1, we learn to recognize the Quality of the game we catch and the crops we grow, the clothes and the tools we fashion, the homes, buildings, and communities we construct. We learn how we can adapt and repurpose all of these to our needs in varying degrees of success. We learn in this understanding that time is periodic, as seasons change and recur. As part of the nature of creating tools and structures such as erecting and taking down tents for nomadic living, we learn that the measure of time involved in some processes and in some forms of mental creativity is bi-directional.

The mental capacity of the human mind to understand, invent, design, build, and use manmade forms and processes for intentional ends in conjunction with naturally understood forms and processes of analogous intentionality, demonstrates a capacity to formulate universal ideas and logical structures, giving us an ability to recognize ideal natures, like the ideal Trigon as an archetypal form distinct from the nature of the material forms observed directly by the senses. From this perspective on the field of observation, the field of recognized ideal intentional Forms and Processes is extended to become coterminous with the observed universe of material, physical space over time.

```
                    2Q
              ┌──────────┐
                  Field
               Topology:
                Extension
              Time Direction:
               Bi-Directional


                Quality
            of Intended Form & Process


             Formal Capacity
              of Ideal Natures


       1Q                      3Q
```

Recognized Quality of The Essential Trigon

Form L.2.1

The focus of the love of a child for its mother and of the mother for its child is integral with the forms and the interactive processes of both, yet distinct from the material particles embodied in the interactions of their biological, carbon-based life-forms. The ideal natures—qualities such as an appreciation and recognition of love or justice, of color or sonority, of harmony or balance—these natures are essentially formless and at the same time intimately associated with material forms.

Both the sky and sea are variable hues of blue in which the state of blueness resides in its entirety in neither the sky nor the sea nor even the eye and mind of the specific observer. Recognized qualities in general, while associated with forms and processes as observed in the material natures, themselves function as a formless capacity to understand, name, and define the relationships between forms and processes.

Recognition of these qualities in turn are the result of communion with the essentially formless, intentional capacity to initiate the creation and evolution of conscious and self-sustaining life forms and living processes through a direct perception and understanding of spiritual natures. Metaphorically, the term 'spirit' means breath, as that which is necessary to sustain life, while remaining unseen and yet ever present from birth to death, co-existent with the oxygen in the atmosphere we breathe. Breathing is essential. Breathing is spiritual.

As indicated in Form L.2.2, itself timeless, Life is the intentional source of all living and inanimate forms and processes, chief of which is the process of self-replication. It is that process which images itself in all its three capacities, intentional, formal, and inertial, and in the soul natures as individual capacities and foci of intuitive, logical, and innate intent, as individual—one might even say quantum—souls.

While essentially formless and spiritual, the Soul is the agent of change in the material forms and processes, especially as humans through the innate capacity to observe and recognize opportunity and risk, the intuitive capacity to sense and respond to motivations of essential love and existential fear, and the logical capacity for effectiveness in responding to ignorance and through wisdom as part of the purposeful creative, material process—as Life, designing and building world after world after world.

Communed Life of The Essential Trigon

Form L.2.2

The topology of the field of Life is a source of time in which the Soul Nature shown in Form L.2.3 as Change is always in the current moment. As an agent of change in these worlds, an enlightened human soul is always focused on a mix of liberal fostering of opportunity, love, and wisdom, and of conservative mitigation of risk, fear, and ignorance. Such souls are not chiefly motivated to join in any earthly battle between good and evil as such a battle is customarily understood, since one group's notion of evil is another group's notion of good. From the divine spiritual perspective there is no adversarial power than can stand against the Soul's capacity for Love, Wisdom, and Opportunity to pursue happiness of each soul, when that capacity is properly understood.

The integrated depiction in Form L.2.4 of these four creative capacities of intentional form & process are themselves timeless.

They are aspects of a unified Living Field which self-initiates and differentiates as Existential components, specified in time and space by that self-initiation. At the beginning of a creative period, the Essence as Undifferentiated Potential on a cosmic and sub-cosmic scale, differentiates as shown according to the ordered sequence of angles.

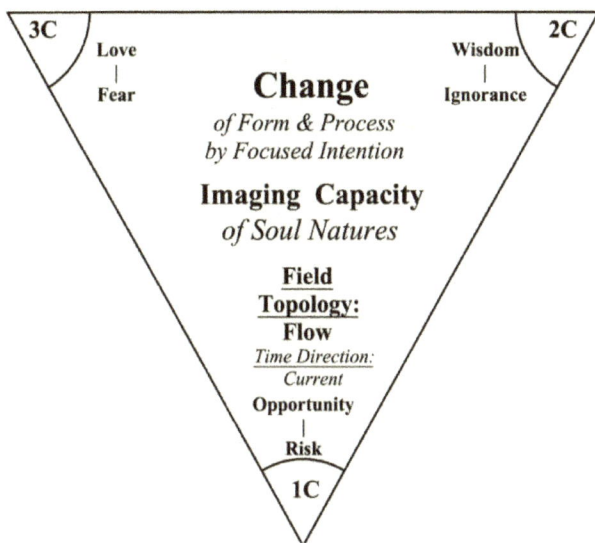

Change Agency of The Essential Trigon

Form L.2.3

The three essential capacities are aspects of that Field—the Intentional as Spiritual, the Inertial as Material, and the Formal as Ideal Natures recognized as Life, Appearance, and Quality, with one Quantitative focus of intentionality as an Imaging Capacity of Soul Natures. The Soul Natures operate as quantized, localized, logical agents of Change—from the fundamental unit of matter that is recognized in this modeling as a dual form of the neutron/proton-electron, through the mineral, plant, animal, and human kingdoms up to the creative Hierarchies of Saints and Masters, the Kingdoms of Cosmic—and Comic—Purpose.

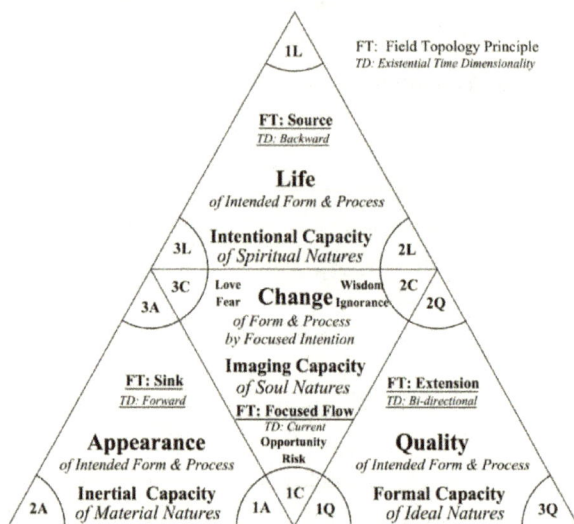

Four Capacities of The Essential Trigon

Form L.2.4

1L—The inherent integrity of the Source of all Life, intentionally creates human images to the Soul Nature as units of Innate Capacity with instinctive understanding of corporal intelligence @ 1C, of Logical Capacity for rationally navigating in the phenomenal world of natural risk and opportunity @ 2C, and of Intuitive Capacity in recognizing the ideal Forms observed in material nature, applying those Forms to technological innovation and communing with other souls in the community @ 3C.

2A—The Inertial Capacity of an undifferentiated continuous topological space @ 2A, with surjection—projection onto that space—from the Formal Capacity of a geometrically defined metric Form @ 3Q, quantizes and transforms that undifferentiated space with the emergent appearance of inertial units of energized, elemental matter. This is necessary for the material construction of solar and planetary environments for creation of durable and reproducible biological forms and sustainable processes for a living ecosystem as observed on Earth, intended for human habitation. Through the soul's interaction with its bodily and environmental Material Natures @ 1A and the vital, emotional, and mental Ideal Natures @ 1Q, and aware initially, if only remotely, of its source @ 1L, the Soul's understanding of its place in the universe grows in accordance with the logic and reasoning reflected in the Soul Nature @ 2C.

3Q—The Formal Capacity @ 3Q, through simultaneous activation and surjection @ 2A, results over time in the creative differentiation of Qualities as named and defined on the forms and processes of the Material Natures recognized @ 2Q in the Ideal Natures of forms and processes. This becomes understood by reflection of the Qualitative process in the Intuitive Capacity of the Soul Nature @ 3C as it is observed to operate in the appearance of the Material Natures @ 3A.

With the growing understanding of the Divine Nature of the Soul—of Love @ 3A & 3C-3Q for the Material and Soul-Ideal Natures of Life and of Wisdom @ 2Q & 2C-2A in operating in the Ideal and Soul-Material Natures—the individual soul begins entry into a direct communion with its Spiritual Nature, initiated by that Source of Life @ 3L and 2L, to complete the process of Spiritual Communion started with the creation of the soul @ 1C. When that process is completed successfully, the soul enters a communion with all four of the Essential Capacities as a liberated soul as understood in Vedantic thinking and as a resurrected soul as referenced in the Abrahamic faiths.

All modeling of systems, in fact all conscious rational thought as distinct from conscious instinctive and intuitive processes, is an operation of the human Formal Capacity of Ideal Natures in both the quantitative and qualitative analysis of the observed phenomena of Material Nature. Understanding of sources of change beyond the observed phenomena belong to the Intentional Capacity of the Spiritual Natures, to Essential Principles as Omnipotence.

Responding to childlike notions of Divinity, modeling of physical phenomena avoids a discussion of sources of change that are understood to originate outside the observed material nature. Instead, physical modeling focuses on observable, measurable, interactive change, understood as functions of conserved quantities of energy in transformations rather than energy production over time as a measure of power from an undefined source. As such, power is generally understood as energy stored as in a reservoir as a secondary source of potential energy, though it does not preclude an understanding of power axiomatically as a primary source of energy with an invariant transformation rate of focused dynamic change defined as work.

This indicates an essential difference between the Material and the Ideal Natures. The material nature is governed by inertia and requires work to effect change, understood as a force displacing a material form or interacting in a material process over a length in space and over time, whereas the ideal nature is ostensibly capable of instantaneous change, requiring little to no effort to move mental forms and their interacting processes around in one's head—though it may seem hard sometimes to change ones thinking. Interaction of material forms are governed by a one directional sense of time, while interaction of mental forms are bi-directional and ideal Forms are inherently timeless. Spiritual nature, on the other hand, is essentially intentional, formless, conscious, volitional, and purposeful; spiritual

360

nature weighs all the ideal options and selects the feasible material courses of action—ideally.

THE EXISTENTIAL TRIGON & THE ESSENTIAL TRIGON

The Existential Trigon of Form L.3.0 is an expansion of the Imaging Capacity of the Soul Natures of Form L.2.3 viewed against the Essential Trigon of Form L.2.4 due to the initiation of a creative process of Life. The three trapezoidal border areas between the three boundaries of the initial, central Imaging Capacity and the three corresponding boundaries of the expanded Existential Trigon— within the three essential Capacity Trigons, 1L, 2A, and 3Q—signify the focused interaction of the Existential Capacities of the Soul, Innate - 1C, Logical - 2C, and Intuitive - 3C.

These intersections of the expanded Imaging capacity within the three primary essential capacities produce the creation and observation of actual material forms and processes in 1A & 3A of the Material Natures within the Inertial Capacity of 2A, recognition by definition of actual mental forms and processes in 1Q & 2Q of the Ideal Natures of the Formal Capacity of 3Q, and Communion with actual spiritual forms as beings and processes in 2L & 3L from the Spiritual Natures of the Intentional Capacity of 1L.

The numbered angles of the Essential Capacities in Form L.2.4 are expanded for the Imaging Capacity to the thresholds of integrated interaction of the three Existential Imaging Capacities indicated by the three solid arcs. The limits of each of those Capacities are dashed arcs, with the range of growth potential of the soul of each capacity between these arcs.

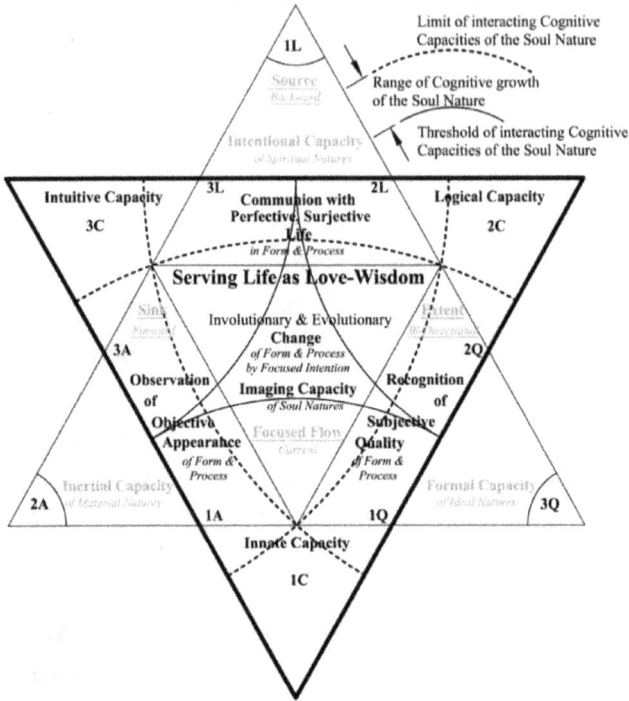

The Existential Trigon expanded overlay on the Essential Trigon

Form L.3.0

The area of the central Hexagon represents the manifest cosmos as the intersection of Essential and Existential Trigons. The Existential Trigon is a threefold imaging of the Essential Trigon along three paths from the impetus of 1L by;

1. CCW rotation of 60°, 1L to 3C, 2A to 1C, & 3Q to 2C,

2. CW rotation of 60°, 1L to 2C, 2A to 3C, & 3Q to 1C,

3. inversion through the middle axis of 3A - 2Q, resulting in 1L to 1C, 2A to 3C, & 3Q to 2C.

This indicates that the Intentional Capacity of the Spiritual Natures—of Life—in 1L is imaged to all three of the Imaging

Capacities of the Soul, 1C, 2C, and 3C. The Inertial Capacity of the Material Natures—of Appearances—in 2A is imaged to 1C once as the Innate Capacity and twice to 3C as the Intuitive Capacity of the Soul, giving weight to the notion of the left-hand side of the Trigon as the female side of the Trigon. The Formal Capacity of the Ideal Natures—of Quality—in 3Q is imaged to 1C once and twice to 2C as the Logical Capacity of the Soul, giving weight to the notion that the right-hand side of the Trigon represents the male side. If we were to think of this as a symbolic mapping of the human brain, looking out at us from the page, these male and female sides would be reversed. This is the case in most mappings of the intuitive and logical hemispheres of the brain.

The arcs from the prior Form L.3.0 are flattened in Form L.3.1 to produce an inner image of the Essential Trigon as indicated by the recapitulation of the stated Capacities at 1L, 2A, & 3Q, and an inner image of the Existential Trigon co-terminal with the Imaging Capacity of the Soul Natures in the Essential Trigon, at the three vertices, 1C, 2C, & 3C. The inner dashed trigon represents a completion of the growth potential of the Soul Nature through the focus of either of these three Imaging Capacities with thorough Observation - 2C, Recognition - 3C, or Communion - 1C of these Soul Natures, so that focus and pursuit of one of these approaches to completion, starting from one of the vertices of *C to the opposite side, represents the same cognitive growth as starting from either of the other two vertices.

The three Imaging Capacities located in the dashed trigons outside the Essential Trigon is subject to misinterpretation representing a mental illusion of the Soul as a personal ego. In truth nothing, and especially ego, has existence outside the Essential Trigon. The illusion of ego is annihilated as a result of advanced initiation. The inner star representing the entire manifest universe therefore resides within the Boundless, Limitless Unmanifest Essence, with the Power to so manifest Itself without end. Thus, the liberated Soul, with Lord Krishna, can state, "Having pervaded the entire universe with a fragment of myself, I remain."

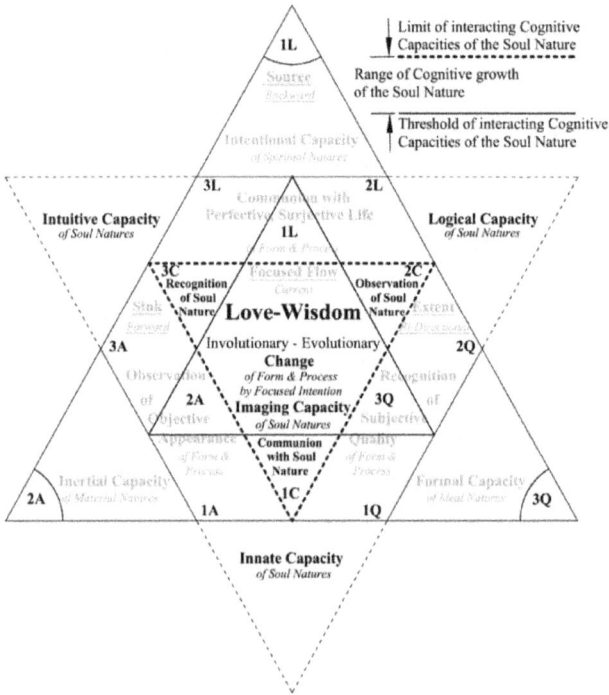

The Existential Trigon expanded overlay on the Essential Trigon

Form L.3.1

We can see in the trigon of Form L.3.2, the relationship of a Platonic formulation by the differentiation of the Essential Truth into the Intentional, Formal, and Inertial Capacities of the Spiritual, Material, and Ideal Natures, and of the creation of the Existential Universe through the process of Imaging those inherent capacities of the Tripartite Soul onto Itself. This creates what is traditionally recognized in a Star of David as a symbol of the Hebrew tradition, within an Essential Trigonal formulation. This depiction can be understood as a common foundational core of Neo-Platonic Hellenistic thought, Vedantic thought of India, and the three Abrahamic religions of the Middle East.

In addition to this model serving as a philosophical and theological tool for understanding the Intentional—the Teleological—Capacity of the Spiritual Natures and as a foundation of the Formal Capacity of the Ideal Natures, it can also serve as a foundation for understanding the Inertial Capacity of the Material Natures as an axiomatic, theoretical basis of physical phenomena and for providing greater detail in the Formal Capacity and in the Living Capacity of the Soul Natures as applied to the fields of political economy.

The Existential Trigon within the Essential Trigon

Form L.3.2

The bold outline of the Essential Trigon represents a knowledge of the entire field of Life—of Being, Awareness, and Bliss—as in the case of a Christ or a Buddha or a Krishna or any of the uncounted other numbers of enlightened souls who have completed this journey and participate still in the building of this and countless other celestial systems.

Form L.4.0 within the bold boundary represents the focus of the Logical Capacity of the Soul at 2C on the Material Natures observed in space and time in what we will call the Omnipresence of the Inertial Capacity, 2A. Here the observed reality as material Truth is comprised of the existent components—of what consist as rest mass and their photonic interaction in the current scientific worldview—apparent to the senses, interpreted intuitively @ 3AEx, logically @ 2AEx, and instinctively @1AEx. We can surmise that corollaries of these material components might exist as more rarified versions of the inertial capacity as in the reported cases of the more subtle vehicles of the soul, as in the dream state.

Form L.4.0 represents a logic-based interpretation of observed experience applied to instances of these material natures embedded in the matrix of inertial capacity that is directly unsensible, represented as a vacuum of space at 2AEs. The inclusion of 2AEs in this focus indicates the teleological notion of a non-random first causal principle responsible for the three interpretations of *AEx, in addition to the inherent or created existence of *C as a function of interactive sentience of the Soul in space and time. As outlined by the bold boundary, 2AEs might be thought of as the domain of a creator Diety or the invariant Laws of Nature or both.

Self-defined as materialist worldviews of the four-fold Natures that might be associated with Form 4.0 are: Darwinism, steady state, non-Big Bang based Standard Models of Particles and General Relativity.

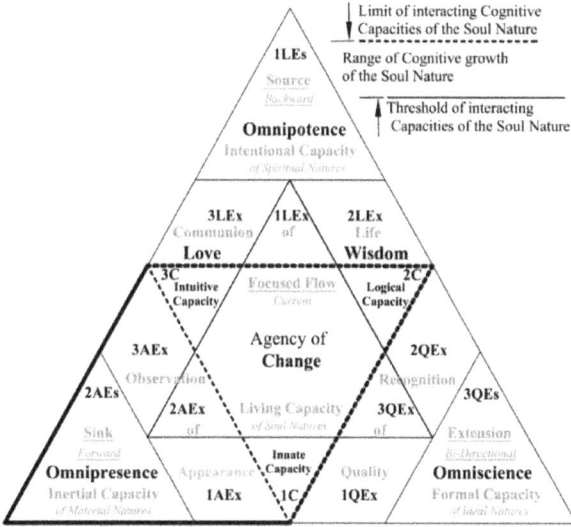

The Existential Trigon within the Essential Trigon

Form L.4.0

The truncated parallelogram of Form L.4.1 within the bold outline represents this same general world view but without the underpinning of a causal first principle represented by 2AEs and is therefore a stochastic interpretation of causality as with a materialist science with no understanding that the Ideal Nature has an essential ontology separate from the thought processes that are deemed to 'live' in the human brain. The inverted trigon of the Soul Nature as the Agency of Change in this view is considered an epiphenomenal aspect of biological evolution that is randomly focused on the stochastically evolved existential material world in *AEx. The essential nature of the material world understood as an Omnipresent inertial capacity to retain material form and process independent of causal impulse, for example as a wave bearing inertial substrate from which quantum particles emerge under well understood constraints, is not part of this view.

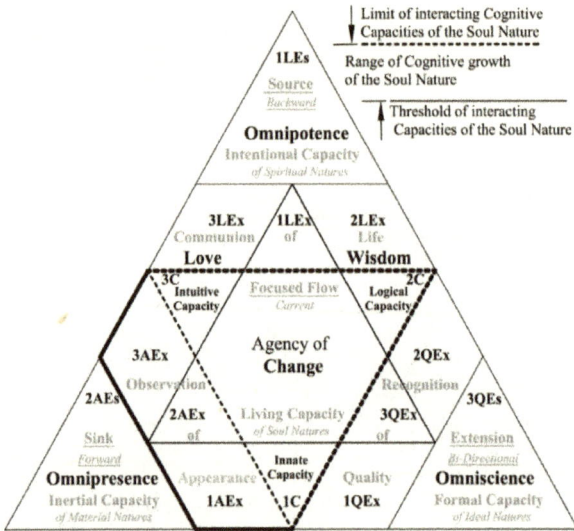

The Existential Trigon within the Essential Trigon

Form L.4.1

As a result, the logical capacity of 2C which is necessary for the establishment and economically effective application of the insights of the modern scientific world view is in existential denial of three essential axiomatic insights. These can only be found in an understanding of the omnipresent dynamics of space and time in 2AEs, through the application of the omniscient formal capacity of mathematics and geometry and axiomatic logic found in 3QEs, under the axiomatic imperative of an omnipotent source of power to drive all change found in 1LEs. These three axioms are evidenced by the material world of physical phenomena in *AEx, recognized as axiomatically necessary by the logic of the soul in 2C.

As distinguished from Form L.4.0, this form is essentially atheistic and epiphenomenal, which is said not as a statement of any opprobrium but as a comment that this world view as imaged by its practitioners lacks any logical axiom for explanation of events other than a recording of what is happening at the current moment, without understanding and reasoned expectation that it might happen again. Even a reliance on a reading of recorded past events requires an historical interpretation of those events based on an axiomatic logical mechanism to 'make sense' of the recorded data, especially if the intent of the readback is to forecast events going forward.

Considering the inherent capacities represented within the bold boundary of Form L.4.1, there is nothing inconsistent in thinking of the Soul as a source of the innate, logical, and intuitive capacities that provide an understanding to the material world in which the human being finds itself, but it fails to acknowledge the essential three invariant capacities of the world around it, and the best it can do is to create a stunted image of its self.

Self-defined as materialist worldviews of the four-fold Natures that might be associated with Form L.4.1 are Darwinism, Big Bang based Standard Models of Particles and General Relativity.

Form L.4.2 is perhaps a more accurate interpretation of what is happening in much of the world view of those that define themselves as atheistic or agnostic materialist yet still navigate the world with an ideal moral and aesthetic compass. The bold boundary here includes the focus of the intuitive capacity of 3C and the innate capacity of 1C in a soul's attempts to understand and navigate the world of experience. In the mental world of ideas and formal logic @

2QEx, in its interaction with other souls @ 3QEx, and its intuitive approach to solving problems in the material world @ 1QEx, the soul recognizes the independent capacity of its ideal natures. Based on observed and recognized experience of material forms and ideal Forms, it may even entertain an appreciation for the possibility of the revelatory experience and communion with the spiritual realm @ 1LEx based on its innate capacity @ 1C. As a result, it may even glimpse the adjacent natures of divine Love @ 3LEx and Wisdom @ 2LEx as in Form L.4.7.

The Existential Trigon within the Essential Trigon

Form L.4.2

We might envision that the two lower unmanifest trigons of omnipresence and omniscience would be included in a logical and intuitive appreciation for those who are theists or enlightened agnostics, those with a belief in some notion of a transcendent Life, who have not yet experienced what they would consider a verification of that perspective. With that inclusion, Form L.4.7 represents a growing number of the enlightened community.

Self-defined materialist-idealist worldviews of the four-fold Natures that might be associated with Form L.4.2 are: agnostic forms of scientific and social modeling using stochastic methods including Darwinism, Standard Models of Particles and General Relativity, Freudian and related psychology, sociology, and economics.

The Existential Trigon within the Essential Trigon

Form L.4.3

While Form L.4.0 may be used to represent the focus of the soul for a spiritual aspirant functioning along the path of Karma Yoga or Christian service, the area within the bold boundary of Form L.4.3 represents the focus of the intuitive capacity of the soul @ 3C on contemplation of Omniscience to be found within the Formal Capacity of the Ideal Natures, in the process of Jnana Yoga, pursuing insights through the study of scripture—of the Bible or Koran or the

Bhagavat Gita—or other inspired spiritual sources, with the goal of enlightenment of a specific or a general nature in mind.

In the process of such focus, in the dream state, in meditation, or in a period before birth /after death, in which there is a lack of focus on the material world, the state of Form L.4.3 is represented.

Self-defined idealist worldviews of the four-fold Natures that might be associated with Form L.4.3, with the inclusion of *AEx are theistic forms confined to psychological analysis and understanding.

The Existential Trigon within the Essential Trigon

Form L.4.4

Form L.4.4 represents this same state, but in a condition which lacks a recognition of the omniscience of the Formal Capacity in the emergence of ideal natures of forms and processes, though the intuitive capacity of the soul at 3C still has a grasp of specific ideal qualities represented within an existential or historical context. Such lack of recognition is evidenced by the notion that contradictions can be found in 2QEx, 3QEx and 1QEx that are inherently irresolvable.

Omniscience in this sense understands that contradictions found in deductive conclusions are the result of contradictions embodied in the axioms of an argument, which from a monistic foundation is free of contradiction. As a result, such contradictions when encountered, should be a clue and cue for further examination of the axiomatic root from which the idea was formulated. Lack of pursuit of an understanding of that contradiction is evidence of disbelief in the possibility of omniscience, of the capacity of contemplation to formulate ideas and solutions to problems, difficult though they might be. This does not mean the solution to a problem will likely be what the soul initially thought it might be. It means, however, that there is always a solution.

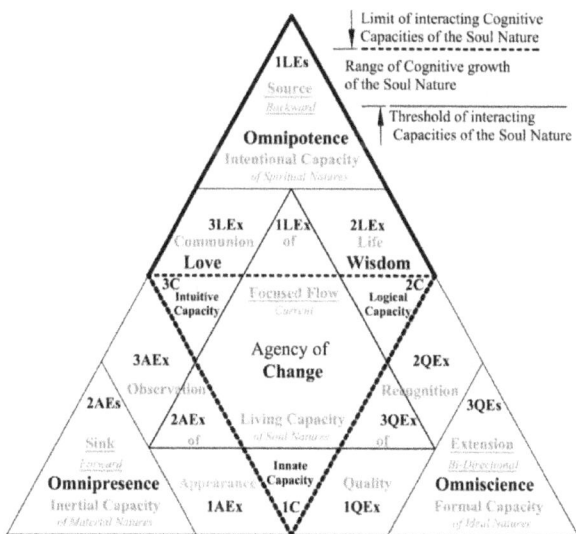

The Existential Trigon within the Essential Trigon

Form L.4.5

The area within the bold boundary of Form L.4.5 depicts the Innate Capacity of the Soul @ 1C, focused on what it understands is the Omnipotence of its source through that source's Intentional Capacity to populate the Spiritual Natures, along with the material and ideal natures. It represents the path of devotion, of Bhakti Yoga of the Bhagavat Gita, of salvation through Jesus Christ of the Gospels, and of adherence to the teachings of Mohammed in full deference to Allah. The path of devotion is followed by the majority of human beings across the spectrum of religious adherents.

The Existential Trigon within the Essential Trigon

Form L.4.6

As with Forms L.4.1 and L.4.4, Form L.4.6 indicates an approach to spiritual natures that envisions spiritual entities as the principal sources of intentional capacity or divine purpose rather than as conduits and expressions of a single Omnipotent source for all Life. This is the essential distinction between a monotheism that sees

374

God as the supreme Deity viewed by a soul in need of supplication and a monism that sees God as a Life spring from which the soul is the stream even as it recognizes itself as part of a greater Stream that is the Soul.

The Existential Trigon within the Essential Trigon

Form L.4.7

Form L.4.7 represents the completion of the Great Work referred to in some teachings, in which the soul has come to fully understand the inertial, formal, and intentional capacities in terms of the material, ideal, and spiritual natures of its experience, so that the soul recognizes itself as love, wisdom, and opportunity, without the risk, fear, or ignorance that attaches to an egoic interpretation of those natures. The omnipotent, omniscient, and omnipresent aspects of the three capacities are understood to continue outside the hexagon and the Essential Trigon, even as the imaging capacity of the soul nature remains eternally at blissful peace even in the midst of existential turmoil, as actor but not a character in the play of Life.

BALANCE OF SCIENCE & FAITH IN THE ESSENTIAL TRIGON - I

We can create a dynamic version of Form L.4.7 as a model for understanding any form or process involving the four principal capacities and their spiritual, material, ideal, and soul natures using a virtual three-dimensional spirit level.

A spirit or bubble level is a part of an engineering level used in the construction process. The level sits atop a tripod which rests by three stanchions, generally placed on uneven ground. The three stanchions are joined together at the top by articulating connections to the bottom side of a flat equilateral baseplate on which the level is firmly mounted. In this modeling the baseplate can be represented by the Essential Trigon. In the construction process, the stanchions are adjustable, allowing the baseplate of the tripod to be closely approximated to a true level with respect to the earth by adjusting the three legs. Here, we will assume a tripod with fixed length legs that give us an accurate reading of the ground elevation in the top level of the baseplate at each of the fixed stanchions, representing the spiritual, material, and ideal natures of the trigon.

The working part of the level with the bubble, called the alidade—which usually has a telescopic sight to read and transfer benchmark readings—is represented by the large hexagon within the bold border of Form L.4.7. In Form L.5.0 and the related following Forms, the 'on the ground' existential condition is indicated by a reading of the Valued Good 'in the bubble' located at the center of the smaller hexagon, as indicated by 'Dynamic Balance' in Form L.5.0. The alidade is attached to the baseplate by three adjustable leveling screws, one underneath each of the vertices of the dashed trigon of the soul natures at the innate, intuitive, and logical capacities. We assume that the current condition 'on the ground' is read 'in the bubble' at the center of small hexagon in all cases. The purpose and function of the three screws is to understand the operation of those screws as required to level the alidade and return the central Valued Good represented in any Form to the central position as is the case with 'Dynamic Balance' in Form L.5.0.

The three leveling screws represent the operation of the three capacities of the soul nature, intuitive, logical, and innate, in the attempt to maintain equilibrium in Life. The screws are symbolized by '*>|<*', where '|' represents level equilibrium of the hexagonal alidade and '*' is a wild card for the variety of qualities which will be stated later, one at each of the three vertices.

The reference plane 'on the ground' which we are reading as reflected to our tripod level 'in the bubble' is comprised of a two-dimensional reference grid with four arbitrary directional senses in the circle, with arrows pointing to the central condition of balance in the first two Forms. A third dimensional reference, not shown, is determined along a gradient toward the center of gravity, into the page or screen in these Forms, opposite to the direction in which the spirit bubble is always positioned, toward its source in open space. That spirit in the bubble is always pointing to the high ground, to get out, to be free, so to speak.

The direction of the four essential natures are spread from their positions in the Essential Trigon in which the Soul Nature is centered between the other three, counterclockwise as four tendencies: the Spiritual, toward the top of the sheet of paper or screen in keeping with the notion of supremacy and intentionality; the

Material, to the left in keeping with the inertial capacity and the intuitive capacity of the soul nature; the Soul, toward the bottom as the position of the its innate capacity; the Ideal, to the right in keeping with the formal capacity and the logical capacity of the Soul. These four tendencies, centered around a point of equilibrium, circulate about the large hexagon in response to existential conditions 'on the ground'.

As seen in Form L.5.0, those natures are named by their logical relationship in the existential frame of reference of forms and processes based on a tendency of each to change along a spectrum, continuous or discrete depending on the context, toward a central point of 'Dynamic Balance' or equilibrium. We are using the most generic terms possible in this first instance for the four directional senses or tendencies.

'Universality' is the axiomatically formless potential at the spiritual nature end of the vertical, primary spectrum, beyond yet still pervading all space and time, so that any observation, recognition, or communion of a form or process in time and space is a perspective on a universal macrostate. At the other end of that spectrum is the 'Particularity' of the form or process, defined by the specification in time and space of material, ideal, and soul natures, so that every particular is unique at that lower end as an ensouling entity, be it a neutron or a galaxy. Such particularity is related to the innate capacity of the Soul for individuated focus of decision making as an actual microstate reflecting all four natures, since the spiritual pervades the other three, if only in the most rarified manner.

'Station' at the inertial capacity and material nature end on the left as a finite maximum or indefinitely extending asymptote indicates a fixed position, quality (or physical property), or place over time of the horizontal, secondary space-time spectrum, while at the formal capacity and ideal nature end of that spectrum of similar maximum or asymptotic termination, 'Motion' indicates a constant variation in position, quality, or place. The end at 'station' is undefined with respect to change in position over time as being timeless, just as 'motion' at the other end of the spectrum is undefined with respect to a change in time with position in space as being undefinable in space.

The primary balance between universality and particularity and the secondary balance between station and motion or invariance and change is 'Dynamic Balance' as an ideal mix which we observe, recognize, and commune with as a harmonic characteristic or condition of Life.

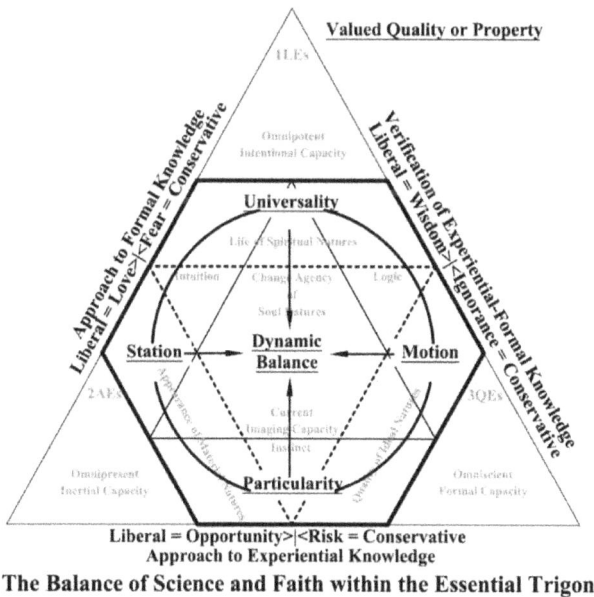

The Balance of Science and Faith within the Essential Trigon

Form L.5.0

In Form L.5.0 and related forms, captioned as 'The Balance of Science and Faith within the Essential Trigon', the screw labeled 'Liberal = Opportunity>|<Risk = Conservative' as primary, located directly below the current placement of Particularity is used to level the bubble by optimizing opportunity (>) or minimizing risk (<) by a turn of the screw as a function of the Innate Capacity of individual soul or community decision making. This function is essentially schooled by mother nature and the native culture into which a soul is born and raised.

Labeled 'Liberal = Love>|<Fear = Conservative' at the intuitive capacity is Faith operating as a secondary screw in balancing the bubble. At the logical capacity as labeled by 'Liberal = Wisdom>|<Ignorance = Conservative' is Science operating as another secondary leveling screw. It is the balance between the use of these two leveling screws that shifts the balance along the secondary spectrum which controls how souls and the community respond to existential events in time and space.

These responses are initially effected through the exercise of a liberal or conservative approach to correct some problem that is first seen as an existential concern amenable to innate understanding and intervention by the soul or community. This is attempted by balancing the alidade and bubble between a universal collective and a particular individual solution to that problem based on the soul/community perception of the mix of opportunity and risk inherent in that problem.

Liberal versus conservative is not a condition of a soul or a community. Most human beings are liberal in the approach to solving a problem that offers opportunity to an individual or affiliated group and conservative in the approach to solving a problem that threatens risk. Virtually all problems represent a mix of opportunity and risk, which if the scientific logician is sufficiently wise will be reduced to a percentage in totality equal to 100%. If the intuitive faithful are sufficiently loving—open to Life solutions—and authentically insightful, they will act according to that insight and not from irrational concern.

The primary problem for every soul and its community is understanding first, the true mix, and second, the immediate and long-term effects, of the soul or community's action. If this understanding is accurately pursued, there will be little if any difference between a liberal and a conservative approach to a problem. Any use of these two terms in political discourse, especially if combined with invective, is an accurate admission of ergodidiocy, returning to the use of a portmanteau from earlier, and they need to do some more thinking and perhaps praying. The negative approach to a problem is generally both anti-liberal and anti-conservative, in that it tends to denigrate opportunity and hype risk in the pursuit of short-term, personal gains.

The two terms used in this modeling are meant to be instructive of understanding the limitations of innate approaches by the body politic to matters of existential concern along with an enlightened approach of Science and Faith in arriving at nuanced solutions for addressing those concerns. 'Liberal=*>|' and '|<*=Conservative' represent a focus on the wild card quality, '*', intended to move the screw in the direction required to level the bubble based on a perception of the opportunity or risk embodied in that concern.

In Form L.5.0, the valued good is Dynamic Balance. No matter what the existential conditions might be at the time, from a cosmological perspective the Universe as a whole always remains in dynamic balance, even if the Milky Way was to undergo a galactic supernova, individual curds and whey notwithstanding. From the perspective of an individual soul in the midst of apparent chaos, that condition appears anything but balanced. Particular instances of chaos in space and time do not indicate that there is not a harmonious universal purpose everywhere extended. It means that an individual soul that perceives such chaos by focusing on chaotic events in space and time, and makes that chaos their own, does so by choice, instead of establishing harmony by focusing on their innate connection to the Soul <u>within</u> themselves, and thereby to other souls within the community.

The Balance of Science and Faith within the Essential Trigon

Form L.5.1

Within, if they have not already, they will discover their Soul Nature as Love in action, as Wisdom, which transcends their ego, which is but a transitory, adaptive mechanism of the soul. Some will recognize that Soul Nature as that of Christ, some as the nature of Buddha, and some as their personal connection to God as one source of Love. As souls—as that Soul—we are a multitude of spokes in the same wheel of the divine Life.

Form L.5.1 represents a lack of wisdom due to isolated focus on particularity. It is the individual soul's mission to find that Dynamic Balance within themselves and facilitate finding that Balance in other human beings and within the community.

We will use this Form in three other contexts, with the appropriate change of nomenclature for the Valued Goods of the community. First of these is a series in a spiritual natures context that is appropriate for monist and monotheistic faiths in Form L.6.0. That will be followed with a series in the context of the material natures in Contemplation II on the Appearance of Physical Phenomena starting with Form A.1.0, and then with an extended series on Contemplation III on the Quality of Political Economy starting with Form Q.1.0 in the context of Plato's Republic.

In Form L.6.0, the primary spectrum of the spiritual nature of the soul's intentionality runs from the notion of 'Predestiny' in which the cosmos is held to operate under the universal control of a Calvinist God or the stars or natural law operating through DNA to 'Free Will' of any faith or even a materialist view, in which the soul accepts free agency for their actions and any repercussions of those actions. Some notions of free will differ little in the implications of the belief across various faiths. Perhaps the biggest difference is found in the notion of one incarnation and chance of salvation for a Free-Will Baptist versus the notion of multiple incarnations and chances as the necessary road to eventual success for Vedanta and some western schools of thought, including the early Christian view of Origen.

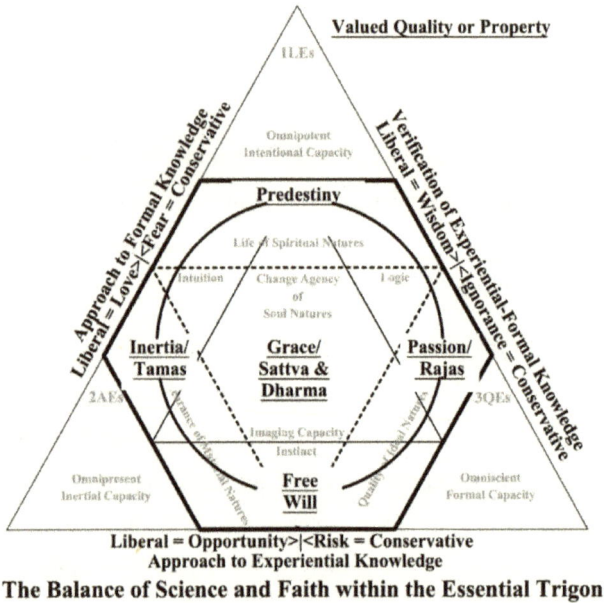

The Balance of Science and Faith within the Essential Trigon

Form L.6.0

The secondary spectrum is similar in quality to that of Form L.5.0 starting with the material nature of the inertial capacity with 'Inertia/Tamas' and extending to the emotional component of 'Passion/Rajas' at the other extreme. In the middle is the dynamic balance of 'Grace/Sattva & Dharma'.

The second term after the forward slash of each of the three valued goods of this spectrum is the Vedantic term for the gunas, or primary qualities. In that school of thought, Tamas, Rajas, and Sattva are woven together in varying degrees of proportion by the soul's experience to produce the particular position of that soul. With

384

respect to the center position of balance, in addition to the concept of Sattva, translated as harmony or goodness—here as Grace—Dharma is a balance along the secondary spectrum between Inertia and Passion and along the primary spectrum incorporating both free will and predestination as the enlightened soul's choice to follow the divine path by yielding, by submitting to the Will-to-Good of the divine Life. Dharma, if followed, becomes an act of Grace.

There is much writing over the centuries of how one enters a state of grace, whether it is something over which the soul has any control or merit, whether there is a way to curry favor with God. There is a way. Stop thinking about it. Be grateful to Life. Grace is gratitude to Life, regardless of chaos. Love Life. Live Love. When in doubt, repeat. Keep doing it.

The Balance of Science and Faith within the Essential Trigon

Form L.6.1

Form L.6.1 echoes the 'Particularity' of Form L.5.1 in depicting the notion of 'Free Will' as the innate focus and central Good of the community or soul. It might be the understanding of a tyro or novitiate who has focused on Free Will as individual freedom from all the other minor truths—or lies masquerading as truths—and revels in that choice with little thought of further responsibility other than constantly reaffirming that choice. It thus runs the risk of missing the divine universality of the moment in which the soul is enmeshed, being instead preoccupied with a fear that all the other particular agents of free will are conspiring against that soul—as a vulnerable ego—who feels such agents might be determined, and in fact predestined, to seduce or harm the soul. As a result, such ego replaces the notion of universal Good as Love, with a universal fear of adversity, the Devil.

The Balance of Science and Faith within the Essential Trigon

Form L.6.2

Form L.6.2 represents a condition of torpor, of ignorance toward the soul's environment. It should be noted that ignorance is not a condition of confronting the unknown for the first time; rather it is defined as the soul's refraining or refusing to recognize and perhaps to deal with a material condition with which the soul is already familiar on some level.

The Balance of Science and Faith within the Essential Trigon

Form L.6.3

The use of a circle in these forms emphasizes that the focus of the soul 'in the bubble' is thought of as being naturally constrained radially in equal measure from the central position of balance. This is to distinguish a state from any pathological condition that might be deemed to exist at the extremes of any two of the four valued goods of a similarly centered square, in the four corners outside the confines of the circle. For example, free will implies some degree of motion as with passion as an emotion, as an emotive impulse. This free will becomes restricted as the focus moves toward inertia, which at the extreme end is stationary. Inertia and free will therefore involve a degree of contradiction, as do passion and free will on the other hand as depicted in Form L.6.3.

We will make use of this pathological depiction in the discussion later in the Contemplation III section as in Form Q.1.6. The idea that a soul is exercising free will when they are mired in inertia or ignorance on the one hand or passion and emotion on the other is problematic. Free will of an addict along an arc to either extreme is relinquished as the addiction takes hold, though a universal lifeline remains.

As the focus of the soul bounces around the lower half of the circle, in the process of trying to achieve some balance through the turning of the two leveling screws—raising 'Wisdom>|' andor lowering '|<Fear' for the condition of fear induced inertia represented by Form L.6.2 and raising 'Love>|' andor lowering '|<Ignorance' for the ignorance enflamed passion of Form L.6.3—the soul will inevitably find the need to recalibrate at 'Opportunity>|<Risk' to move the bubble back to center @ 'Grace', and in the process relinquish any obsessive preoccupation with 'Free Will'.

We are not showing the condition in which 'Predestiny' is the focus of the soul, but it might represent a condition of kismet, which is beyond the ken of any but Allah to understand and control. One might think that even if such focus were to apply, one would not be in a position to recognize or claim it in the public sphere. Of course, there have always been those that thought otherwise, when in fact it was an exercise of Free Will.

At first glimpse we might say that the photo above is an expanse, an extended field of just one thing, water – perhaps we think ocean. Then we notice the appearance of the troughs and peaks of the waves; the lighter blue on the lower left may indicate a shallow bottom or at the middle or the upper right, the entrainment of air from a previous crest collapse; there are small white caps and foam from their breaking scattered on the surface; bubbles follow the eddies and main currents beneath; there appears to be a mist floating above the churn driven by the wind. Analyzing further, it is obvious that there is an atmosphere above the water, where the mist and spray formed of small droplets of water is suspended for a time before sinking back and merging into the sea; so the expanse of the ocean itself must be comprised of countless numbers of such droplets.

As a result of further study using microscopes and other devices that allow us to 'see' beyond what is visible, we understand that the drops are in turn comprised of molecules and elemental atoms bound together by electromagnetic interactions; that in turn these atoms appear to be bound states of individual wave-particle electrons (leptons) and nucleons – well they don't really appear at all, its just that the only way we can explain their behavior is to attempt to visualize them, to model them in our minds using quantitative logic, mathematics, and analytical geometry to predict their activity in space and time – and the nucleons, to be modeled as bound states of three individual wave-particles called quarks which join together according to well-ordered quantum mechanisms now referred to as the standard model using various types of quantum field theory. This last step, if we really think about it, means that all the quantum particles are joined to each other by extension as fields of one quality or another, of electromagnetism, of gluonic or strong force structure, or of gravitation, so that all we can say about the quantum wave-particles themselves is that they are the focus of maximum field intensity, as the maximum probability of having them crest at a given locus of space at a given time.

Like the photo above, these wave-particles are modeled as the appearance or emergence of crests and troughs in the waves of a quantum generating ocean as a type of quantum foam at a microscopically small size; a scale—the Planck scale—that is as small compared to the size of an electron or nucleon as those illusive wave-particles are to the size of the sea represented in this photo; that under ill understood conditions these Planck scale quantum crests and troughs spring into extended existence, perhaps life, for an astronomically long time.

This means that the space in which this all happens is a cosmic continuum and not an empty container of some type of hard, inert particulate substance of some other origin, of some other quality with some other properties. Such a continuum must be an extended field, which must be flexible if it is extendable or expanding as it appears to be, but it must be generally inert, since it appears to be expanding very slowly. Since it is flexible, it is either plastic or elastic, but must be elastic, at least in some regions, if it shows evidence of being wave bearing, as it so appears.

So if cosmic space is an inertial, wave bearing continuum under expansion, we should look to some mechanism for the emergence, the appearance first, of quantum fluctuations in the wave-bearing substrate—(however, we will not have to look to the microscopically small Planck scale for that emergence as is the current fashion, but rather to the neutron scale)—and second, for the localized emergence of oscillation and maintenance of a discrete sustained rotation of that oscillation to produce quantum half spin angular momentum and spin energy, a magnetic dipole, quantum gravity, all recognized as an expression of the neutron, and with continued cosmic expansion, a drop in inertial density and mechanical impedance and the subsequent ejection of a minor portion of wave energy recognized as the electron, with beta decay and a spin flip and drop in spin energy of the neutron to that of the proton.

The materials documented under this topic are found in the several monographs and links on the UniServEnt.org website to YouTube videos menued chronologically under this category, starting with the most recent at the top, from August of 2019, and going back to the first presentation of October, 2006. They are the result of the quantitative application of these axiomatic conclusions drawn from various qualitative investigations under the category of Essential Principles over 30 years starting in earnest with my matriculation at Duke University. In the process of writing down some of my thoughts of a general philosophical nature, I was compelled to address my lack of understanding of fundamental physics. This lack was in part a reflection of the general state of misunderstanding of that field of study at the academic level, in that

391

there is no physical understanding of how the cosmic spatial continuum, customarily treated mathematically as a 4-dimensional spacetime of general relativity (GR), interacted or coupled, with the massive (principally nucleonic) or energetic (photonic) quanta of the standard model of particle interactions, such coupling being a necessary condition of GR.

In pursuit of this understanding, I assumed an application of classical mathematical methods using Newton's gravitational law to two neutron at the femto scale as might occur in a helium nucleus, while disregarding the theoretical interaction of the two protons. The computations are included in the excerpt following the video below on the website.

The effect of the coupling of space and quanta, which is modeled as a localized oscillating, twisting of the spatial fabric, is shown in the videos linked on this page. It is a more detailed depiction of the stress and strain shown on the Projects page.[5]

Though I suspect few physicists would recognize it and fewer still agree with the statement, the scientific study of physical phenomena is founded on certain axioms that must be taken on faith, and in fact speak to faith as a fundamental tenet of rational thought. Among these are the notions of certain qualities and ideas, or properties and laws as they are referred to in physics, ideal Forms as they are referred to in the thinking of Plato.

Qualities are the nouns for which the mathematical systems of numbers are the quantitative adjectives. Even in the systems of abstract algebra and number theory, all numbers reference or imply a

---

[5] Text in Italics taken from the UniServEnt.org website

qualitative thing upon which any mathematical operation must work, as with addition or division, if only as a qualitative placeholder or wildcard. One can only add or subtract items of like kind or quality; 2 apples to 3 apples to equal 5 apples, 2 oranges to 3 oranges to equal 5 oranges, or 2 apples to 3 oranges to equal 5 fruits. In contrast, one cannot divide or multiply like qualities.

Though this is perhaps not well understood, the number '1' that is generally thought of as a square root and the number '**1**' that is the square of '1' are qualitatively different numbers, (where the figures in single quotations are printed with different fonts to make this distinction). **1** can be thought of as the square area of 1, made by multiplying 1 length in one direction by 1 length ninety degrees to the first to get **1** unit of area, understood as **1** unit of square–length equal to 1 unit length squared; (1 unit length running north to south) x (1 unit length running east to west) = **1** square unit.

This means that only part of any number, such as '*one*', is objective and the rest of that part is contextual, meaning subjective based on an understanding of what quality is quantized by that numerical representation. In truth, what is 'objective' is simply a matter of 'subjective' agreement—of 'intersubjectivity'—arising from the nature of the quantizing process, intentionally quantized or not.

We can take the matter further if we reverse the understanding of qualitative numbers by taking the square root of the number '**-1**', generally understood to be of the imaginary sense or sign, 'i', applied to a linear number as '$i1$', indicating $i1$ x $i1$ = **-1**. But if we use the number **-1** to quantify a piece of ground or fabric as a unit area, what does the minus sign mean? Perhaps it is indicating a reduction in the area of an original piece. How would you make the cut?

To deduct an area, you might measure back from a square southwest corner of the piece along the edge -*1* east and -*1* north, but we soon find if we check by computing the area by entering it in the computer that the total is actually **+1** based on customary mathematical notation, which would add to the total area of our piece. Instead, we might understand and use a convention in which the so-called imaginary sense, *i*, actually means '90 degrees from another length used in computing a negative area'.

For those who are not familiar with the 'cross product', as indicated by the 'x' used in the equation above, -1 can represent more than just a negative area. In certain contexts, it represents a torque, a resulting force operating in a direction at 90 degrees to the area indicated by the square of two *i1* forces operating—multiplying—one on the other. The twisting force of the two *i1*, then is equal to the **-1** of the resulting force, where the direction of the force is determined by which of the two *i1* is operating on the other using the right-hand or left-hand rule.

Imaginary numbers appear naturally in the formalism of complex wave mechanics, but they are often discarded when they show up in some calculations of observed phenomena as an anomaly. While it is understood that rest mass particles—by which we here mean neutrons, protons, and electrons—are in some sense constituted as waves, they are dealt with in mathematical treatments of mass as discrete and invariant globs of matter, albeit with a quantum field influence principally of an electromagnetic and strong nature acting between particles.

Under more or less well-defined conditions, a neutron glob spits off a portion of its mass as an electron, leaving the mass and various other properties of the proton behind where the neutron once was. In the process, however, the mass or mass-energy of the proton plus the electron is less than the original neutron by an invariant missing amount. This missing amount of mass-energy cannot be accounted for by current modeling, but it can be accounted for using the modeling of complex wave mechanics to understand the electron-proton configuration as stress-strain torsion waves.

The nature of the two components quantified using the imaginary sense, il x il, is a characteristic twist or torsion associated with the emission of the electron from the neutron and accounts for the missing mass-energy, Δm, permanently bound in the -1 twist of the proton but not recognized by the mathematics of the conventional modeling.

Some essential or axiomatic qualities that feature in classical physical thinking are energy, mass, momentum, action, force, and power among many others that are modeled as bodies and discrete particles interacting in a field of observation and, when and where possible, a field of controlled experimentation. To this we can add several unit (quantum) instances of many of the same properties, plus unit (quantum) spin angular momentum as Planck's constant, called h-bar, and the speed of electromagnetic wave propagation, generally called the speed of light, along with many other notions of mechanisms governing the unitization (quantization) and interaction of the related unit (quantum) particles.

These various qualities can be reduced in our understanding to three axioms of fundamental, natural capacities and one axiom of change mediating those three; the three natural capacities are Power as a kinetic energy potential, Inertia as a reactive force differential, and conservative continuity of Form and Process, all mediated by the capacity to sense and direct—to register and redirect—a change in Stress of a material unit within the field of observation and interaction.

While it is well known publicly and better understood in the various fields of expertise that these units have wave characteristics in certain contexts, the units are generally conceptualized as particle fields which are in turn conceptualized in fuzzy fashion as points or loci of maximum focus of energy or mass along with other properties of an otherwise diffuse extension of the unit fields. The fuzzy nature of this unitization is why I am switching as indicated in the two paragraphs above from the use of the term 'quantum' to 'unit', since there has been no clarification in fundamental understanding over the past century through the use of the term quantum in quantum theory despite the technological application of the notion. The term gets passed around as if it contained some deep recondite understanding instead of the unknown mystery that it is for most people, expert or not.

My own approach to this subject for over twenty years has been to try to understand the same properties of the units, especially with respect to unit spin, quantified as ½ spin, as a type of localized, discrete wave phenomena in which what is generally thought of as the fabric of spacetime is modeled in a wave bearing matrix as a continuous substrate comprised of variable inertial density. This approach has come to fruition over the last 25 years, starting with a derivation of Newton's gravitational constant as a unit wave source of gravitational force, reaching substantive conformation around 2006 as a model of emergent units as unitized by a gauged cuboctahedral lattice potential of the energy density through the application of classical complex wave mechanics, and has culminated in the past year with understanding of this unitization of the inertial matrix via densification of the cosmic extra-galactic filaments.

This last paragraph will no doubt be a nonsensical concept to most readers, including most experts, but the modeling is well defined and worked out in graphic detail in the material on the UniServEnt.org website and verifies the observation of various invariants that are found in the standard model of particles (SM) and general relativity (GR) as ad hoc and free parameters, but in this modeling arise naturally and consistently from the axioms of the model. One of those principles is Continuity of Space and Time which features in the current modeling of SM and GR as conservation of energy/mass. Space and Time are variable qualities of this principle, much as those qualities are in the combined quality of Spacetime of SM and GR, and they are necessarily continuous in this modeling. However, spacetime in the case of SM and GR is discontinuous as indicated by the notion of a point source Big Bang and a threshold of unit scale at the Planck scale in those models. There is no axiomatically understood modeling in SM or GR for quantization of particles from a point source discontinuity of a Big Bang other than an undefinable exogenous, source of material Power, a God. Belief in a Big Bang, along with the related understanding of the Planck scale—short of personal experience as with God—is a matter of faith.

In the modeling presented on the website, that same Power is endogenous, continuity of space and time are inherently Present and Prescient, and unitization is gauged by an Inertial Invariant, the Hebrew letter tav, ת. Tav represents one of the principles at the interior center of all things in certain Qabalistic teaching, and is a constant of the wave bearing field of space and time in this model.

Tav is equal to h-bar, the primary invariant of current quantum or unitary theory, over the speed of light, the primary invariant of relativity—which is axiomatically important in that h-bar is a time derivative of the moment of inertia, whereas tav is an invariant that is not a function of time. From the invariant of this modeling and various qualitative geometric parameters—which can be deduced from various observable phenomena—the fundamental unit properties of material interactions are derived.

The significance of this line of modeling, of thinking, because that is what modeling is, the logical and consistent control of human thought processes, was apparent to me some 25 years ago after I was able to derive Newton's constant using only the first principles of classical mechanics. With this model as a foundation, the potential for the viable development of cold fusion as a source of clean, cheap energy became apparent after I became aware around 2015 of the continued interest in the 1989 reporting of anomalous heat and the production of helium by the chemists Martin Fleischmann and Stanley Pons in the electrolysis of deuterated palladium. Under the revised moniker of LENR as Low Energy Nuclear Reaction—a change in name in response to the ill understood nature of the mechanism behind the initial claims of tabletop temperature cold fusion—an international assortment of experimentalists with their financial backers has been pursuing a variety of independent attempts at replication, with claims of positive confirmation of the results, to better understand the interactions and to determine if they are truly nuclear.

What has been missing from these investigations is a theoretical basis for this understanding, in particular a more informed understanding of the coulomb force, the interaction between the proton and electron, and the electroweak and the strong interactions between the proton and neutron, that hold these systems together in the SM. Both of these interactions are present in the deuterium atom and in the fusion of two deuterium atoms to make a helium4 atom. A deterministic wave analysis of this modeling adds clarity to this process as indicated in the link to the video animation on the UniServEnt.org website.

A clear understanding of this process is worthy of pursuit. If the process of cold fusion can be technologically controlled and implemented for useful work, cleanly without production of gamma emissions and on the scale of a personal electronic device, it will be a significant breakthrough. 1% of the hydrogen in the water of the earth's surface is deuterium. There is enough of the element to provide the current human energy consumption of the world for tens of millions of years. The cost of production of the element for industrial use would be less than $10 per year to run a home or an automobile. It will be highly disruptive of the political and economic status quo. However, it is worth pursuing for all but the vested interests that might be averse to progress.

The unified modeling of inertial, material interactions and processes offers the possibility of understanding and implementing the process of cold fusion and other processes and deserves further public discussion and vetting. It is one of the major motivations for adding the three Contemplation sections of this addendum instead of sticking to rock & roll, drugs, & sex.

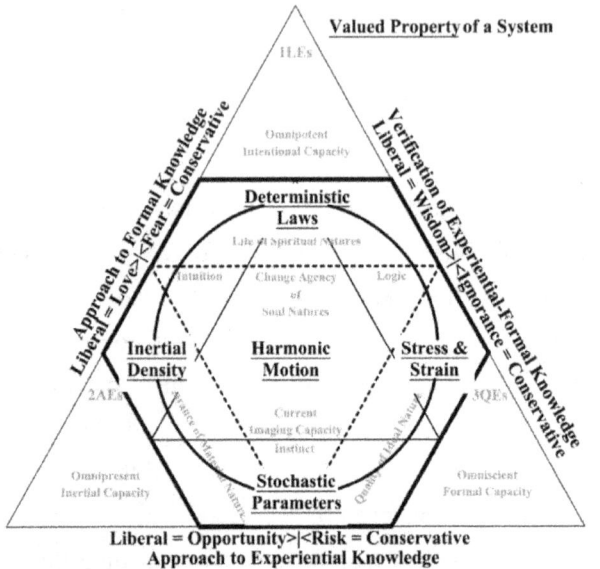

The Balance of Science and Faith within the Essential Trigon

Form A.1.0

From the prior section on Life as Essential Principals, Form L.4.7, the omnipotence of the Intentional Capacity understood as a matter of Faith finds expression in the constraining power and invariance of the 'Deterministic Laws' understood as Science in Form A.1.0. These understandings are different articulations in which faith is the intuitive apprehension and science is the logical comprehension of the same observed experience. Once they are properly understood, faith trusts in the laws of Nature's God and science trusts in the laws of God's Nature.

In Form L.4.7, free will as the innate capacity of the multitude of individual soul natures reflects the omnipotent intentional capacity of Supreme Being. In analogous fashion, the

'Stochastic Parameters' operate as free quantum particles—as in Brownian motion for example—reflecting the deterministic conservation laws recognized by science. 'Inertial Density', or mass as popularly conceived, is obviously related to the inertial capacity of form and process on the left, while the 'Stress & Strain'—tensors of energetic interactions in transmitting force in energy of motion—is a function of the formal capacity on the right. The balance between the vertical and horizontal spectra is 'Harmonic Motion' understood as an elaboration of uniform circular and simple harmonic motion. That elaboration exists over the range of observed phenomena from the cosmic extension to the level of the hydrogen atom, and obviously includes the bodies of human beings, whose existential presence is essential to a recognition of Life and the nature of the Soul which does the observing and recognizing and communal understanding and creates ideal models of that understanding.

In a dialectical process that Plato would appreciate, understanding of both science and faith requires balance in the approach to gaining experiential knowledge through the careful observation of material nature, in order to enhance formal knowledge by the recognition of ideal forms and processes in the material natures, with the intention of verification or amendment of that knowledge synthesized as ideal Forms and Processes, and finally, alteration of the material forms and processes through the agency of the person of science and/or faith who is a conscious soul inquiring into some aspect of Life.

In the interest of gaining experiential knowledge on any subject, the enlightened soul takes a liberal approach toward opportunity and a conservative approach toward risk in interaction with the material nature. It takes a liberal approach of openness to inquiry and Life opportunity—which is a form of love—and a conservative approach in mitigating fear and ignorance of Life risks as wisdom in weighing the application of formal solutions in an understanding of material problems. It exercises a liberal approach in the application of authenticated wisdom and a conservative approach in the application of yet unverified or apparently unverifiable determination of a solution to a problem. Hence my problematic situation as a prophet of enlightened scientific investigation in a field that is dominated by faith in scientific canon grounded in ad hoc principles.

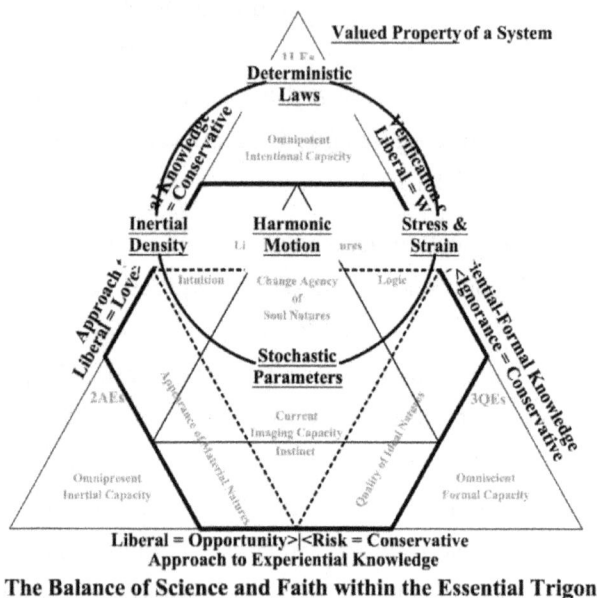

The Balance of Science and Faith within the Essential Trigon

Form A.1.1

Given the independence of the formal capacity in scientific investigation, it is perhaps not difficult to understand the current theoretical impasse in some physical, political economic, and theological thinking, in which the balance of harmonic motion, social justice, and divine grace are shoved to the side, replaced 'in the bubble' in this Platonic thinking of 'Particularity' of Form L.5.1 by the predominance of stochastic parameters, individual freedom, and free will. Scientific modeling does its best to remove the human element from its understanding, and yet, from the ascendance of the notions of free will in certain religious thought and freedom in social and economic notions, we see in physical analysis its reflection as stochastic functions governed by the interaction of 'free' particles and parameters which are—like much human interaction—axiomatically ill defined.

From this focus as shown in Form A.1.1, the axioms of 'Deterministic Laws', such as those governing Newtonian physics and even General Relativity, are sidelined and not integrally examined together for their foundational effect on the observed requirements for Life which resulted from the emergence of quantum phenomena, generally seen as a random effect of a big bang. A fascination with the concepts of black holes and time travel have led in current theoretical thinking to a focus on the extremes of 'Inertial Density' and event horizon 'Stress & Strain' at either end of the secondary spectrum, possibly connected by a wormhole. This unfortunately bypasses a careful investigation of 'Harmonic Motion', from which one can in fact derive a Unified Field Theory by engaging in a thorough study of Simple Harmonic and Uniform Circular Motion.

In keeping with the same logic from the last section on Life as Essential Principles in Forms L.5.0 to L.6.3, the scattered focus and understanding represented in the lower and upper semi-circles from 'Inertial Density' to 'Stress & Strain' is resolved in an understanding of 'Harmonic Motion', and shows a consistency with the axiomatic foundation of the 'Deterministic Laws' as a basis for understanding the particularity currently observed and recognized in the standard model use of 'Stochastic Parameters'.

This bypass of the last century is due to the same axiomatic failure to recognize a Universal Potential, as an essential principle with the Inertial Invariant, as a wave bearing capacity of the inertial continuum of space, from which all particles emerge as determined by well-ordered and understood conditions. Part of this oversight comes from the developments of General Relativity, that while recognizing the concept of an inertial energy-stress density, appears as yet to not understand that a change in stress of a continuum also involves a variability of strain on a microscale, even though the notion of a warpage of spacetime is readily recognized on a macroscale.

Stress is a measure of force operating on a unit of area. Strain is a ratio of change in length, area, or volume of some material measured against a unit of that same material. Such strain occurs in response to a change in force operating on the material so that it results in a change in the unit of that material. General Relativity does not appear to consider strain on the scale of an atomic nucleus, because it started its investigation and verification of gravity on an astronomical scale.

A capacity for strain, however, is the nature of an ideal elastic wave bearing continuous material and includes a propensity to undergo torsion or twisting based on the density and force operating on the continuous material of space. The energy required to create and maintain oscillation of these twists as responsible for the emergence of rest mass quanta is the missing mass-energy difference between the neutron and the proton–plus–electron resulting from the process of beta decay, Δm.

It is said that more than two equations in a book meant for a general readership will kill a publication, so here they are for those with a desire for technical information.

First, the following is a quantum version of the field equation for general relativity in a flat spacetime and showing only the space components of the stress energy tensor, $T_{\mu\nu}$, as a function, T_{ij}, of the expansion strain of the Hubble rate, Λ, where g_{ij} is a metric tensor.

$$T\left(\Lambda\right) = 2T_{ij} = g_{ij}\Lambda$$

The oscillating force components, τ_{ij}, of the expression $2T_{ij}$ can be represented by a double matrix as face centered and for the two opposing sides of a unit cube under isotropic stress and strain, where the negative sense of the second matrix equals the additive energy of the opposite sense of the first or

$$\tau_{ij} = \begin{bmatrix} -d\tau_0 & \tau_0\cos\omega t & \tau_0\sin\omega t \\ -\tau_0\cos\omega t & -d\tau_0 & \tau_0 \\ -\tau_0\sin\omega t & -\tau_0 & -d\tau_0 \end{bmatrix} - \begin{bmatrix} d\tau_0 & -\tau_0\cos\omega t & -\tau_0\sin\omega t \\ \tau_0\cos\omega t & d\tau_0 & -\tau_0 \\ \tau_0\sin\omega t & \tau_0 & d\tau_0 \end{bmatrix}$$

The symmetric components of the matrix, which are the diagonals running from upper left to lower right of each of the two matrices in brackets are responsible for quantum gravity and form the basis of Newton's gravitational constant. The anti-symmetric components, which are the remaining six terms in each of the brackets, are responsible for quantum spin angular momentum, inherent spin mass-energy, and the electro-weak and strong force of the grand unified theory. The two components together are the unified field theory that Einstein was looking for.

This form is responsible for the creation of the three principle leptons, the electron, e, the muon, μ, and the tau, τ, (not to be confused with the τ_{ij}, above), and two baryons, the neutron, n, and proton, p. This happens not from a big bang, but from a densification of cosmic space into the filaments and webbing from which galaxies form, a process generally conceptualized as involving dark matter. The sum of the mass-energy values of these five particles and their relationship is <u>exact</u>, within the standard uncertainties as the reader can verify for themself from the internet CODATA values, so that

$$5n = 3p + e + \tau + \mu$$

This statement is parsed as a breakdown of the above according to the following logic:

(1) A neutron mass is equal to that of a proton plus an electron plus the missing mass-energy in brackets incorporated in the twist between the two particles with emission of the electron.

(2) In a duplication of the first parsing, the two protons are isolated from the two electrons and two missing masses which are bracketed together. It should be clear that each instance of beta decay involves a twist in the form of Δm.

(3) This indicates that the remaining two neutrons from the left side of the above equation in the third line are equal to the value of the two remaining particles on the right side, the muon and the tau, but we must subtract the total of the bracketed terms from (1) and (2) from the third as shown.

1) $n = p + e + [\Delta m]$

2) $2n = 2p + [2e + 2\Delta m]$

3) $2n = \mu + \tau - [2e + 3\Delta m]$

Further analysis suggests, based on the analysis of beta decay and Δm in (1), that each Δm represents a twist incorporated in a decay from the more energetic state of the neutron to that of the proton as with beta, so that the muon and tau, which are more energetic than the neutrons, appear to be precursors to the neutrons. Considered as a waveform, we can think of the energy of a transmitted wave as the equivalent differential stress-energy required at the surface of a precursor, such as a neutron, to induce the wave decay transmission, which in the case of beta decay is equal to that of the electron, e, as in (1) and (2). With (3), it is well known that the muon and tau are short-lived particles; as isolated particles, the tau at 300 femtoseconds decays, 2/3 of the time into a hadron and 1/3 of the time into a muon or electron, the muon at 2 microseconds, decays into an electron. In free space a neutron has a lifetime of 14 to 15 minutes. This supports the idea that the muon and tau are precursors to the two neutrons. More significant is that the mass of the muon is much smaller than the neutron and the tau much larger, but the two together are equal to two neutrons plus two wave transmission force and three decay twists.

Muons and taus are principally observed to occur from the collision of relativistic protons, referred to as cosmic rays, with atoms in the earth's atmosphere. In that context the tau and muon are not represented as being generated in tandem, though the tau will decay to emit a muon 1/6 of the time, but the context of (3) suggests a different conclusion.

An alternative modeling posits the following process:

- Non-particulate potential energy density on a cosmic scale concentrates in large filaments and webs which support the emergence of discrete quantum waves as rotational torsional oscillation on a femtometer scale at the differential density boundary. Volumetric regions outside the filaments and webs are unsupportive of such emergence in the same frequency.

- Differential isotropic stress, e, at the boundaries of the filaments and webs, results in a form of torsional wave spalling at the femtometer scale to produce the neutron, the proton-electron as protium, and deuterium, both gaseous and ionized, as the fundamental components of the quantum system. It does this through an intermediate process of generating the tau-muon couplet that decays in a matter of a few hundred femtoseconds into a profile of two neutrons, two proton-electron pairs, or one of each.

- In order to conserve energy, it does this with respect to (3), by a 180 degree twist as a spin flip equal to Δm between the tau and muon with a transfer of energy to the muon, followed by an emission of an electron and a spin flip from each of the two waveforms as $e + \Delta m$. This is done in the process of wave spallation at a density differential as a type of internal friction response as indicated above and developed and posted elsewhere.

- The spallation process results in the close-range binding path of generated neutrons and protons to produce the lightest elements, ionized or not, principally hydrogen as protium and deuterium, and helium.

- Gravity is the quantum function of the symmetric components of the above matrix resulting from the rotational oscillation of these unit waves—the centripetal force of the oscillation—principally the neutron and its proton-electron derivative, from which we derive Newton's constant. In the absence of a quantum function to produce gravity, there is no gravitational interaction of dark, non-particulate matter.

- Spin is the quantum function of the anti-symmetric components of the matrix which produces an angular momentum and a magnetic moment with a quantum field effect. The transverse wave force of the oscillation is the strong force that binds these nuclear forms together.

- These light elements congregate via the quantum gravitational force to form gas, stellar, and galactic systems, for the eventual evolution of the heavier elements.

In summation of this Contemplation, a conservative fear of exposure to a professional risk of addressing the problem of free parameters and being seen as foolish in the process inside the physics academy, coupled with ignorance of an opportunity for axiomatic insight from outside, is responsible for this long-term bias. This risk conflicts with the perception of a liberal opportunity for progress on the part of free thinking by those outside the cloister, encouraged by public knowledge suggesting innovative breakthroughs and the notion of open debate, but hampered by ignorance of a common lexicon for communication. This is my perception of the state of things with respect to several of these potential breakthroughs on the part of my own thinking and others over the past 30 plus years.

— o —

A link to the UniServEnt.org website for research in this section with an animation of the fundamental rotational oscillation with related videos is linked here:

https://uniservent.org/physical-phenomena/

The following links provide access to unpublished monographs on this modeling.

- **Unification** Addressing the Fundamental Problem of Theoretical Physis link is here:

https://uniservent.org/pp02-addressing-the-fundamental-problem-of-theoretical-physics-2/

- **A Condensed Matter Model of Fundamental Particle Genesis as a Function of an Accelerating Cosmic Spacetime Expansion**

Fundamental Rest Mass Quanta as Simple Harmonic Rotational Oscillations of the Spacetime Continuum,
Driven by Cosmic Expansion
with
Application of the Analysis to the Experimental Field of Cold Fusion

By Martin Gibson

August 6, 2019, with Addendum September 6, 2021

A link to the paper is here:

https://uniservent.org/pp01-condensed-matter-model-of-fundamental-particles/

A related animation of torsional displacement followed by rotational oscillation is here:

https://uniservent.org/work-in-progress/

A video with animation of the fusion process of palladium catalyzed deuterium is here:

https://uniservent.org/lenr-video/

Some notes on the cold fusion process can be accessed here:

https://uniservent.org/pdd-he-initiative/

410

- **Simple Harmonic Motion in Classical and Quantum Phase Space**

  Fundamental Rest Mass Quanta as Simple Harmonic Oscillations of the Spacetime Continuum Driven by Cosmic Expansion

  By Martin Gibson

  August 1, 2013

  https://uniservent.org/pp03-simple-harmonic-motion-in-3d-phase-space/

- **A Dimensional Analysis of the Dimensionless Fine Structure Constant**

  By Martin Gibson

  December 14, 2010

  https://uniservent.org/pp06-fine-structure-constant/

- **Excerpt of Appendix D – Exponentiation and a System of Natural Logarithms from**

  A Classical Complex 4-Wave Foundation of the Cosmic-Quantum Mechanism

  Fundamental Rest Mass Quanta as Simple Harmonic Oscillations of
  the Spacetime Continuum
  at Resonant Frequency and Wave Number, Driven by Cosmic Expansion

  By Mart Gibson

  October 14, 2006

  https://uniservent.org/pp08x-excerpt-from-appendix-d/

- **Construction of the Natural Numbers from a Real Exponential Field**

By Mart Gibson

July 19, 2007

https://uniservent.org/pp09-construction-of-the-natural-numbers-from-a-real-exponential-field-2/

THE BROWSER ECONOMY EXECUTIVE SUMMARY

An effective state is fundamental to the operation of free markets, as essential as their ready and willing buyers and sellers. More than a necessary expense, the state is an integral institution of an economy's capital and like all capital must be adequately maintained for the efficient provision of final goods and services. The question for anyone with an interest in policy effectiveness in such provision is simple; along the spectrum of possible governmental scope of operations, from basic policing to provision of infrastructure, to a comprehensive safety net, to public ownership of components of the productive apparatus, where should we place our policy target? We take it for granted that any implemented policy should be amended or discarded, if deemed ineffective. We feel some urgency in the determination of this target, given the recent global recession with its anemic recovery. We use the myth of a pre-market Browser Economy to elucidate the oft-unrecognized disparate nature of utility and value in current economic thinking.

It is the premise of this piece that the principal goal of policy in a modern economy must be to insure "life, liberty, and the pursuit of happiness" for its citizenry and welcome guests. It need not attempt to guarantee that happiness, in fact it cannot, but it should not allow that pursuit by one club to impede the pursuit by others. In a market economy in which virtually every good or service consumed in the satisfaction of this goal involves a monetary exchange and in which the pursuit of this goal by some private parties results over short time horizons in an upheaval of production, trade, and employment that for many is the only access to money for such exchange, maintenance of the necessary liquidity cannot be assured by private funding and is the ultimate responsibility of the public sector. In fact, it is the responsibility of Congress alone according to the Constitution to "coin Money," and "regulate the Value thereof", though the general consensus has permitted the creation of money through the issuance of private banking debt since well before that document's creation.

We find in this study that for a given level of liquidity, as quantified by expenditures on final consumption and on capital goods and services, where capital expenditures include both public and private sectors, an optimum equilibrium ratio of 0.618... for

(1) final consumption to total expenditures is equal to that of

(2) capital to final consumption expenditures.

Conditions favorable to overall economic growth, meaning a rise in the general standard of living, are indicated by ratios somewhat below the optimum for (1) and above that figure for (2).

Examination of World Bank data for the period 1970 to 2013 shows a ratio range for the world economy of a few percentage points below (1) and for the OECD nation average of a similar range, before rising above (1) in 2009. Some notable economies trending several points above the target for this duration are Greece, Mexico, and until 2004, Brazil and India. The U.S. trend rose above (1) in 1982 during the Reagan administration with the implementation of supply side policy and has risen gradually, with the exception of most of the Clinton tenure when it stabilized, to a current level of approximately 7 points above the mark.

With this optimization level in mind, we analyze the Z.1 Federal Reserve September, 2014 data of U.S. sector and combined accounts, comparing the annual values for 1975, 2005, and 2013 as a percent of GDP and total asset value, with respect to structural changes based on those percentage differences between 1975 and 2005, 1975 and 2013, and 2005 and 2013. As compared with 1975, as of 2013 there was a 16.1% sector swing in percent of domestic net worth to households at 11.1% and ROW at 5.0%, from the business and public sectors, most noticeably in a percentage reduction of Nonfinancial Noncorporate business of 3.9% and Federal government of 7.8%. We might expect this from supply side policies over this period, though the NN business figure is perhaps surprising, but what is more surprising, given the prognostications and promises of the Hayekian school, is that the return on total domestic wealth as measured by GDP as a percentage of Personal Sector asset value, decreased by 5.9% from to 21.0% in 1975 to 15.1% in 2005 before the financial crisis, before recovering slightly to a 5.4% differential in 2013 at 15.6% after modest market intervention. The differential figures using Personal Sector net worth are 0.2% less.

In final summaries of consolidated accounts, we add figures for land, infrastructure, and human capital to the national balance sheet to demonstrate the unfounded concern among some parties about the size of the national debt and to emphasize the lack of wisdom in failing to maintain public infrastructure and human capital. We also state why, in the context of free competition in the production of commodity final consumption products, labor is reduced to a commodity level, defined as compensation to abundant, fungible labor for no more than paycheck to paycheck costs of living. As a result, employers producing commodity goods for the global competitive markets cannot compensate such labor, regardless of skill set, for sunk education costs or long-term medical and retirement costs.

In light of these developments, United States policy recommendations are made for restructuring of business and personal taxes so as to target costs of common or public goods and services use and to get rid of arbitrary income taxes and thereby all loopholes with replacement through the use of electronic fiat currency as a Universal Basic Income equally for all citizens as a right of citizenship, to decouple long term social from immediate product costs in worker compensation, and to provide for a clear separation of basic public and premium private provision and insurance in health, education, property and finance, such as FDIC coverage. This latter matter indicates a separation of private and publicly backed banks and an end to "too big to fail" status. The intent of all envisioned policy is to free up entrepreneurial efforts to grow and succeed or fail on their own as private concerns and to provide for a rational, comprehensive public safety net, secured against ill-advised privatization.[6]

My early interest in economics and politics was renewed in the early 2000's with the collapse of the dot.com bubble, geopolitical events in the wake of the 9/11 attacks, and the financial meltdown of

---

[6] Text in Italics taken from the UniServEnt.org website

the fall of 2008, none of which were a surprise. Having briefly witnessed the vapidity of centralized economic planning and control of the Soviet system in the guise of egalitarian communism in the early 70's and having lived for over forty years since the start of the Reagan administration with the neoliberal system of laisse faire capitalism driven by the equally spiritless notions of greed and rank consumerism, I was looking for an understanding and articulation of a middle ground that served the individual interests and freedom of the soul along with its collective responsibilities to the community.

In the U.S., the common observation of the increasing concentration of wealth in the control of the few was paradoxically attributed on the one hand to the successful wisdom of the system of private enterprise, while the social costs created by those private interests, unrecognized by the market system and passed on to the community—the 'externalities' as the economists are so fond of calling them—on the other hand were deemed incapable of being addressed by the public sector through taxation as being too expensive. That is except for the needs of maintaining the military-industrial complex designed to protect those private interests.

The vacuous, trickle-down notion that the private system, if left to itself, would take care of all the needs of the public sector—the needs of the community—reminds one of the old adages attributed to harsh times in the Soviet Union during the Great Patriotic War, fought by the Red Army, but paid for in large part by the solidarity of the Working Women of America in the war effort.

A group of workers in the midst of the fray sent a request up the appropriate ladder for resupply of food. They received a reply from the party after some time instructing them to just tighten their belts, to which the workers of course responded, "Comrade, please send belts."

The response of elites, be they Soviet style communists, welfare state socialists, state capitalist autocrats, or free market capitalists, has often been couched in a common misconception about the nature of wealth, generally valued in terms of monetary transactions, based on the myth that such wealth exists primarily in equivalent monetary stores of value in banks. The concept that wealth principally resides as financial (FC) and real (RC) market valued capital assets over a varying range of distribution between the public and the private sectors is an ergodidiocy, aggravated by the fascination with money as tokens of satisfaction—a satisfaction found only in the eye of the individual beholder and holder of that money.

Financial and real assets considered as wealth is a secondary fact; the principal store of wealth is the community of human beings, and therefore human souls from which such asset value is derived. It is human ability and effort as human capital (HC) in concert with the resource base of Mother Nature that is the source of all derivative financial and real capital; first, in the ability and effort of the community, materially and ideally, to produce those real assets in a sustained manner as required to meet the ongoing needs of that community, and second, in the spiritually guided wisdom of that community, collectively and individually, in assigning financial asset and market value to those capabilities and efforts. In terms of national accounting practices such as the US Federal Reserve and World Bank systems, said *capabilities* are referred to and valued in general market terms as Stocks—Forms—and said *efforts* are referred to as Flows—Processes—where the Stocks are the net accumulation of Flows as of the current accounting periods after deduction for current depletion

418

of those Stocks and current consumption from those Flows which occur in the process of producing them.

In caricature, the left views the money in private accounts as a public good that has been taken by exploitation and 'externalities' from those that have been reduced to living paycheck to paycheck at the level of commodity labor, and the right views the money in public accounts as a private good that has been expropriated by taxation for unnecessary public projects that should have been in the ability and effort of the private sector to allocate and would have been, had it not been for the intrusiveness of the state in valuing those abilities and efforts. In contrast, in the enlightened terms of the principle of human capital, the left focuses on the largely unrecognized and insufficiently nurtured wealth of non-market valued human capital (NHC) while the right focuses on the recognized, sustained wealth of the elites as market valued human capital (MHC).

The true wealth is a measure of the natural resources of the planetary biosphere, as raw and produced materials—including the sun that provides it with light and heat and the moon that provides it with a minor level of reflected solar light and the gravitational effects of the tides—along with human resources, natural and developed, currently available as Stocks used in the production of current Flows to the community. The only assets that show up in the Fed and World Bank figures are for financial and real capital, with no recognition given for human capital, market or non-market valued.

This gross oversight and the well-known trend in the concentration of market valued capital and income over the past forty years led me to research this trend in 2013. I was motivated by public press observations of structural changes in the national accounts in the U.S. since the advent of supply side thinking with the start of the

Reagan administration, and while there were general comments of shifts from domestic to defense spending, I was interested in finding out the details. I was spurred on by a brief email thread a few years prior with an author of a recently published book on the application of mathematics, which was the author's field of expertise. He had asked me why, as an economist, for all the advances in the standard of living over the past century, the average living wage of a semi-skilled worker adjusted for the cost of living had not increased.

The answer to this question is straightforward, although I have no idea how well understood it is in the academic economics community, based on some of the published thinking of that community. In a market economy with abundance of fungible labor of any skill set, absent any wage support legislation, the cost of that labor will be determined by the cost of the goods and services required to get that worker to their place of work on a week-to-week basis, perhaps month-to-month if they are salaried. In other words, competition in a labor market in which there are more workers needing such jobs than jobs available will limit a worker's pay over time to commodity levels. All the cost of living for the technological advances that we associate with an increase in the standard of living over that century—for automobiles and fuel, for home electrification and communications, for prepared food products, and the rest—are built into the costs and wages of getting that fungible laborer to work every day, but no more. There is nothing in those wages for private safety net investment unless legislatively required.

If we value a product that we produce based on the amount of time it takes to produce it, and we put a price on our time based on the value of the product, as the overall productivity of the community increases, the time-based price placed on the product will decrease. Initially one basket of goods required to sustain a soul takes 8 hours to produce and so we pay ourselves ℏ8, but after developing a new technology it only takes us 4 hours to produce that same basket or one of equivalent utility, so we pay each member of the community ℏ4. The community then gets to play four more hours or to build and repair their cottages or their tools at no charge to themselves. This was the general scenario during the Middle Ages in Europe in which agrarian economic activity was the primary mode of production, in which the primary technologically based change in productivity was the ebb and flow of the seasons.

In an increasingly industrialized community, the agrarian sector of the economy based on the seasons, with its seasonal periods of relative leisure decreases, and increasing numbers of the non-farm community are increasingly free to work longer and faster under more arduous conditions—such as in the coal mines of Wales and in Pennsylvania in which my Welsh great grandfather died along with three of his sons in the Avondale Mine fire of September 6, 1869— to keep up with the needs of increasingly productive machinery in answering the appeal of the mercantile elites for a sustained exchange of cash flow for products in their businesses.

Since the workers only need enough food & drink, enough shoes & clothing to be warm & dry in their home and to stay healthy & productive at their place of work from day to day or perhaps week to week, they only need ℏ4 pay—based on the productivity of the agrarian sector—on a day to day basis to free up enough of their time at their work to produce 8 or even 12 hours of product for the mercantile elites, aided by their elite professional agents, in exchange for the ℏ4 needed by the workers.

This exchange works particularly well for the fast-food workers of the world, except for the fact that it doesn't allow them much time to build or repair their cottages and tools, such as the cars needed to sleep in and get them to work, since the elites don't have need for or want to pay for mass transit or tents that might clutter the landscape. It doesn't allow the workers much time or cash to go to their health, childcare, & educational professionals on a pay as you go basis, since their isn't a lot of excess cash in the ℏ4 to pay for the doctor, childcare, and school, and the elites of the community think it is better to let the market take care of those general welfare needs based on their perception of what those needs might be.

If this sounds a lot like a sarcastic Marxist observation, that's because a thing is what it is. Unfortunately, the materialist analysis of Marx with respect to the exploitative nature of capitalist production when controlled by the elites enamored with neoliberal, laissez faire capitalism is as true now as it was in 1871 bourgeois Paris and 100 years later in the Soviet Union, though ingeniously obscured by the introduction of 'externalities' and Madison Avenue. Whether under capitalism or fascism or socialism or communism, elites exploit the working people because they find themselves in some position to maximize upside opportunity for their own material benefit or to minimize the perception of downside risk by clinging to the ideals of the status quo as the right thing to do, and not because they want to serve humanity for the spiritual benefit of one and all by doing what is just. From that position they must make a choice among the offerings as they feel so motivated by greed and selfishness, by fear and loathing, or by love and wisdom—or as might be stated in this last choice, by the apostle Paul, by faith, hope, and charity. Unfortunately for many, the easiest of these choices is not the last.

The Soul within the Essential Trigon

Form Q.1.0

I am a monist, I suppose I would properly be called a neutral monist according to Wikipedia, though I am still working on that definition. There is the concept of dual-aspect monism to be considered, but logic suggests that in truth we must go beyond two and even the traditional concept of a trinity to the concept of a quaternity monism as introduced herein and shown in Form Q.1.0. My understanding of history, of faith and science, suggests we embrace the three as the material, ideal and spiritual capacities of Life, along with Its inherent capacity to replicate, to image those three essential capacities as souls in a distinct but interconnected manner, as the basis for understanding and addressing the needs of the community.

Marx well understood the past, that material conditions cannot be changed or explained away by incantations and appeals to bourgeois sensibilities devoid of collective actions to address the material needs of the entire community. Plato well understood the future, that the social world of mankind—of mind-kind without regard to sex—was naturally heir to the same ideal processes conveyed in the dialectics of Socrates concerning the ideal Goods of the Republic, the Goods of Justice, of Honor, of Prosperity, of Freedom, and of Power, in dealing with the material conditions presented by the environment and human nature to the community, by the ideal Philosopher King and Guardians of the Republic. Christ well understood the ever present now, that the spiritual expression of a Philosopher King of both Plato and the Hebrews is ever as a Moral Authority to establish Justice in the community Here and Now rather than as a vision of an earthly and material kingdom to come. It is the vision of that Moral Authority of Christ that leads to the material realization of the end of class division glimpsed in the social vision of Marx through the implementation of the ideal of Justice in the community in the vision of Plato and his Republic—now.

As in Form Q.1.1, when Justice is central to the community and to the individual soul, then the remaining Goods will be in balance, of Honor and Prosperity from the left to right and of Freedom and Power from the bottom to top. Then the true capital of the community, the human capital, along with the necessary real and financial capital they generate, can be properly nourished and protected from the cradle to the grave and allowed the free and independent initiative of best serving the community and the individual souls, without allegiance to any of the above listed 'isms', so vaunted or denigrated by the current affiliations and self-identifications of their elites and beguiled followers.

In much of the current global popular culture, the first three capacities and their corresponding natures are considered and understood as unrelated to each other. In general, an understanding of religion and theology are pertinent to the top trigon as the spiritual nature; of physical and biological sciences, to the left-hand trigon as the material nature; and of philosophy, social science, and the arts, to the right-hand trigon as the ideal nature. For cultural and historical reasons, the spiritual nature has tended to remain disconnected, particularly within certain portions of the Christian community, but the material and ideal natures are increasingly understood to be interrelated.

An unbiased study of the material world is impossible without an understanding of the ideas of the ideal nature, but there appears to be insufficient axiomatic rigor used in attempts to understand the interrelationship of the two natures, in part because the two are not understood by many to be distinct—or if so, precisely how. Even less well understood is the essential integrated reality of the material-ideal duality with the spiritual natures. This is due in large part to the predominant reliance on the sense of sight in the observation of the material natures and in formulation of models of their interactions. This predominance is to the slighting of the other senses and feelings, since spirit is generally deemed to be invisible to human sight, if not essentially formless, while still being sensible to well-tuned human capacities as a presence or energy field or emanating communicable quality such as love or good humor.

The human reliance on the sense of sight in navigating the existential opportunities and risks of material nature predisposes the soul to categorizing forms and processes literally viewed as pleasurable or painful, in broad terms as good or bad, and in the broadest of these in which that pleasure or pain is recognized or fantasized as resulting from a moral or intentionally hostile act, as good or evil.

The distinction between bad and evil is important. The general judgement is that a risk which is likely to end in a bad result should be mitigated, while a risk that is likely to end in an evil result should be eliminated. The costs of eliminating a risk deemed as evil are likely to exceed, often greatly, the cost of mitigating that same risk seen as a bad bet. It behooves us to use caution in deciding what is evil rather than what is simply bad, beyond a narrow consideration of elimination and mitigation costs. From the monistic perspective, evil is not recognized as a distinct nature, but rather as an ideal Quality that in form or process has yet to reach fruition or is moribund—as in past its prime—in either case as unripe fruit.

Hence for those who have some biblical literacy, we have the allegory of the Garden of Eden—and it is just that, an allegory—in which eating of the fruit of the Tree of the Knowledge of Good and Evil results in more than a soul's exposure to the peril of eating fruit that might be unripe or rotten as recognized by the taste as being either good or bad. This allegory is not meant as a lesson in what things are good and what things are bad for the soul. In the Garden of Eden before the Fall, Adam and Eve still know to eat the sweet fruit and spit out the bitter. This knowledge of good and evil is not based on a gustatory revelation to individual souls of a pleasurable or bitter experience, of good or bad meant to counsel repetition in pursuing opportunity or avoidance of encountering risk of such peril going forward.

Such knowledge carries the inevitability of knowing that even good tasting fruit that may itself seem harmless, can still be existentially evil and unfit for human consumption. It carries with it the naked knowledge of having caught oneself acting in a perverse manner—of doing something that it understands is contrary to authoritative wisdom. There is no implied connotation of anything

426

sexual in this idea of nakedness, rather it is the recognition of conscious isolation as a separate self, of knowing oneself as an independent agent capable of doing something contrary to its own nature for which the action has consequences—of knowing oneself as an 'ego', Latin for the core singular personal pronoun of being, 'I', for which the first person pronoun used by the Diety of the Garden is not 'I' but 'we'. 'Let us make man in <u>Our</u> image,' thus saith the Gods and Goddesses, which is the Elohim speaking with One voice.

To cover up the recognition of being an ego, the soul must either deny the independent agency of that activity—first Adam with, 'Eve made me do it', then Eve, 'the Serpent made me do it'—or it must convince itself that the action is neither contrary to its nature nor consequential. To perform this cover-up, the soul creates a 'persona'—a mask as a character in a classical play—a fig leaf to hide the risk, the fright, and the illusion of independent—naked—existence.

Thus, the fruit of the Tree of the Knowledge of Good and Evil is denial or feigned ignorance of any perception of the soul's innate, but heretofore unself-conscious agency. The penalty for what becomes a habitual denial or ignorance of the soul is the continued realization of self-conscious activity as an existential expulsion from Eden—whether it is an authentic or an illusory expulsion—even as that soul struggles to redeem itself from the illusion by concentration on doing good work and to avoid the evil of ongoing toil and tribulation to hopes of regaining entrance to the Garden.

The historical record states that in the world of Orthodox Christian teaching after the Second Council of Constantinople in 553, the pre-existence of souls was removed from the Judeo-Christian Church teaching, making the Old Testament allegorical basis of original sin problematic. In the Greek teachings of transmigration of souls, the memory of past lives is obscured for what should be obvious reasons of preventing distractions of recollection of what might be the joyous or horrific affairs of the past, in order to facilitate concentration on the circumstances of a soul's current corporal, familial, and cultural embodiment.

Those who grow up thinking of themselves as existential beings defined principally on their personal histories and relationships, focused here-and-now on the recreational–educational sense experience offered by the opportunity and risk represented in the material and ideal worlds, may or may not be aware of any prior lives or even think of themselves as souls. Such lack of awareness need not be seen as a detriment as long as the soul has a moral compass and does not follow the senses into uncharted risks, which can carry a peril with it into the afterworld. In time, a soul that comes to recognize—first as just a glimpse—their spiritual nature within, will tire of the allure of the senses and seek a greater truth. Those who have begun the conscious rise to the enlightened level of logical–intuitive initiates come to understand that they are here to share in the growing recognition of a divine plan and purpose, to facilitate their education along with their recreation, for themselves and those who are still engrossed in the world of material sensation.

Whether starting out as 'fallen' or simply new to the journey, as an independent soul, enlightenment to the spiritual nature cannot be completed through doing good work and avoiding evil alone as an isolated, psychologically naked, self-conscious ego. That soul must begin to understand that they are a focus of Life experience as part of a collective Soul Nature, inherently connected to other souls in or out of material embodiment and they must make and embrace a conscious recognition of that Truth.

Through the committed practices of harmlessness and contemplative, dispassionate detachment—by learning to replace existential fear with love in understanding life and to displace ignorance with wisdom in the conduct of one's behavior—the soul begins to lose the sense of naked self-consciousness and the associated need for clothing the ego by a denial of the ability of choice. They begin to give up the unconscious need for a binary personality mask in navigating the opportunities and risks of the community as if viewing a cast of good and evil characters in order to pick a part, and instead start to recognize the roles through the skill of the actors in the play.

Until the need for recognition and affirmation of the ego is overcome, the perception of vulnerability to <u>illusory</u> threats from the environment, other actors, and oneself as evil will prove an impediment to the growth of Love and Wisdom of the soul. Fueled by mortal fear and ignorance, founded on an inability to skillfully gauge the mix of opportunity and risk in any change of circumstance with confidence, the soul defaults to assumptions of risk as the manifestation of malevolent intent and to the known methods for dealing with such malevolence.

If malevolence is truly the case, there is even more reason to respond to a peril wisely based on rational understanding of the circumstances and not out of an instinctive fight or flight mechanism. There are circumstances which call for instinctive action, but when time permits, circumspection is better, allowing in the same event a more conservative overview of risk and a more liberal vision of opportunity.

Opportunity and risk of a given subject are the two sides of the same coin, though they are rarely evenly weighted. Current use of 'conservative' versus 'liberal' as political terms, employed with invective and scorn, are attempts to instill fear of unsubstantiated or spurious risk and ignorance of unrecognized or veiled opportunity.

The conventional polite political terms used in the public literature for the wings of the geopolitical spectrum, liberal and conservative, are of course 'ismized' to become liberalism and conservativism, as if this ismization lent any understanding to the discussion. Even were we to extend the politeness to liberal-leaning and conservative-leaning it would not help. Using left and right or left-wing and right-wing only adds to the confusion, as this political perspective depends on whether you are referencing a party you are looking at or one you are looking out from.

The charts that follow incorporate my perspective of the way this terminology arises based on an initial condition of material natures on the left and ideal natures on the right, which in turn can be attributed to conventional thinking of concrete left-brain logical and fluid right-brain intuitive functions as developed here. The left and right brain functions are assigned as if one is looking out of the page from the chart, so that Prosperity shows up on the right side of the chart from that perspective and Honor on the left. As we shall see, that has nothing to do with the true nature of liberalism and conservatism, which are instead rightly understood as an attitude in the approach to weighing some quality with respect to its mix of opportunity and risk.

From moment to moment the focus of the soul is subject to an evaluation of existential conditions with respect to *any change* in a current condition of opportunity–risk. Opportunity–risk is appropriate instead of the customary 'Opportunity & Risk' because existential conditions should be understood as embodying an inherent bi-potential element in any choice, whether we choose to retain the current condition or choose to make a change. In any such choice, we retain or engage an opportunity and a risk of experiencing a change for the better or for the worse, however we may want to define better or worse.

This does not mean that choice is a zero-sum game. For example, if the general opportunity–risk with respect to the probability and payoff of a choice is 90%-10%—in practice, probability and payoff are rarely the same—and a community has a conservative tradition of risk avoidance and is looking for a 99%-01% payoff, the community choice will be trending at an undocumented, perhaps unaccountable loss, to the tune of 9%. If that same community has a liberal tradition of opportunity assumption looking for an 70%-30% payoff, the community will be trending at a gain; the 30% loss expectation will be more than compensated by the 10% actuality, for a perceived net of 20%.

Communities are not monolithic in that loss and gain are not spread evenly across the community. The 9% loss doesn't make it to the top nor the 20% gain, to the bottom of any ism, though the second case at least has the potential for some redistribution of the opportunity gains under the Christian concept of Charity or the Platonic concept of Justice. Non-conservative segments of the community looking for 99%-01% payoff end up with an accountable loss assigned to the bottom tiers, while the non-liberal segments looking for 70%-30% are happy to take literal credit for the 20% gain.

In addition to the Soul's innate and instinctive capacity for dealing with opportunity–risk are the Soul's intuitive capacity for dealing with love-fear and the logical capacity for dealing with learned wisdom-ignorance. Liberal–conservative therefore, is the bi-potential attitude of every soul in dealing with opportunity–risk, love–fear, and wisdom–ignorance. As such, for an astute, skilled soul, this indicates a liberal attitude intended to enhance, increase, or affirm a condition understood to offer opportunity, love, and wisdom, and a conservative attitude intended to diminish, decrease, or avoid a condition understood to offer risk, fear, and ignorance.

The problem facing the soul and the community lies in learning to skillfully assess the percentage of opportunity–risk—which should as nearly as possible equal 100%—innately recognized in any circumstance we observe in our environment, of our love–fear in our intuitive response from and to the circumstance, and of our wisdom–ignorance in logically dealing with that circumstance.

This necessarily implies a couple of things that run counter to conventional wisdom. Personally, and politically considered, liberalism is not the opposite of conservatism and vice versa. An anti-liberal attitude is one that fears and ignores a well-understood opportunity, just as an anti-conservative attitude is one that loves and counts as wisdom pursuing an exhilarating, ill-conceived risk. Both anti-attitudes can end in a pathological condition for both the soul and the community.

Enlightened understanding concerning some condition is conservative in its inclination to diminish the elements of a perceived risk, along with publicly illuminating the fear and ignorance associated with that condition, while liberal in its inclination to increase the aspects of opportunity, through the exercise of love and wisdom in the community. For a given condition, all other things being equal, decreasing risk increases opportunity, decreasing fear and ignorance about that condition gives light to the capacity for love and wisdom; increasing opportunity decreases risk, increases the capacity for love and wisdom and lowers the atmosphere of fear and ignorance.

The application of these dual inclinations in the other direction, increasing risk, fear, and ignorance in the name of conservatism or decreasing opportunity, love, and wisdom in the name of liberalism—of freedom—is a recipe for dissolution and disaster. Liberalism, as the notion of the pursuit of individual freedom for even the least of those among us through the enhancement of opportunity, love, and wisdom within the community, is fundamentally wedded to the notion of protection of that freedom for those least among us. That is done conservatively by mitigation of the risk that rises from neglect and predation by the powerfully positioned, through relief from fear and alleviation of ignorance within that same community.

In Plato's Republic, Justice is the principal Ideal or Good of the community, where Justice is defined as each soul pursuing a livelihood for which they are well suited and from which they derive the greatest happiness—this being a utopia, after all. The point here is not for the creation of a state or government that decides who does what in the community. Rather it is the utopian notion that the community should provide the means and opportunity for each individual soul to reach the position within the community that offers the best service to that community <u>and at the same time</u> the greatest happiness and realization of <u>expertise</u> for that soul. To Plato, the inhabitants of the community are souls and not simply mortal human beings, so they are deemed to have the capacity to grow in responsibility and learning over the course of their lifetime(s).

We can extend this understanding of the Essential Trigon to the work of Plato's Republic in hopes of providing some insight concerning the current global state of affairs. In very brief restatement and uncited form, Plato devised the concept of an ideal Republic or Just City State, a community ruled by an aristocracy of learned experts as philosophers, led by a Philosopher King and his/her Guardians of the City. The guardians are selected by the community at a young age regardless of sex and educated in the required fields of study for eventual service of the interests of the community. From among these guardians—who live a Spartan existence—a Philosopher King is selected to rule the community, the chief responsibility of the rule being to ensure the valued primary ideal Good of the community, which is Justice, as just defined.

Honor of the cohort in service to the community, Prosperity of the family through capital accumulation, Freedom of the individual soul to pursue happiness, and Power of the tyro to grab the reins of the system when everything appears to be going haywire, all are alternative Goods of the community when Justice of the Guardians of the community fails in dispensing civic responsibility as discussed in Plato's Republic. The work of Plato seen through the dialectical example of Socrates depicts the devolution of the utopian Republic, from rule by a non-hereditary philosophical Aristocracy supported and educated by the community, to a moribund Tyranny ruled by uneducated elites under the guise of an authoritative execution of divinely sanctioned purpose.

From the ideal Republic, Plato describes a process of decay in which the Just Community devolves through a series of stages in response to natural and social stress and strain within the community and among an environment of other city states. In the process of the devolution of the Republic, in response to foreign invasion or domestic turmoil a Timocracy of military elites and their affiliated cohorts inspired by the ideal of Honorable Service come to rule the affairs of the community and to some degree the ideal of Justice suffers.

Under this rule, skillful commercial production and trade is fostered with a resulting hereditary accumulation of human, real, and monetary wealth, and the ascent of the ideal of developing Prosperity comes to rule the community through an Oligarchy. As a result, less skillful and less hereditarily positioned souls are moved to the sidelines of the community and the ideal of Justice suffers further.

In time, the sidelined and disenfranchised souls, motivated by the desire for greater freedom in pursuing their own interests in the community come to rule as a Democracy by enfranchisement or revolt, though affairs come to be led by public personas through appeals to the crowd. As education of the polity is allowed to languish in the civic climate of short-term interests, the ideal of Justice suffers yet again.

In such climate, amid crises and with members of the community having lost the initial vision of the Guardians, tyros of the community vie for position and from their melee a Tyranny, with a Tyrant to rule autocratically, emerges with the perceived Power to solve the crisis. With the material and social motivations of a juvenile, lacking true understanding of the spiritual and ideal natures of the soul, Justice becomes the capricious rule of the tyrant and chaos reigns in the community. Only a reinstitution of timocracy or oligarchy, and in time the advent of a new philosopher king and guardianship, can sort things out.

The history since Plato bears out many of the dynamic components of the political and economic narrative found in his writing, so evident in current global events. We can provide a better understanding of this dynamic in keeping with the previous forms, by placing the Community of Plato within the Essential Trigon in a manner that relates the five Platonic ideals of the community to the material, ideal and spiritual natures of the souls within the community.

BALANCE OF SCIENCE & FAITH IN THE ESSENTIAL TRIGON - III

Neo-Platonist Balance of Science and Faith within the Essential Trigon
Science: Technology Uses Material-Ideal Natures along Prosperity — Honor spectrum
Faith: Intuitive Logic Uses Spiritual-Soul Natures along Power — Freedom spectrum

Form Q.1.1

With respect to Form L.5.0, as seen in Form Q.1.1, 'Power' is placed in the omnipotent 'Universality' position of the intentional capacity of Life; 'Freedom', as 'Particularity', is assigned the innate capacities of the individual souls as a reflection of the imaging capacity of the that Life through the soul natures; 'Prosperity', as

'Station', assumes the intuitive capacity of the soul to recognize and utilize the formal capacity of the mind in implementing the inertial capacity of the material natures for the benefit of the community; 'Honor', as 'Motion', in the logical capacity active in the community to protect and serve at the risk of individual loss, in the interest of the entire community; all of which if done, as shown as in 'Dynamic Balance', by and for the benefit of all, resulting in 'Justice' for the entire community. Justice is based on the central Guardianship of the Philosopher King, however that guardianship is envisioned, constituted, and personified in the rules and regulations of the community. It may be as simple a guardianship as the competent education and maintenance in the public mind of an enlightened constitution and legal enshrinement of the Just civic values of the community.

On this basis, we can associate the ideal Goods of the community with the corresponding constitution of that community. When the community is in balance, Justice is the central Good of the soul and the community, and the remaining four of the public values are kept in the proper perspective and place according to the material, ideal, and spiritual natures of the soul as recognized in the community.

In the Form Q.1.2, Justice, the point of balance in the center of the circle, has been displaced into the upper capacity of the spiritual natures as Freedom and popular Democracy are moved by the bubble to the center of the small hexagon as the current condition, indicating an imbalance in the community. This means the level of the platform at the screw at the innate capacity vertex is elevated above the other two vertices. It is not at its optimum position vis a vis the other two and needs to be lowered in order to bring the Justice bubble back to center.

The Community of Plato within the Essential Trigon
Individual Freedom as popular Democracy or Anarchy

Form Q.1.2

This statement of imbalance may at first appear to be counter-intuitive, but Freedom in this context is the result of a culture that is focused on the freedom of the individual at the risk of abdicating responsibility to the community. If the individuals are mature and have developed responsibility within the community, they will undertake to enhance opportunity and minimize any risk to that community. In our level metaphor, this is accomplished by increasing Opportunity> and reducing <Risk by turning the liberal-conservative screw to level the platform, which will bring the bubble of Justice back to center. Increasing opportunity in this case means widening access to opportunity for the *community*. Decreasing risk means increasing the responsibility and decision making of the *community*.

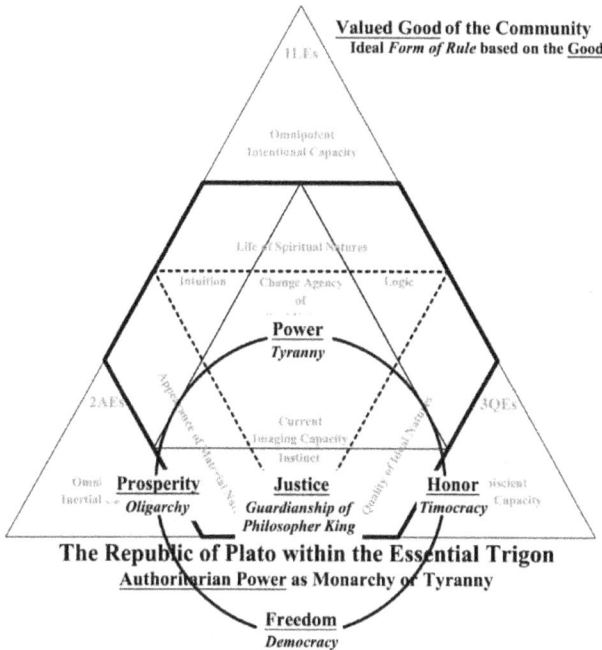

Form Q.1.3

If the bubble appears as in Form Q.1.3, with Power positioned in the center of the small hexagon and with Justice in the control of the innate capacity of the souls, dependent on the development level and innate capacity of a tyro and followers, below the level of the two intuitive and logical capacities, tyranny results in the community as shown. The same turning of the screw in the opposite direction will once again increase Opportunity> and reduce <Risk for the community and the souls within it.

Form Q.1.4 shows Honor at the center of the community in a Timocracy, a military meritocracy, perhaps as a form of socialism, indicating the level of the screw at the intuitive vertex is lower andor the logical vertex is higher than the innate vertex. Increasing Love and reducing Fear while reducing Ignorance and increasing Wisdom in the conduct of community affairs is required to move the bubble back to center. This echoes the comments concerning Form L.6.3 and the balancing of the motivations of the passions.

The Republic of Plato within the Essential Trigon
Honor of the Cohort as Timocracy or Communalism/Socialism

Form Q.1.4

On the other side of the baseplate at Form Q.1.5, in the central place of Prosperity, an Oligarchy has a similar prominence. In both cases, it is an insufficient extension of Love and Wisdom beyond that recognized in the family to the community at large, with an allowance of a surfeit of Fear and Ignorance outside the family that produce the imbalance shown. The reversal of those trends are required to rebalance the community by enhancing a liberal attitude toward the development and growth of Opportunity, Love, and Wisdom while fostering a conservative attitude for reducing Risk, Fear, and Ignorance in the public realm for the entire community.

The Republic of Plato within the Essential Trigon
Family Prosperity as Oligarchy or Private Capitalism

Form Q.1.5

In Form Q.1.6, we show the four extremes of political economy found in the global community. Motivation in the extreme pursuit of the utopian ideal Goods of Freedom and Prosperity result in the notion of Laissez Faire Capitalism; of Freedom and Honor, in the notion of Democratic Socialism; of Honor and Power, in the notion of Authoritarian Socialism; and of Prosperity and Power, in Authoritarian Capitalism.

In all these extreme examples, Justice is shoved to the sidelines for all but the elites of their communities. In the first, Form Q.1.7, those that are not adequately positioned to participate in the community are deprived of Justice. In the second, Form Q.1.8, the most creative and entrepreneurial thinking souls run a similar risk. In the third, Form Q.1.9, those who are not in the elite are left with the injustice of living in ignorance about their ability to excel as souls. In the fourth case, Form Q.1.10, those not in the elite ranks suffer the injustice of living in endemic fear of economic ruin and depravation.

Globalism & the Community of Plato within the Essential Trigon

Form Q.1.6

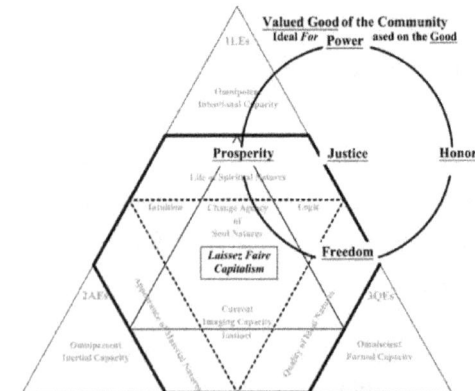

Globalism & the Community of Plato within the Essential Trigon
Extreme effects of Prosperity & Freedom on Laissez Faire Capitalism

Form Q.1.7

CONTEMPLATION III — the Quality of Political Economy

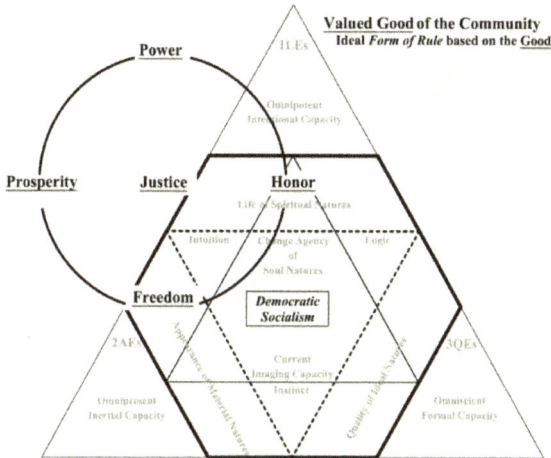

Globalism & the Community of Plato within the Essential Trigon
Extreme effects of Honor & Freedom on Democratic Socialism

Form Q.1.8

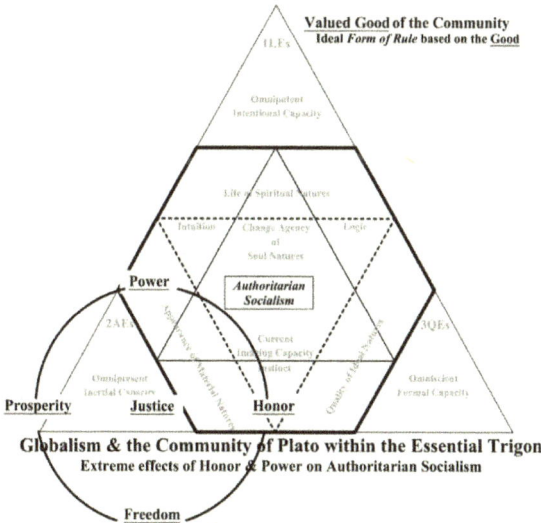

Globalism & the Community of Plato within the Essential Trigon
Extreme effects of Honor & Power on Authoritarian Socialism

Form Q.1.9

443

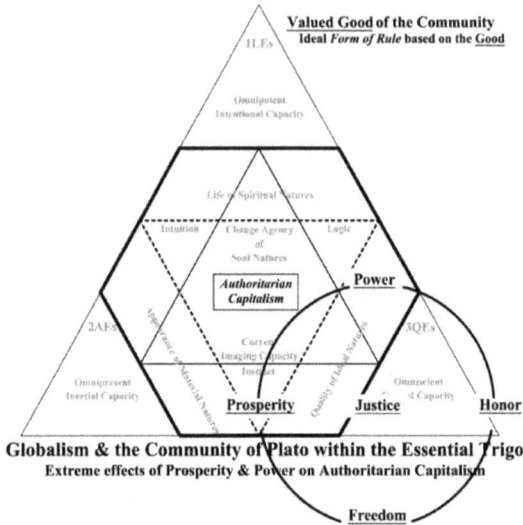

Form Q.1.10

ANALYSIS of DOMESTIC & GLOBAL STRUCTURAL CHANGE

To gain a greater insight into the operation of the U.S. and global economy through an understanding of the structural changes in that integrated system, in 2013 I researched global trends of the last 50 years or so, a period which has encompassed my adult life since my initial exposure to the field of political economy. A review of World Bank consumption spending as a percentage of the total and of US Federal Reserve accounts of Stocks and Flows has led me to the following statistics with respect to the structural changes in the global economy.

This research with documentation has been written up in working paper form and published on my UniServEnt.org website at https://uniservent.org/political-economy/ in a flip book as The

Browser Economy – An Analysis for determining the Optimization of Investment and Consumption Allocations according to their Valuation in a Market Economy. The Executive Summary for that work is included at the top of this section, Contemplation III.

First with respect to the consumption figures, I came to the realization that an optimization factor exists in a market system, in which the ratio of valuation of capital to consumption goods expenditures is equal to the ratio of consumption to total goods expenditures, where 'goods' means goods and services. This ratio is that of the golden ratio, 61.8%, a well-known mathematical form related to the Fibonacci series recognized in nature that optimizes the growth of some natural systems such as the spiral forms of seashells and growth of rabbit populations. Such growth rate is verified in the global World Bank figures for the past 50 years. It indicates a marker for policy goals. I have not found this factor noted in any publications as of the time of writing this piece.

The inverse of this figure or 38.2% is the optimum ratio of capital goods to total goods expenditures. Percentages greater than this figure indicate a level of capital expenditures in excess of what is needed to sustain an equilibrium position going forward, and therefore are indicative of growth, while lesser percentages indicate a level insufficient to sustain that equilibrium and growth. In 1975 this factor for the U.S. was near the optimum at 38.8%. By 2013, the factor had fallen to 31.5%, along a steady decrease of investment in public infrastructure and real and human capital.

With respect to capital, the U.S. accounts for 1975 state a 10 to 1, real to financial capital ratio, reduced to roughly 6 to 1 in 2013. Human capital in the U.S. extrapolated over this same time period and based on a 2010 Commerce Department study by Michael

Christian[7] is comprised of about 30% market valued human capital and 70% non-market valued human capital. Based on this study, human capital was close to 20 times the value of real capital, 200 times the value of financial capital in 1975, and in 2013, was 100 times the value of financial capital and 100,000 times the value of all the U.S. monetary gold at 11 billion dollars or $35 per citizen; hence the wisdom of fostering the development and maintenance of that human capital, Human Life, from the cradle to the grave, not as a source of exploitation for private profit, but as a solid basis for a high quality of spiritual life for the whole community.

U.S. Sector Net Worth as % of Total	1975	2013	Diff
Households & nonprofits	62.4%	73.5%	11.1%
Nonfinancial Corporate Business	19.5%	17.8%	(1.7%)
Nonfinancial Noncorporate Business	12.3%	8.4%	(3.9%)
Financial Business	1.7%	(0.5%)	(2.2%)
Federal Government	(2.7%)	(10.5%)	(7.8%)
State & Local Government	7.7%	7.2%	(0.5%)
Rest of the World	(0.9%)	4.1%	5.0%

Structural Changes expressed as percentages of U.S. Sector Net Worth between 1975 and 2013 show the effects of supply side policy implementation over this period.

---

[7] Human Capital: "Human Capital Accounting in the United States, 1994-2006", a report by Michael S. Christian, published by the U.S. Department of Commerce, Bureau of Economic Analysis, http://bea.gov/scb/pdf/2010/06%20June/0610_christian.pdf

With respect to the Fed figures, the breakdown of structural changes indicates the ascent of private equity, sovereign wealth, and other ROW accounts to the detriment of public corporate, mom and pop business, non-leveraged financial, and especially federal government spending. An in-depth dive into these figures in The Browser Economy gives more insight into the current income distribution figures.

This was followed up with two related postings from investigations of 2020 and 2021. The first of these was written in response to an invitation for papers under the Capital as Power Essay Competition posted by Blair Fix, for which I am quoting his response of the review board from April 2, 2021.

> *" Hi Mart,*
>
> *Thanks for submitting a paper to this year's Capital as Power Essay Competition. The reviewers thought your paper was interesting, but were unsure exactly how it relates to capital as power (as they understand it). In particular, the reviewers thought the relation between capital as power and ergodicity economics needed to be clarified and explained further. For that reason, they decided the paper did not warrant a prize.*
>
> *You are welcome to revise the paper and resubmit it to RECASP if you wish.*
>
> *Thanks again for the submission.*
>
> *Regards, Blair"*

Rather than revise that submission, I thought it more appropriate to revise the title to 'Capital as Position in Ergodic Economic Modeling' which is closer to the truth, in my opinion, of what economic power really is—the vital position of an economic producing-distributing-consuming entity in the production-distribution-consumption decision making process. That position, located ergodically by a mix of de jure and de facto determinants within an environment of productive resource, weighted by the vitality of the decision-maker, is what is recognized as the power of capital. Ergodicity economics weighted by the positioning in the distribution of rational decision makers is discussed in the following paper.

A Critique of Neoliberal Economics, Part I –

Quantitative Analysis & Assumptions, Capital as ~~Power~~ Position in Ergodic Economic Modeling -:- Hierarchical Position and Focused Rationality in an Analysis of Stocks & Flows[8]

From this paper, Part I & II, we have the following:

AXIOMS concerning ECONOMIC ACTIVITY & CAPITAL

The word, capital, is from the Latin for 'head', caput; related to a common Latin stem for 'roomy, the ability to hold', capax, related to 'capacity', the ability to receive, contain, perform, or function in a position or role, both physical and mental. The word, power, is also from the Latin, posse or potens, by way of the Anglo-French, poer, as 'to be able, to have power'. It is therefore somewhat redundant, if not tautological, to state that social power and the cultured ability to direct the energy coming from any natural potential as economic activity, comes to be represented by way of

---

[8] U.S. Federal Reserve 4Q 1989 & 4Q 2019, Household Income and Net Worth Data

cranial capacity as the experienced mental ability of collectively engaged human beings.

*In an economic context, **capital** is the rationally and emotionally effective productive capacity and potential, the **power,** of human beings working with the natural resources at hand, by their individual and collective **labor**, to maintain their place of **living** in the world. An economic interchange among human beings involves an expenditure of energy and incorporation of material in the supply, production, warehousing, and distribution of the final consumable **goods and services (G&S)** required for living; as an integral corollary this includes the percentage of that energy and material that is required for the creation, maintenance, and replenishment of any intermediate goods and services necessary for production and distribution of the final consumables. All these intermediate goods and services are forms of real capital and necessarily include the creation, maintenance, and replenishment by way of the sustenance required of and for the human beings involved in the living experience.*

*A portion of these interchanges between human beings are performed within the context of a market mechanism as a trade of G&S for ostensibly equivalent **tokens of satisfaction ($)** as instruments of financial capital in the form of money, promissory notes, certificates of extant stock or future flows of assets, or other tabulation of accounting **value**, so that such portions of both intermediate and final G&S have a representational, stock-valued human entitlement as **market-valued human capital (MHC)**. The remaining portion of the interchanges that are productive of intermediate and final G&S are assignable as **non-market-valued human capital (NHC)** which can only be estimated based on broad equivalences between market and non-market components. These*

449

NHC interactions are the earthly product of Nature's bounty, God's grace, however you may choose to designate God as the endless, supreme potential source for change, and community nurture that must be sustained from cradle to grave by means of both MHC and NHC; this NHC as might be indicated with "all men (and by implication, women) are created equal, ... endowed by their Creator with certain unalienable Rights, that among these are Life, Liberty, and the Pursuit of happiness" in the U.S. Declaration of Independence and which we might deem applicable internationally.

Certain accounting in the U.S. economy of recent years puts the ratio of MHC:NHC average in a range of 0.43:1 to 0.33:1, where 1 is an implied statistical average of NMC. From this thinking as we will detail, MHC of 0.43 to 0.33, or 0.38+/- 0.05, can be theoretically distributed along a spectrum with each individual's percentage of the total market valued capital of an economy, all greater than 0.0 (since a negative as debt would indicate involuntary servitude or Shylock's pound of flesh), while the NHC is simply the per capita average of the total NHC accounted as 1.0.

*Capital then, all of which is an intermediate good or service, can be viewed and valued as: **human**—consisting of the physical and metaphysical skills and capabilities of people both MHC and NHC; **real**—consisting of the physical resources, both natural and technologically developed, available for human utilization through productive human effort; and **financial**—consisting of various methods devised for directing and accounting for the past and future production, distribution and consumption of goods and services required or otherwise desired by society.*

*The referenced power can be viewed qualitatively as: **social**—consisting of the skilled capacity, expertise, or position to* *organize and direct a desired productive enterprise;* **energy source**— *consisting of the available, technologically developed and thermodynamically defined capacity to fuel useful work, both mechanically and through the ecological and nutritional needs of human living; and individual* **labor power**— *consisting of the mental and physical ability to provide and sustain useful and necessary, thereby meaningful, work.*

Labor can be viewed along a spectrum as: **self-initiated**— *consisting of the employment and direction of the work of oneself and/or others;* **employed**—*consisting of the voluntary provision of one's own work effort at the direction of others; and* **involuntarily servile**—*consisting of wage, penal, chattel, or ensnared bondage under conditions of coerced toil.*

Living can be viewed along a spectrum from a **risk of enslavement** *to material wretchedness due to personal behavior or the depravity and disregard of others up to an* **opportunity for liberation** *of spiritual perception and intuitional creativity.*

Capital and labor, both as an expression of power, is at work under any condition or state be it; tribalist, feudalist, capitalist, socialist, or communist; monarchist, oligopolist, liberalist, or anarchist; browser, hunter-gatherer, agricultural, industrial, or cybernetic. This dynamic of capital production and use is not confined to 'capitalism'; nor absent under 'socialism'. The political organization of that state is determined in proportion and valued degree by those who are positioned to exercise the power inherent in the instruments of both capital and labor over a range of **hierarchical structure** *and* **decision making**. *That decision making is characterized herein as a choice defined by the motivation, expertise, capability, and position of the individual or affiliated group as a* *function of focused rationality, even if that reason is confined to the daily decision of how or whether to continue with a meaningless job, with no apparent alternatives in sight, in order to survive.* [9]

From a review of the data from this research and analysis using weighted ergodic modeling comparing the U.S. Fed data for household income and net worth for the 4th quarters of 1989 and 2019 abstracts, we have the following tables:

Income	Top 3.1%	15.6%	31.3%	31.3%	15.6%	3.1%
4Q 1989*	24.9	34.8	24.7	13.0	2.5	0.1
50%	23.7	39.5	26.4	8.8	1.5	0.1
Divergence	+ 1.2	− 4.7	− 1.7	+ 4.2	+ 1.0	
4Q 2019*	33.9	37.5	20.1	6.9	1.5	0.1
60%	32.8	41.0	20.5	5.1	0.6	0.0
Divergence	+ 1.1	− 3.5	− 0.4	+ 1.8	+ 0.9	+ 0.1
*As adjusted for comparison with the model						

Income Table – Conformation of Fed Income data with weighted ergodic modeling of corresponding percentages

Net Worth	Top 3.1%	15.6%	31.3%	31.3%	15.6%	3.1%
4Q 1989*	36.5	37.0	22.6	3.4	0.5	0.0
60%	32.8	41.0	20.5	5.1	0.6	0.0
Divergence	+ 3.7	− 4.0	+ 2.1	− 1.7	− 0.1	
4Q 2019*	46.0	34.7	17.9	1.2	0.2	0.0
70%	44.4	39.2	13.8	2.4	0.2	0.0
Divergence	+ 1.6	− 4.5	+ 4.1	− 1.2		
*As adjusted for comparison with the model						

Net Worth Table – Conformation of Fed Net Worth data with weighted ergodic modeling of corresponding percentages [10]

Each table, Income and Net Worth, present data from each year in three rows. First of the rows are the values from the Fed data adjusted to fit the same percentiles as the probability distribution of 5 flips of a fair coin, weighted according to the percentage factor of the

---

[9] Text in Italics taken from the UniServEnt.org website
[10] https://uniservent.org/capital-as-power-in-ergodic-economic-modeling/

first column, computed in the percentiles of the second rows. The divergence in each percentile of the Fed data from the weighted ergodicity is then shown in the third row.

Some items of interest in these figures are the following: There is a 10% increase in the weighting of the skew over thirty years in the distribution from 1989 to 2019.

There is a 36% increase in income and a 26% increase in net worth for the top 3.1% over those thirty years.

There is an 8% increase in income for the second 15.6% over that period but a decrease for all remaining percentiles. All remaining percentiles show a decline in net worth for that period.

There is a 10% increase in the weighting for each of these years between the income and net worth distribution skews.

The second 15.6% percentiles of both the income and the net worth show an approximate 4% negative divergence of the Fed figures from the ergodic model. We would surmise that this might be due to in large part to the function of tax redistribution from this column to the adjacent percentiles on either side, to the 31.3% in the bottom half of the Income table and to the 31.3% in the top half of the Net Worth table. These two divergent figures are related. The flows to the lower 31.3% in Income are an offset in part to the negative divergence from the Net Worth.

Any further attempt to clarify and explain this quantitative analysis can be found in the qualitative analysis of the second essay that follows in the link below.[11] This essay is a qualitative analysis of Capital as Power in Ergodic Modeling in terms of three naïve

---

[11] https://uniservent.org/a-critique-of-neoliberal-economics/.

assumptions of neoliberalism stated therein as the private sector fetishization of Money as fantasized Omnipotence, of Decision Making as fantasized Omniscience, and as Freedom as fantasized Omnipresence, through a dialectical lens on the philosophical work of Marx, Plato, and Christ.

A Critique of Neoliberal Economics, Part II –

Qualitative Analysis & Assumption, Capital as Money, Focused Rationality, and Hierarchical Position -:- The Ideals of Omnipotent Money, Omniscient Decision Making, & Omnipresent Freedom bound by Material Conditions, The Dialectics of Neutral Monism in the Historical Philosophy of Marx, Plato, and Christ

This work incorporates my first reacquaintance in some time with the work of Plato in his Republic and the dialectics of Socrates, which we can see echoed in the philosophical discourse of Marx and the moral, spiritual imperatives of Christ. The five principle Goods of the Republic can then be reconsidered, not in the customary manner as an ideal linear decay of Plato from the Good of Justice under the rule of the Philosopher King to the Good of Power under the rule of the unenlightened Tyrant, nor of a material linear ascent of Marx through the experience of class struggle born of contradictory historical conditions of material constraint and capital excess, nor of the eschatological instant emergence of the Kingdom of God and resurrection of the dead. Instead, we merge the ideal-material dynamics of Plato and Marx with the ever-present moral, spiritual imperative of Christ to extend charity to the 'least of these my brethren'.

Finally, there is a short slide show of the Basic Income Study with links to a downloadable Basic Income App created in Filemaker at https://uniservent.org/basic-income-study-slide-0/

This app includes an interactive spread sheet which provides a comparison of three alternative ways of providing for the necessary funding of the public sector in order to maintain the non-market value of human capital, through taxation, borrowing at a variety of interest rates, and direct issuance of fiat currency, all with a variety of mixes. In line with the optimization factor discussed above, this includes the ability to tailor the expenditures between outlays for public, private, common, and club stocks and flows. From this research we have:

- the use of the Basic Income App or interactive application constructed along a similar logic for reviewing the alternative mixes of funding of public, private, common, and club stocks and flows,

- the optimization ratio as a guide in judging the effectiveness of economic policy initiatives, public and private,

- a recognition of the significance of non-market valued human capital and the need for inclusion of that capital in the national accounts in order to protect and enhance the value of that capital across the entire community and not just in the vested, highly market valued human capital components in the community, which is already readily maintained by market forces and requires little additional direct investment beyond that of the final statement. Every statement in the public record of net worth breakdown should include the recognition of this NHC,

- a recognition of the vapidity of discussions that link personal income tax as necessary to the vital funding requirements of public policy rather than an alternative enlightened discourse concerning the issuance of fiat currency in keeping with Modern Monetary Theory (MMT) and Universal Basic Income (UBI) for optimization of educational investment and use in a mix of public and private employment.

A link to the UniServEnt.org website for research in this section with an animation of the fundamental rotational oscillation with related videos is linked here:

https://uniservent.org/political-economy/

- **The Browser Economy**

   An Analysis for determining the Optimization of Investment and Consumption Allocations according to their Valuation in a Market Economy

   Mart Gibson

   February 10, 2015

https://uniservent.org/the-browser-economy-3/

- **A Critique of Neoliberal Economics Part I –**

   Quantitative Analysis & Assumptions

https://uniservent.org/capital-as-power-in-ergodic-economic-modeling/

- **A Critique of Neoliberal Economics Part II –**

   Qualitative Analysis & Assumptions

https://uniservent.org/a-critique-of-neoliberal-economics/

- **Basic Income Study with app**

https://uniservent.org/basic-income-study-slide-0/

- **Ergodid Economics with supporting documents and spreadsheets**

https://uniservent.org/ergodidiocy/e-economics/

The distinction between a soul and its ego is significant, especially when the reference to 'ego' is really to 'nos'—where 'I' is really a 'We'. From a spiritual perspective, the purpose in a multiplicity of souls bound together by love is not the evolutionary opportunity for the development of a gratifying sense of excellence by a single ego or even a group of egos—much less a clump of fancy DNA—at the collateral costs to the rest, even in a hierarchical context of implementation of a divine plan. Neither is that love intended to serve the mutual benefit of individual souls alone. Rather it is the necessary wisdom of differentiation of a collective Soul Nature into individual foci as souls in the service of a divine creative purpose, for which that wisdom is the defining logical connection and our love, the intuitive method of communion for that concerted effort.

While it would be reasonable, up until the time of Copernicus and the astronomical observations of Kepler and Galileo that followed, to equate the scope of a divine creative purpose and plan with what was known of the universe in the European world as filtered through the Judeo-Christian scriptures and canon of the Roman Catholic church, that scope has changed greatly with the developments of the scientific revolution. Eastern teaching has had its own scope of understanding of the cosmos for the last several millennia, equally recognized to be divinely created and overseen by the same divine Source and Agency, but with a vastly greater scope of space and time, differently named but still recognized by Christ in referring to "other sheep...not of this fold: them also I must bring, and they shall hear my voice; and there shall be one fold, and one shepherd"[12]

The teaching of Vedanta of the size of space is that it is essentially limitless, or at least undefinable except by God. That teaching of the time scale of a year of the supreme creative God, Brahma, is 3.1 trillion human years, for which a day in the life of Brahma is said to comprise 8.6 billion years, with a nocturnal 4.3 billion and a diurnal 4.3 billion years, about the earth's age if God confined their work to the daytime. This is interesting if we interpret the first chapter of Genesis in a similar manner as the divine creative process transpiring over 6 days of God instead of 6 days of mankind. It should not be surprising if the rabbis of the Levant and the priests of the Indus valley shared a commonly sourced tradition from Mesopotamia, or that a day of God for the creative program in each case was symbolic and representative of a very long time, meaning over 50 billion years if we applied the cosmic clock to the story of Genesis.

The point we are after is not that Genesis should be considered technically accurate in quantitative detail. It is interesting enough from the perspective of the creative period of a solar system or a galaxy, in that the Abrahamic and Vedantic authors appeared to have been intuitively tuned to the general scope and scale of the creative enterprise in astronomical terms as we currently view that scope rather than the 8,000-year-old earth of some of the latter-day interpretations of Christianity. More interesting, if we use a qualitative categorical translation of the first few verses of Genesis, that might be, 'At the start of a creative project, creative Spiritual Potential initiated and differentiated its Material Nature into the vast

---

[12] John 10:16

rarified portions as space and the dense portions as undifferentiated material without form, with obscurity upon the interface of the spatial abyss between the rarified and dense portions. And the creative Potential initiated oscillation in the interface of the abyss, creating light.'

This sounds a lot like the differentiation of cosmic space into the vast regions devoid of rest mass and the relatively small, dense volumes of filaments and webs associated with dark matter from which occurred the emergent generation of rest mass wave particles and photonic energy as light in generated plasma primarily in stars on a cosmic scale, but apparent on a galactic and stellar/planetary scale as well. The appearance of such phenomena is the necessary requirement for the emergence of self-replicating intelligent life forms similar to ourselves, observed, recognized, and communed with as human souls.

It is the development of individual egos, self-isolating through pride, ignorance, and fear in responding to opportunity and risk, that obscures the recognition and communion of a mutual love and hampers connection within the community in the wise pursuit of their efforts. It is a soul operating 'in character' that creates an ego as a fig leaf/mask in response to a perception of facing an existential risk, real or imagined. This mask leads the soul into stereotypical categorizations of such risks in the behavior of others as evil rather than just bad, thereby creating an antagonist, villain, adversary, this last of which is of course, satan as antichrist, bad actors who can be found operating in any errant and perverse ego.

It is one thing to take a part in a play; yet another to believe the role is real, though this is generally more the case than not before the soul approaches the threshold to enlightenment. The soul may create a protean mask for any number of roles that it may wear from day to day, or it may settle on a caricature role, false face for the duration. Roles become reinforced by culture and habit, which once committed to heart become indistinguishable from the soul's transcendent, but illusive sense of always being present in the ego's personal life-or-death drama. Beyond the body, the ego does die—it must if the soul is to become and remain free. For logical reasons, no one can be born into the same role and drama in all details twice. It is this death that is referred to in the scriptures as the second death, which is a death of the ego necessary for the release of the soul from its cravings and attachments to material and ideal forms and processes.

It is to this end that the enlightened soul attempts this release prior to physical death through spiritual practice, again not to escape rebirth but rather to be better fit for any future role in the production of the divine play. It is the reason for the path of initiation for those who have made themselves ready, because it enables and results ultimately in the death of the ego, with release from the illusions of good and evil that binds the ego as a protagonist to its antagonist. This ego death is not instantaneous, happening over an extended period as determined by the soul's dharma, which means the soul's correct and Just path in Life.

Completion of this process, referred to as moksha or nirvana in the eastern teaching, is a release from existential concerns, resulting in a state of grace, peace of unsurpassed understanding. Referred to as annihilation in some Buddhist texts, it is annihilation of the ego only, the false sense of self, and in time results in an end to the flood of mental images and emotional processes that beset the soul from time to time, sometimes in great measure, while either quick or dead. Such death produces an awareness of the ever-present bliss of being, of Life without pause, beyond the usual dichotomies of opportunity and risk, of love and fear, of wisdom and ignorance.

Three Paths of Yoga to Enlightenment within the Essential Trigon

Form C.1.0

In Form C.1.0, the inner hexagram and the surrounding six parallelograms forming the hexagon represent the manifest universe perceived by the Soul as residing within the Boundless, Limitless, Unmanifest Essence, 1LEs, 2AEs, & 3QEs, along with the Imaging Capacity to so manifest Itself without end. The smaller hexagon in the center of the larger hexagon represents the Living Capacity of the Soul which is unmanifest even when that Soul itself is the manifesting existent agency of change. The three Imaging Capacities of the Soul at 1C, 2C, & 3C are operating in the manifest world as indicated by the ring of Existential components, 1AEx, 2AEx, and 3AEx as observed as the appearance of material forms and processes, 1QEx, 2QEx, and 3QEx as recognized as the quality of ideal forms and processes, and 1LEx, 2LEx, and 3LEx as communion with the spiritual purpose behind all life forms and processes.

Each of the three capacities of the Soul has two adjacent Essential Capacities with which they laterally interact and one with which they intrinsically interact as imaged reflections, as indicated by the shared ordinal number of each capacity.

The Innate Capacity of 1C interacts directly with the material natural appearances 1AEx as they are recognized to embody various ideal natural qualities 1QEx, according to the intrinsic imaging of the intentional, spiritual natures of 1LEx in 1C. This is the primary course of what has been called the Path of Return of the Soul to its Source, in the Abrahamic theology as the Resurrection into the Kingdom of Heaven or as the devotional path to liberation of Bhakti Yoga in the Vedantic traditions.

The Logical Capacity of 2C interacts directly with the ideal natural qualities of the mental, Formal Capacities such as found in mathematical, mechanical, and geometric Forms of 2QEx, as direct expressions of Living the axiomatic imperatives of 2LEx and realized intrinsically through imaging of wise activity of the Inertial Capacity of 2AEx in the Soul Nature at 2C. This represents an active life of service in Abrahamic thinking and the path of enlightened activity, of Karma Yoga in Vedanta.

The Intuitive Capacity of 3C interacts directly with the communion of Souls and First Principles in 3LEx and in the material appearances of 3AEx, through the intrinsic recognition of the qualities of the ideal, the mental, nature at 3QEx imaged in 3C. This is the path of spiritual knowledge of Christ or the Buddha, as self-realization of Jnana Yoga in Vedanta.

Success in one of these three is success in all, here indicated by the three bold lines converging on the Living Capacity of the Soul, all of which then lead from this convergence, up and through the dashed horizontal line that separates the soul from full communion with its source as the Will-to-Good, representing the Resurrection to eternal consciousness Living of its spiritual nature as Love and Wisdom.

The Path to Resurrection within the Essential Trigon

Form C.1.1

We can use the Trigonal Platonic analysis in Form C.1.1 as a foundation of Christian Trinitarian cosmology. The Intentional Capacity as the Timeless Source of all Life is God the Father. The Material and Maternal Nature is the formless, undifferentiated, matrix as inertial wave bearing potential, the proverbial Virgin Sea—or in Latin, 'Mare'—the Virgin Mary. The Formal Capacity of Ideal Forms, of Ideal Goods or Truths, is found in the Spirit of Truth as the Holy

Spirit, the Logos. The Imaging Capacity of the Soul Natures is found as the union of the Father and the Holy Mother of Catholicism, the Virgin, in the immaculate conception of the Son of Man, realized through the anointing by that Holy Spirit as Jesus Christ.

The crucifixion is represented by the horizontal boundary, between the Father in the Heavenly Kingdom and his Divine Son of Man, where the vertical pillar represents the path of Ascension connecting those realms of death encountered in the corruptible lower Existential manifestations of the Material and Ideal Natures with the upper realm of Eternal Life via the Resurrection into the Spiritual Nature, where the Son as Soul comes to live and reign at the right hand of the Father. With the union of the Holy Spirit and the Virgin Mary through the Assumption—another instance of Ascension—the Spirit of Truth is recognized as One with the Spiritual Natures.

The Idea of the Resurrection is generally associated with revivification of a physical body, the corporal form, based on some interpretations of the Gospel accounts. While such an event in itself would be significant, it is secondary to the related and more essential concept of the Ascension, of being "caught up" unto Heaven. It represents the elevation of the consciousness of the soul as a 'Son of Man', the Image of God, above the phenomenal world of material observation and ideal recognition into spiritual reunion and communion with the Eternal formless, omnipotent source of Life.

In Form C.1.2, the Trigonal framework can be looked at in a parallel manner with the teachings of theosophy and the outline of 'The Dream' section mentioned previously in the notion of the three outpourings of the Divine Life as it informs, reifies, and validates a creative plan and purpose. The First Outpouring—the Female, Maternal Aspect of Divinity as the Mother of all Living—gives form and process by way of the Active Intelligence of that Inertial Capacity to the Material Nature in all the animated life forms with their necessary supporting solar and planetary environments as indicated in 1-3AEx.

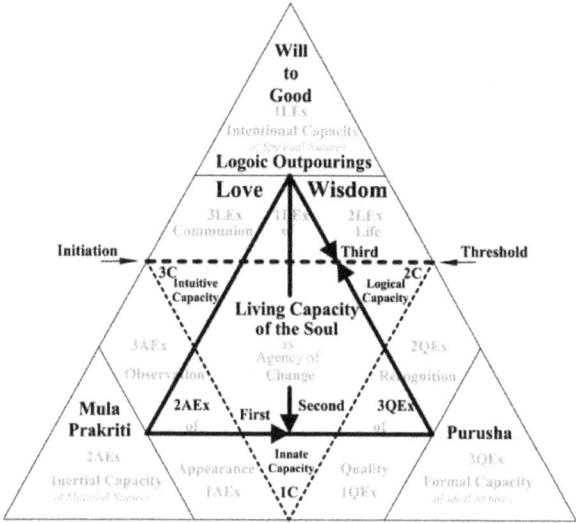

The 3 Outpourings of Theosophy within the Essential Trigon

Form C.1.2

This Outpouring is met over time by the Second Outpouring—the Androgynous Aspect of Divinity as the Son of Man—as the Innate Capacity of the Soul in 1C in its integrated observation of the objective universe. From this point the Soul begins its journey of ascent through the process of embodiment for education and service in the Formal Capacity of 1-3QEx by developing an understanding of the Ideal Natures through a recognition of Ideal Forms and Processes, including an intrinsic reflection of 3QEx in 3C to its Intuitive Capacity for observation at 3AEx and communion with the greater Life in 3LEx, and finally through understanding of the Logical Capacity of 2C.

The soul is then met by the Third Outpouring—the Male, Paternal Aspect of Divinity as the Father of all Living—at the initiatory threshold prior to entry into the Divine Hierarchy, the Kingdom of Heaven, in 1-3LEx.

This initiation takes place on inner spiritual levels, registered in the dream state by the application of the rod of initiation by the appropriate Hierarch. This energizes the appropriate psychic center, which in the final case is the crown chakra. Initiation also takes place under the direct supervision of a guru in material embodiment.

This event is initiatory and not the completion of the induction process. In this process, it opens the Soul to the influx and direct contact with the vital, emotional, and mental forms and processes, including the kundalini, some of which can be extremely stress producing, until the Soul learns to effectively deal with the emotionally energized mental forms and processes. Over decades this leads in the final process to egoic transparency, understood as previously discussed as a destruction of the personal ego and release of the Soul from personal attachment to the physical body going forward.

This release is a liberating state of sustained equanimity, liberating the soul from existential concerns, peacefully pleasurable, without being self-consciously distracting and intense. Contrary to some eastern teachings, this does not preclude re-embodiment for hierarchical purpose and service to the divine plan as an end of rebirths. In truth, such bliss is an innate condition that any soul experiences whenever they are unconcerned and happy; for the enlightened soul this realized state becomes unremitting as the ego slowly dissipates over time.

This brings us to the concluding section of the Paros Commune — 2021 & Beyond. The true nature of the Soul is not realized in any identification with one's own personality or any role it may assume in the great Play of Life, as satisfying as that part may at first appear. It is not realized by playing the part of a capitalist or a socialist or a fascist or a communist; a republican or a democrat; a conservative or a liberal; a man or a woman; a gender or not; a woker or a dreamer or a populist schemer; a christian or a muslim or a jew or a hindu or a buddhist or an atheist or agnostic; or any actor that is concerned about flubbing their lines after ignoring the director and failing to show up for rehearsals.

The true nature of the Soul is Love and Wisdom; Love, realized by confronting fear, not with bluster, but with a willingness to understand that fear in oneself and others, and Wisdom, realized by confronting ignorance, based on an understanding of those fears and a realization of that Love, both of which are exercised in addressing the opportunities and risks present in the Community. Love is first, for without such Love based on an all-encompassing vision of Life, there can be no pervasive Wisdom in the community.

Wisdom is not exercised by sowing discord and dissension in the community or between communities. It is not found in laying on a mantle of authenticity as being a good soul and labeling an antagonist as an evil one, desiring their annihilation, regardless of how bad their conduct might be. Wisdom confronts bad conduct to the full extent required of any turpitude, without indulging in the fantasy that the confrontation stems from a superior position that is essentially free of corruptibility. All flesh is corruptible, and so the soul that craves the flesh becomes corruptible in and for that craving, particularly when that craving is for Power over others, even if those others are seen as evil.

The innate nature of Soul embraces a conservative approach to Risk and a liberal approach to Opportunity. Confusion in this regard arises whenever the nature and the mix of risk and opportunity on a matter of concern to the community is not clearly understood, or when the risk is clearly understood by one part of the community and the opportunity is clearly understood by the other, so that a means to the solution to a problem is misunderstood or if understood, misapplied due to disagreement over method. In light of this confusion, particularly in the U.S., we will consider a few of these in brief form; 1) public versus private problem solving, 2) abortion and religious liberty, 3) guns, and 4) race and a public safety net.

PUBLIC versus PRIVATE PROBLEM SOLVING

Private problem solving tends toward a conservative approach as it is managed between private parties to a solution with 'skin in the game', while public problem solving tends toward a liberal approach which is often not readily addressable by those with very real concerns, but without clearly defined 'skin' or even 'game' as with those suffering the effects of externalities. Why? Practically speaking, problem solving takes money. Money is a financial instrument-of-demand held for future exchange of goods and services, some of which have yet to be produced and are therefore presently unavailable and of unknown value in the community. Much of the public envisions that same money as instruments-of-satisfaction which have been received in past exchange, having value for goods and services already produced, to which they are entitled to exchange in future demand for those same or equivalent goods and services based on that valuation, even though some have yet to be produced and valued.

The inherent problem with money is that the future value of that money is a function of the stability of the political economy—the community—as attested to by the current bout of inflation. And the stability of the community is a function of two principal things; 1) the level of technological understanding in the production of intermediate and final goods and services, and 2) the required population of souls with the necessary skills to implement that technological understanding. It is readily understood that those skills are evidenced in both the material and the ideal forms and processes of the community; think hardware and software, electronic and mental decision-making as real and human capital. Current supply of resource and production is a factor, but it is the technologically developed, understood, and implemented skill of the community that ensures stability and the value of money over time.

What is less well understood, if it is acknowledged at all, is that the paramount determinant in ensuring the necessary stability through periods of dislocation and misalignment of the necessary levels of material and ideal skills in the community are the necessary spiritual skills of Love and Wisdom—Goodwill—as inclusive compassion and the exercise of that Love, as we have tried to outline in these contemplations on the Essential Trigon. In this Eden which we call Earth, the development of those spiritual skills, like any living change in form and process, is fueled by the sun, supported by the stable ground with the precipitation and flow of water laden with life forming minerals, and nourished incessantly with the exchange of carbon dioxide and oxygen in the atmosphere. But it lies in the domain of the Soul and its Natures to choose when and where and what to plant, when and where and what to build, when and where and what to produce, and when and where and how to live and treat others. When dislocation and misalignment of access to material and ideal resources occur, the first inclination for finding a solution to the problems that have created the mess is to reach for the money, instead of looking for the human, and to a lesser extent the real capital required for the solution.

Money is an artifact, starting historically as a token form of satisfaction for storing human value used in the occasional exchange for goods with others, to eventually become the present technological process for directing virtually all human activity in the production of intermediate and final goods and services required for living. By itself, money does nothing. Money did not produce the sun or the earth or the water or the air or any living form and process including those involving human beings. God did. Divine Purpose as the source of all Living did. As long as we fail to realize That Intentional Capacity is operating as Divine Love and requires our deference and the checking of our ego at the door of in any struggle with our fellow souls, looking for existing pools of cash will not serve us well.

Private problems generally involve money, often just a little, which is under the control and administration of private parties. They tend to be seen as having conservative solutions due to the inherent risk of running out of private money if it is deemed to be in short supply. Public problems often take a lot, a liberal amount of money, much of which is increasingly under the control of a few private parties, where many of the souls involved in and impacted by the externalities requiring a public solution have little of their own. A major issue for solution to a public problem then is not enough money in the hands of the many private individuals dealing with the weight of the externalities. With insufficient understanding of the monetary system and lack of access for the majority of human beings to any private means of acquiring that money in a market driven increasingly by commodity production and consumption, there is neither a conservative solution to an ever-increasing risk of doing nothing nor a liberal solution for providing any opportunity to solve the problem that humans have created as now understood.

Problem solving generally requires agreement. Private solutions take a few agreements between a few souls, while public solutions require agreement between a lot of souls. That is unless and until one private party or soul takes it on themselves to decide on a solution that affects others unilaterally, be that problem private or public. As we have seen, this can involve the tyranny of an unskilled tyro, which generally leads to greater problems unless the tyro is spiritually gifted; it can involve the legitimate decision-making of an elected official which may or may not have the necessary insight; or it may lead to the impromptu action of an experienced soul, deferred to and based on their recognized wisdom in the community.

Allowing private solutions to problems between private parties is generally seen as a liberal attitude if we are thinking about liberal as in free-market and independent decision-making. A problem occurs when these liberal agreements between private parties in search of opportunity result in the realized risk of external costs to the community outside the boundaries of the private contract. In an authentically conservative response, this leads to attempts to lessen the risk by assigning the public external costs to the private parties responsible for those costs in order to balance the books, if they have the funds to address those costs. Without such funds, this is met with attempts to address these costs as a 'liberal' public problem, by disingenuous private parties, when in origin they are truly conservative failures, since any and all attempts to address the presence of 'externalities' in private contracts is a conservative attempt to lessen risk to the community. The only alternative to such a conservative failure to balance the external books is a liberal attempt to increase opportunities for those souls outside the private contract who are suffering a risk or loss from the external costs by using MMT and UBI.

This appears to be the crux of the debate over public and private initiatives in problem solving—who is going to pay for it rather than how it is going to be technically solved. As it is, the IRS is ostensibly tasked with this solution, but it is largely a straw man, which has outlived any usefulness, as the budget is now rarely balanced and then only with detrimental results. Modern monetary theory along with elements of a universal basic income as a citizenship dividend tied to the value of maintaining non-market valued human capital offers the combination of a liberal opportunity to address the externalities and a conservative mitigation of risk—all by largely getting rid of the antiquated personal and business income tax while preserving only those taxes required to offset the costs of externalities, as costs that are incorporated but not included in pricing a final good or service.

ABORTION & RELIGIOUS LIBERTY

Restrictions on abortion are generally viewed as a conservative right of a minority based on their religiously held beliefs, designed to protect the integrity of the life of the unborn, against the liberal rights of the individual child bearer—necessarily a woman—to have control of her own personal body, which includes the right to decide when and whether to reproduce. Prohibition of abortion is necessarily a prerogative of the state, operating at the behest of the those that hold such beliefs, as stated in the claim that life of a person with rights begins with conception. In the United States of America, the only thing that trumps that prerogative of the state is the U.S. Constitution as stated in the first amendment that "Congress shall make no law respecting an establishment of religion, or prohibiting the free exercise thereof; abridging the freedom of speech, or of the press; or the right of the people peaceably to assemble, and to petition the Government for a redress of grievances."

This means exactly what it says, that "no law respecting an establishment of religion" of one set of beliefs or faith shall enforce a law "prohibiting the free exercise thereof" with respect to people holding another set of beliefs or faith. An exception might be if the "free exercise thereof" involves the enslavement, apartheid, or murder of another person, another human being, as in the days of human sacrifice, chattel slavery, and discriminatory legal regimes. The belief that abortion is murder that applies to a fetus that is not viable is based on two flawed assumptions.

First is the self-contradictory notion that a human being exists as a person prior to viability, defined as having the capability of living, under normal conditions, outside the womb—by breathing on its own. Second, prior to viability, the only basis for any claim to murder for such termination is the assumption of the existence of a soul attached to the evolving fetus from conception by creationist or traducianist religious belief. Creationism holds that each soul is created by divine intent with each conception and traducianism holds that the soul is created as a potential along with Adam and Eve and passed on as an instance of actualization with each human conception. There is no demonstrable evidence admissible in a court of law that either of these is the case, though the presence of a soul in a court room should be proof as of that point in time; the notion of the presence of a soul <u>from conception is simply a matter of religious belief</u>. There is ample evidence to the contrary, that in cases of stillborn and some instances of unconscious infant birth dependent on medical life support systems, there is no soul present, where a soul is understood in most religious and many philosophical contexts as necessary for human life. Viability in these cases becomes a moot point. Somewhere along the timeline from conception to such a birth, the soul must be understood to have vacated the body or else was never present; for a viable birth, at some point the soul takes up residency.

From an understanding of the pre-existence of the soul as found in most eastern religions, in ancient Greek, early Christian, and Neoplatonist beliefs, each human being is an incarnation of a divinely created soul that lives in the ethereal realms or underworld between embodiments, to be born into different circumstances of inherent opportunity and risk for whatever purpose the soul or the divinity intends. Such preexistence is also a matter of religious belief, unless it is a matter of knowledge based on a recollection of prior incarnation, though proof of this in court also remains problematic. For those Christians who believe that life of the soul began at conception, they clearly cannot claim without contradiction that they have personal knowledge of the fact. Proof of becoming a soul at conception, or any time, is a matter of belief unless it is a recalled experience.

Anti-abortion, then, is actually a liberal state solution designed and sanctioned to provide each soul the opportunity-risk upon reaching viability and birth, of reliance on state support for cradle to adult care sufficient to become a viable citizen without the risk of abandonment. But this is currently pursued without regard to the mix of opportunity–risk faced by each soul, making it an essentially anti-conservative risk. Pro-choice, on the other hand is a private, conservative approach to decision making by the parents, particularly the mother, in dealing with unknown risks of childbearing and childrearing of the infant soul often in a community that may not be prepared to foster that soul's growth and development adequately or properly.

As someone who knows about preexistence of the soul from my own experience, who remembers my own entry as a soul into this current material existence at the time of my own birth, I know that we are not created at or by conception—at least I know this 'we' wasn't. I don't speak for everyone in this regard for what should be understandable reasons. As a soul, my life did not begin at conception, because that Life has no beginning and no ending, though every human body has both. The purpose of each human life, between these bookends, is to gain material-ideal-spiritual experience as a soul in order to cooperate more fully with the community in the divine plan and purpose, always forward looking, and not just so we have the opportunity to grow up and buy stuff.

The current anti-abortion solution ignores the nature of opportunity–risk within the community and takes the liberal approach of applying public chastisement and penalization of what would otherwise be a private, conservative solution in weighing the decision to terminate a pregnancy, something only a prayerful mother is in a position to decide. In much of the world governed by neo-liberal economic decision-making with no private safety net, if allowed or mandated this liberal anti-abortion solution would result in births of infants at heightened risk, without the proper access and opportunity to health, educational, vocational, and general spiritual resources conducive to Life, through the turning of a blind eye to basic human care and adolescent education, including the teaching of contraception and sexual understanding of the human soul.

This is not said to avoid a discussion of an enlightened determination of viability. It is meant to address the current liberal motivation of one-upmanship and delight in assigning public retribution for what should be a private, conservative right to a choice that is justly a decision between a child-bearing soul and God. If that soul sees the wisdom of bringing their child to term and raising it with Love and Wisdom, that would be a good thing. Until the liberal anti-abortion solution sees the wisdom of matching their zeal—primarily for retributive justice, and only ostensibly for bringing a child to term—with a proper public foundation for child rearing within the community, they would do well to check their anti-conservative bias at the liberal public door.

What is missing in the context of the current judicial show, on whether to operate on the basis of stare decisis or to set precedent aside in disingenuous deference to the lack of a statement of a right to abortion in the constitution, is any reference to the first amendment. The current liberal anti-abortion movement seeks to make it a crime, by delegation to the states, to terminate a pregnancy even prior to viability as an act of murder of a human being, based only on the religious belief that a soul is created by God at conception. Rather, as a material vehicle created by conception for the eventual habitation of a preexistent soul, at or sometime before birth, there is no act of murder prior to viability. To think otherwise is to operate without true experience or knowledge in the matter and possibly with malice.

The notion of the creation of a soul, and therefore a person, at conception, if honestly held, is an understandable fallback belief against the backdrop of a soulless Darwinian materialism. We all know instinctively that we are souls. But how we got here is a religiously held belief that is not subject to verification. Neither do any of the Supreme Court Justices have this verification or we might have found it communicated in the recent leak. If those citizen Justices wanted to set aside precedent and rightly consult the Constitution, instead of looking for references to abortion, they would have concentrated on the first amendment, again as "Congress shall make no law respecting an establishment of religion or *prohibiting the free exercise thereof;*".

The states right to prohibition of the individual right to choose whether to bring a child to term begins at viability, as murky a threshold as that might be. One would surmise that there is no cynical English case law that would consider a miscarriage or a stillbirth to be a murder on the part of a mother or midwife or doctor, but there is talk of such state law. The prohibition of that right prior to viability is an imposition on the free exercise of an individual's religious faith based simply on the contrary religious beliefs of another citizen, including citizen Justices. That free exercise is a federal right under the constitution, above the purview of any statehouse—unless, of course, we interpret the first amendment to mean that while Congress can't do it, the statehouses still can. But that would mean that the statehouses can also allow, "abridging the freedom of speech, or of the press; or the right of the people peaceably to assemble, and to petition the Government for a redress of grievances." I don't think we want to go there, but then again, that is obviously the intention of some misguided souls.

My personal free exercise of religious faith is Holy Ghost infused, informed by the Spirit of Truth since before my birth, and not dependent on any biblical interpretation. It should be apparent to anyone that is honest, that the decision to end a pregnancy is a spiritual decision, if we believe in free will of the soul and not the tyranny of the state. It can only be entrusted to the individual mother, up until the threshold of viability. Based on that murkiness of the viability threshold, we might think any penalties attached to a violation of that threshold should be mitigated or misdemeanored, and not pursued with the current smug felonious hypocrisy of some people.

Babies are precious. They represent all the potential of human life; under the right circumstances, they are an opportunity for a life of joy; without the circumstance of a supportive community, they are at risk of disaster for themselves and those that love them. That children exist at all is due to the God given ability to procreate, an ability that requires understanding and experience to master in all its implications. It is not something that just happens or that can be left to the state to supervise as the liberal anti-abortion movement would like to do. Taking the moral high-ground in a mission to end Roe v. Wade is both theologically and legally unsound in subjecting the matter to a plebiscite. Prohibiting the free exercise of religious belief as it pertains to the human body prior to well defined viability strikes at the heart of the constitution and the federal government which was designed to protect that constitution, so when we try to trump another religious belief with our own, we amplify the risk of taking the God of Love, Wisdom, and Compassion permanently out of the legal discussion, and that is something no one should want.

GUNS

Gun rights are another interesting source of confusion. The right to bear arms is a liberal approach to avail oneself of the opportunity for self-protection or to hunt, while at the same time being a private, conservative approach to lessen the risk of being assaulted by someone else. As someone who grew up with firearms in the house, I have never been afraid of nor particularly fascinated by them. I have never been afraid that the government wanted to take them away, and I'm not terribly concerned about the idea of restricting access to them by immature souls under certain well-defined conditions. The main point is that the approach to limiting access to guns is a conservative impulse if the aim is to lessen the risk of turmoil in the community, in contrast to the liberal desire to preserve the opportunity of access and the right of sales by the gun manufacturers.

This desire is fueled in the U.S. by the exaggerated fear and perception of a 'liberal' federal government intention to take away private ownership of guns, a fear that is fueled by the acquisitive nature of the gun lobby, which has thrown wisdom to the wind—'a howitzer in every home' appears to be the logical conclusion to their marketing plan. The purposely confused result is that the risk is not well understood to be addressable by a public solution and obscures a real solution in terms of the liberal opportunity–conservative risk framework. Instead, the problem is cast as an anti-liberal attitude against a frontier opportunity for gun ownership and an anti-conservative increase in the risk of open season on anyone in the public square from any soul possessed and directed by their personal demons to rid their world of evil. We could start by recognizing that a gun, like a car as a potential lethal weapon in the wrong hands, should be subject to the same proof of maturity in its use as an automobile. We already know that. We just don't seem to want to fund its enforcement.

RACE & A PUBLIC SAFETY NET

For individuals whose primary identity is with the Soul and the Soul Nature as their essential self, race, sex, ethnicity, and other types of public identification are secondary. These are existential, socially recognized facts with extended meaning, defined by the personal experience of being and navigating in the world. Such recognition generally arises through a positive self-identification with commonly observed markers of a material nature such as gender, skin tone, language and speech pattern, clothing and other personal adornments, and cultural traditions and customs. Such markers also provide an illusive recognition of identity through a combination of that self-identification in varying degree of meaningful authenticity and a negative superficial identification through marker association imposed by others. The carriers of these observable markers, as forms and processes, and the souls that recognize them in themselves or conjure them in others, must determine if that recognition represents an illusory or real threat and if that determination is of significance in their navigation. Attached to such markers are the socially defined names that are assigned and recognized as relevant to those forms and processes, often with a binary value placed on that relevance— conservative & liberal, expert & idiot, good & bad, or evil & good.

The stereotyped 'conservative' might be viewed by a 'liberal' perspective as being driven by ignorance and greed, informed in their utilitarian valuation of others by how 'useful or useless', ultimately by how 'good or evil' they are. A stereotyped 'liberal' might be viewed by a 'conservative' perspective as being driven by fear and conceit, informed in their idealistic valuation of others by how superficially 'educated or uneducated' they are, again ultimately by how 'good or evil'.

As has been developed here, a balanced view as a soul from a liberal–conservative perspective sees all members of the community as being driven by hopes for opportunity and concerns for risk, informed in their just social valuation of others by their level of skill with respect to whatever they happen to be doing at the time. Be it in the public or private arena, perhaps recognized as being 'good or bad' at how well they are doing their job or hobby, if they are forced to make a determination and comment, it would be how well they seem to be following their path in Life, their dharma. It therefore behooves someone who wants to maintain that balanced view to take some care and to use a dose of good humor in addressing the ergodidiocy on either side of a discussion.

Until recently, enlightened souls skilled in the public arena generally refrained from identifying with most of the contentious 'isms' bandied about in the media, not because they are timid, but because they don't make the identifications in their own head that others might anticipate they would or should. They know not to pick a fight with someone who is not listening, and they figure out how best to respond when turning the other cheek. Taking sides in a pointless argument is fruitless until someone is actually shooting at you, and then it helps to know who, what, where, when, and why the shooting is occurring. If you must shoot back, it helps to be judicious in the use of ammunition and to aim well—figuratively speaking, it currently needs emphasizing.

As a soul, in my current incarnation, this body has been given an entry point in 1948, Chattanooga, Tennessee, determined by DNA and a family social niche that has been percolating around in northwestern Europe for the past few thousand years, of Scots, Welsh, and German heritage, from the last few hundred years of the Protestant branch of the Christian world view, from a stock of farmer–shopkeepers, miners, and small business professionals, a mix apparently devoid of excess financial capital, but steeled with strong moral fiber.

These circumstances of birth and development make me—an older married southern white male protestant, though I'm not sure about the proper order of the adjectives—subject in the eyes of some to stereotypical assumptions bordering on being prejudiced—about them being prejudiced about me being prejudiced, not about me being prejudiced about them being prejudiced. Heaven forbid that I might be prejudiced!

We all have prejudice. Prejudice is not a bad thing when you have to make a split-second decision, and you have very little data to inform your judgement. It comes in handy when you are faced with what might be an existential threat, such as being asked to put your hands on the hood of your car for a pat down when you have a couple of joints in the back pocket of your pants, or when you are the law enforcement officer doing the asking, responding to a traffic infraction or a radioed request for assistance. A well understood procedure for both parties is essential in dealing with such an existential risk that calls for a prejudiced response. A citizen who has no perception of having committed an infraction may feel and be justified in asking why they were stopped, but that doesn't mean they have a right to sort things out or should run off rather than comply with a legal request.

Both parties understand that they are at risk; they have both watched too many TV programs and news clips not to have that perception drilled into their brains. If the driver can find an opportunity to quickly dump the weed, he can avoid a lot of time and expense in being fined or incarcerated. Perhaps there is no weed, and the driver is just reaching for his wallet to show his driver license and knows there is nothing to hide. If the officer is not on guard, the driver may pull out a pistol and shoot. So thinks the officer as he responds to a quick offering of a driver's license with a round of fire.

Such moments are best suited for a conservative, procedural approach to lessen the risk in the moment. They do not represent an opportunity for a liberal discussion of civil rights or whether the driver has done anything illegal or not. Granted, the officer may be a bad dude and the driver's life may be in jeopardy, but that will be the case in any event if the driver resists out of fear or indignation. And the driver may be a bad dude as well and the officer will have little time to think about how to respond if the driver draws a weapon out of their back pocket.

We will assume first in this case that things work out okay and the driver goes on their way. Prejudice on the part of the officer that the driver should know enough to comply with the request allowed a safe and expeditious handling of the matter. Prejudice that the instance was fraught with a degree of peril causes the driver to comply with the request and, after the pat down and license check, to go on their way. Note that the discussion about prejudice in this traffic stop to this point has not been about race. It is prejudice on the part of the officer in assuming the driver understands that officer has legal authority and prejudice on the part of the driver in understanding the possible lethal consequences of failure to comply with a legal request.

We have not discussed the skin tone or ethnicity of the officer or the driver based on the DNA or heritage of either. It is not pertinent in the moment, even given whatever reports of similar instances have been circulating in the community. Ethnicity only enters into the discussion later, after the incident has played out, based on the self-identification of the driver, possibly that of the officer, and the recognition of an ethnic marker of both with respect to the part each has played in the incident. Historically and statistically speaking, one assumes that people with darker skin are more likely to be stopped and frisked than light skinned people, based on the anecdotal evidence—whatever your prejudice might be with respect to anecdotal evidence. I don't know that for a fact, simply because I don't have bona fide access to the statistics, and I might be prejudiced, but the time for that discussion is not during the traffic stop.

There are various aggravating factors that might be involved, primarily the result of socioeconomic circumstances, but that should be addressed in a political forum. Assuming an observation and recognition of ethnicity is present—including one that might be indicated by a marker common to both officer and driver—a traffic stop is not a good time to relitigate race or slavery or the civil war or any other marker of social status that an aggrieved soul, rightly or wrongly, might find offensive.

Sometimes the stop goes awry. If the driver is a bad guy, or a good guy in a struggle with a bad cop, and the officer is injured or killed, in most cases the cop will be seen as the victim. Rightly or wrongly, the diversely ethnic driver will become another highly visible instance in the media added to a perception on the part of some of a growing problem with an ethnic diversity dimension. There will be calls to crack down on crime, but the funding to do so in all its components to mitigate the risk will not be found for reasons already discussed, and because in general it does not threaten the elites who control the money—unless it helps bolster contributions to their political campaign coffers. And so, it falls on the traffic officer to become more alert and thereby more prejudicial in dealing with the statistically recognized incidents of perilous risk. It is straightforward—more alertness, more stress, more prejudice.

If the driver, good guy or bad, is injured or killed in the process, because the prejudicial system is set up to facilitate in the operation of justice—and that is what a legal system is in part, a logical system of forms and processes to filter and pre-select or predetermine what breaches of norms and standards warrant adjudication—the officer is assumed to have done the best they could under exigent circumstances. This also focuses on the notion that the driver could have avoided the result if they had simply complied with a legal request by a duly authorized officer of the law. This then results in another media field day with calls for racial justice or to protest racial injustice, some justified, where a cub reporter gets their moment of fame and gets promoted, sometimes justified, and calls go out for more money—that goes once again to bolster some groups political campaign coffers—falling once again on the traffic officer to become more alert and thereby more prejudicial in dealing with risk. Heightened risk involving split-second decision-making heightens prejudiced decisions and the implementation of more conservative response to the risk.

So, no one talks about the real causes of the problem of traffic stops and no-knock warrants and the militarization of police ending in violence and what it would take to change that trend. That would put an end to too much money ending up in political coffers on both sides of any escalating policy debate. The lust for money and the grudging acceptance of its need has always been at the corrupting core of community problems. Maintenance of that core has always been facilitated by keeping whatever money is available pooled in relatively few hands so that it is ostensibly accessible when needed by the community, under the control of conservative private or liberal public interests; this, in a population that generally has a surplus of untapped human capital needing only imaginative funding for its development. The corruption comes when private interests covet public funds, public interests covet the private, and the untapped human capital goes unfunded.

The real solution for calls to end current vestiges of racism and discrimination of all kinds will not be found in de jure policies and programs that rely on bureaucratic means testing based on material or ideal markers to assure their efficacy. Calling for redistribution of wealth or reparations for unjust treatment that happened 50 plus years ago based on superficial means testing, while leaving out of the discussion the needs of several times as many disadvantaged 'whites' who have suffered their own injustices at the hands of indifferent elites, though not so ignominiously, will not get the discussion very far. Reparations are in order, but not along racial lines and not through ham-handed redistribution of existing capital when the realities of modern monetary theory and the potential of universal basic income as a dividend right of citizenship are available.

The market system will never address all the basic needs of society, but that doesn't mean the needs should not or cannot be addressed. Or that the means of addressing the needs can only be met by robbing Peter to pay Pauline. The Internal Revenue Service is not needed to address those needs; for the most part, the IRS is not needed period. Raising children from birth to adulthood is an expense. It is not a profit center by any means. Those expenses still need to be met and can be met with a combination of MMT and UBI, using enlightened public policy and private initiatives.

486

With respect to the U.S., the existence of the IRS is the real thorn in the side of a large number of souls in the community that see it as a means of taking money from hard working people to pay for social programs that are of questionable value, in some cases perceived as antithetical to the values of those hard workers. This perceived grievance is exacerbated by the existence of affirmative action laws and programs designed to help those who have suffered from past discriminatory laws and programs, which after 40 plus years of implementation appear to have done little to narrow the pay gap between racial groups, based on some statistical reports.

This is attributed to a failure of affirmative action on both sides of the issue, though for different reasons. It avoids the obvious existence of non-market valued circumstances of an opaque nature that maintain systemic bias based on historical hierarchical and other position in the political economy and that have a market valued effect on wages and property valuations. Such bias is not addressed by affirmative action policy which is designed to filter by recognizable social markers such as gender, skin tone, language and speech patterns, ethnic culture, and affiliation for policy applicability. While those markers focus efforts on the material nature of bias with the intention of effecting its material mitigation, their primary effects are essentially of a psychological, ideal nature, attaching to the individual soul and affiliated group targeted by the policy as a shared experience. That effect in turn can either emphasize or deemphasize that bias based on the identity reactions of members of the group.

That identity reaction has less to do with the innate capacity of the souls in the group and more to do with the variety of adaptive measures that the subgroups in the group have evolved as a response to what each soul experiences as an individual material–ideal–spiritual condition. Identity is an individual spiritual condition of the soul as a focus of that soul. It is always an operation of individual free will, despite the fact that its essential nature is always collective. It can and generally does defer its decision-making intentionality to what it perceives as the Wisdom of the souls recognized as experts in the subgroup and group, sometimes ignoring signals to the individual of truths which are contradictory to that expressed wisdom. The material conditions of the group may appear and in fact be monolithic, but the material-ideal-spiritual conditions are never monolithic—except perhaps in the mind of an observer that views the group from outside that identity through the observer's own bias.

Ideal conditions, in the Platonic sense, always represent a choice as a competition of ideas which requires a spiritual decision as a judgement. In the most extreme case of deciding whether to continue to fight or to turn the gun on oneself rather than face the perceived lengthy abomination and desolation of a material loss, the material-ideal-spiritual reality of a judgement is such that retiring prematurely from a material skirmish may not change the ideal-spiritual choice that was simply delayed in a preempt to defray the material perception of loss. The response to the opportunity and risk observed in a monolithic material condition is always a material-ideal condition of choice, for which the choice is always made intentionally if only by default, by the spiritual nature. This makes for the existence of a variety of subgroups within what can mistakenly be seen as a materially conditioned monolithic group from the vantage of those who identify as being outside that group.

The price of acting on such a mistaken observation and failure of recognition of the true material-ideal-spiritual state within an exogenous community is currently playing out on the international stage in the destruction of life, liberty, and happiness surrounding the invasion of Ukraine. This miscalculation by an authoritarian state and culture represents a failure to recognize the actual endogenous material-ideal-spiritual conditions within its own domain, as with any authoritarian state that governs itself by reliance on a myth of monolithic materialism through intimidation and/or acquiescence of those whose innate inclination is to identify with the state.

The natural inclination of self-identifying members of a group to defer to perceived experts as leaders of the group is conflicted if they perceive themself to be a member of a subgroup that is being imaged by a leader as being outside the group identity for whatever reason, as in the case of a law-abiding driver interacting with a law enforcement officer on a specious traffic stop. The material condition of the traffic stop is monolithic for both parties, but the material-ideal condition for both the driver and the officer are qualitatively different; there is an inherent hierarchy in the condition of the decision-makers in that the officer has legal authority over the driver.

Let's assume for argument that the 'circumstances of an opaque nature that maintain systemic bias' is weighted, that is biased, according to three related positions into which an individual human soul is born. This condition is investigated in some detail as referenced in Contemplations III, previously under the links to A Critique of Neoliberal Economics, Part I. That position of birth includes, 1) an innate survival capacity, which demands food and water and shelter from the natural and social elements, and introduction and education into a community as a contributing member for the well-being of that soul and the community. That position of birth includes, 2) a logical capacity to learn and operate in such a community in an economic manner that has been determined by a history of material conditions, which in the U.S. is largely under the control of private interests and decision-makers. Finally, that position of birth includes, 3) an intuitive capacity that understands the intentional capacity of the material and ideal natures which finds utility in material resources and the purposeful applicability of ideal Forms and Processes which can lead to technological change and benefit.

The innate capacity is primary, since without access to the means of survival, the human body will die. The material position of the soul at birth is therefore an existential bias of primary concern. This concern does not alter the fact that the innate capacity of a soul to survive appears to have a component of survival strength or will that is not determined by genetics or social position, that under the same genetics, social position, and material circumstance results in different survival outcomes.

The logical capacity is secondary in interest, as the ability of the soul to accustom itself to the community and adapt itself to the economic conditions into which it is born and finds itself as determined by historically developed material conditions. As there is an increasing disparity in the rapidly evolving economic conditions of the soul at birth, there is a bias of development of the soul within the community based on the social position of each birth. For those born into a comfortable position, the situation is generally seen as self-evidently just. For those born into exigent circumstance, the lack of adequate childhood nutritional and developmental needs risks competent natural capacity and guidance of the soul for becoming a contributing member of the community and throws that soul back on its innate capacity in the primary condition in a type of social environment governed by survival of the fittest.

The intuitive capacity is of tertiary interest in some respects, though it is perhaps primary from a perspective of leadership in the community. As long as a soul is able to find a pleasant position in which to work, play, and socialize in a productive manner within the community, most of us will be satisfied. As long as the intuitive capacity to understand and read other souls is motivated by goodwill on the part of the experts and leaders in the community, with an understanding of its technological opportunities and risks, the general members will be intuitively inclined to acquiesce to leadership decisions and the community will prosper. When the leadership has the capacity to 'read' the fear and ignorance of others in the community and is motivated by opportunism, financial greed, and a desire for exploitative power through lying, and seeks to manipulate and enhance any perceived bias arising from fear and ignorance in the community for personal benefit, the community will suffer. They do this by achieving identification between that leadership and a core, self-defining subgroup of the community, thereby enhancing the status of that subgroup to the exclusion of other subgroups, and if unscrupulous, identifying another subgroup as an existential threat.

Such is the 'opaque nature of systemic bias' in the community, which consists primarily in ignoring existential bias with respect to the survival needs and economic conditions of those born in the community along with the treacherous use of logic, biased to motivate those disadvantaged by fear. In truth, this systemic bias is anything but opaque to enlightened souls. To continue to work it requires the curtain and mirrors of the Wizard of Oz to provide cover for such leaders and to deflect and vent frustration on the part of their deferent followers.

Unless the community can address all those within it as souls of equal inherent value by learning to love and not fear each other, by acting with wisdom and not with ignorance and neglect, one party's anti-racism is in danger of becoming just another 'ism' looking for prominence among all the other 'isms'. It is just another deflection for the lack of imagination concerning the nature of money as a necessary means of providing liquidity for all those in the community for the basic right of access to life, liberty, and the pursuit of happiness.

I know that I am Soul, and because I know that for myself— as I have intuited it since birth, apart from a few post-adolescent years of doubt before recapitulation and verification by the brief episode on the ferry from Turku a month after leaving Paros—I know it is true of others. I know that <u>We are Soul</u>. Such knowledge is not a matter of personal endowment or achievement but simply a matter of where we are, along with others in the midst of the great sea of Soul Natures, of where We all are in this great sea of Life. As such I understand that each and every one of us is Soul; not <u>a</u> soul—that too, but more than that—the Soul. We are collective Being, the Divine Child of the Paternal Spiritual Source and the Maternal Material Presence of all Living, in Communion with a Divine Family, a Divine Community.

Those souls among us who are yet to have this understanding are in that position because they are still young in the great chain of being, just as 95%+ of human beings in bodies on this planet are younger than me. Some have not arrived at their destination, and some may be lost for the present. Some are just out having fun as we were back in the day in Paros, neither lost nor yet arrived at our destination nor even aware of the journey. There is no particular political agenda that will solve the problems that currently face the community, other than in working for the balance of Justice under the Guardianship of Plato's Republic, at the center of the extremes between the pursuits of unrestrained freedom and authoritative power on the major axis and between a desire for prosperity defined by material abundance on the one hand and for honoring the ideals of

492

personal service to the community on the other. It behooves us all to follow that moderate example of Plato's Philosopher King, of Christ, of Krishna, of the Buddha, and yes, of the Marx quoted in "A Contribution to the Critique of Hegel's Philosophy of Right", along with many others with the end of Justice in mind and the Spirit of Truth in our heart.

Just as I know I am Human, that I identify as a human being, I know as Soul I am just temporarily here as an older married southern white protestant male, etc., etc., and so forth. The natural tendency is to identify with age, marital status, geography, ethnicity, religion, sex, and some other traditional roles if a stability in material conditions in which a soul is born and raised is perceived to exist. In times of cultural flux, with traditions challenged and the elites of the community indifferent, clueless, or hostile to each other, the current fashion to identify as a gender or a sexual preference, in a racial, religious, vocational, professional, or political culture is understandable, especially under pressure of one's peers and to get the begrudged attention of the elites to which one identifies. Though it is a tell to some of the experts among us, the underlying uncertainty of being a tyro, of having yet to discover one's true nature as a soul, of wanting to figure out what it all means as an ego is okay and can be indulged ... unless it shows a decided shift in community balance away from Justice toward anarchy, tyranny, or both.

Those of us who funneled through the Paros Commune of 1971 were born into such a cultural flux. We were drawn to song and dance, to the intoxication of wine and weed, and to the allure of mutually liberating sexual encounter like a moth to the flame in the youthful freedom and opportunity of the times. I can only assume that for most of us, the intensity of those enticements mellowed as we returned to our homes, back to school and work, and to families of various shapes and sizes.

For the fortunate among us, the rock & roll, drugs, & sex transmutes into a mature mix of low decibel music, lower proof libations, and companionship as we settle like sand into the bottom half of the hourglass of life. Some of us remain stuck in an adolescent search for meaningful identity and stability in the vortex of the funnel, mentally and physically burning out, but that is okay. Everyone figures it out in the fullness of time.

As souls, we carry the socially recognizable markers of our birth in our bodies and into the community, where personal histories are formed. We learn to recognize them in ourselves and others and to interpret them for good or bad, too often for good or evil. Each personal history is unique to the personal experience of that soul, but is subject to the understanding and misunderstanding, the interpretation and misinterpretation, of every other soul in the community.

When we encounter unfamiliarity—unknowns and ambiguity—we project what we have learned about good and evil from our own tradition and cultural flux onto the unfamiliar. At times the risks are interpreted as good, and the opportunities are interpreted as evil due to inexperience and prejudice of a soul in its limited understanding of current circumstance. At such times, tyros of all persuasions can fall prey to the unrecognized fear and ignorance of their own egos in the pursuit of power and freedom, individual and collective. We appear to be in such times now, though my perception is that most souls hunger for moderation. If we fall prey to the enticements of the extremes, if we insist on picking sides, the center will not hold, and we will destroy the community we now have. If we learn to embrace the middle path of love and wisdom as souls in working toward a just balance in the community, we will make it better together.

Life is like a flower, a gift from someone who loves you and whom you love, but a rose with thorns, nonetheless. It should be taken and held with care to avoid the thorns while breathing in the bloom, then placed in water, eventually to root and plant and grow. Some prefer to view and sniff the rose from afar from fear of pricking their fingers, and thereby miss the full fragrance and the velvet touch of its petals. They let it lie on the counter in the tissue wrapping, ignoring its need for water, soon to find it withered, the scent gone.

I have a better idea of what Life means now than when I stepped outside into the broiling sun of the Aegean to join the Paros Commune of 1971 in search of rock & roll, drugs, and sex...and what it all meant. To my own satisfaction, I have completed the quest to understand what it means to embrace and be embraced by the Soul Nature that started on the ferry to Sweden from Turku.

I am now more interested in 2021 and beyond...like 2022. I hope some of those reading this now will follow through and come out tomorrow, like myself in this year of the Paros Commune Jubilee. That is the reason I now embrace 2021, more or less. Though the current year in which we find ourselves is filled with tribulation, for me in the spirit of the Paros Commune of 1971, it is a year of Jubilee.

Echoing a response to those concerned about the current times, from my inebriated fellow traveler on the ferry from Turku, Finland in 1972, I say, "Relax. Everything's alright."

Love Life ... Live Love. We are One Life.

ACKNOWLEDGEMENTS

For being good friends and helping with this endeavor: Molly Gibson, Anne Poarch, Cindy Wiens, Jonathan Scott, Richard Brautigan, the Paros Commune of 1971, including Edward Martin Michael John B. and J.C. Barbee. And to all the rest.

Thanks.

UniServEnt

THE PAROS COMMUNE JUBILEE & BEYOND

If you catch the spirit in which this was written, the following few pages are provided for jotting down your thoughts for your own purpose or for possible response or sharing of links on the nature of Imaging Soul and Community—that's *imaging*, not imagining, since imaging is what the individual soul does, images its understanding of the community onto itself and then of itself back onto the community. We can start coming together now to show that We are that Soul and can begin to build that Community in the image of that Soul, not from the left or the right, but from the center of 'All Things Common'.

This requires no utopian schemes to take other people's stuff, their money and their toys. It just takes some clear-headed understanding of the need for civic decorum so we can begin to address the technical nature of current economic problems using technological policy approaches such as universal basic income based on a citizenship dividend and modern monetary principles in funding necessary infrastructure and human capital replenishment and technological innovation by recognizing the true nature of quantum wave mechanics that can point the way to the development and implementation of economically feasible cold fusion, to rid the world of the dependence on unsustainable energy sources. It requires initiative, public and private.

If you want to help in such initiatives, with time and/or treasure, address your interest to inquiries@UniServEnt.org.

Peace.

www.ingramcontent.com/pod-product-compliance
Lightning Source LLC
Chambersburg PA
CBHW022107020426
42335CB00012B/868